HIGH-PROFIT
IPO STRATEGIES

Since 1996, Bloomberg Press has published books for financial professionals on investing, economics, and policy affecting investors. Titles are written by leading practitioners and authorities, and have been translated into more than 20 languages.

The Bloomberg Financial Series provides both core reference knowledge and actionable information for financial professionals. The books are written by experts familiar with the work flows, challenges, and demands of investment professionals who trade the markets, manage money, and analyze investments in their capacity of growing and protecting wealth, hedging risk, and generating revenue.

For a list of available titles, please visit our Web site at www.wiley.com/go/bloombergpress.

HIGH-PROFIT IPO STRATEGIES

Finding Breakout IPOs
for Investors and Traders

Third Edition

Tom Taulli

BLOOMBERG PRESS
An Imprint of
🐦WILEY

Published by John Wiley & Sons, Inc., Hoboken, New Jersey.
Published simultaneously in Canada.

The second edition of *Investing in IPOs Version 2.0* was published by Bloomberg Press in 2001.

For general information on our other products and services or for technical support, please contact our
Customer Care Department within the United States at (800) 762-2974, outside the United States at
(317) 572-3993 or fax (317) 572-4002.

Wiley publishes in a variety of print and electronic formats and by print-on-demand. Some material
included with standard print versions of this book may not be included in e-books or in print-on-
demand. If this book refers to media such as a CD or DVD that is not included in the version you
purchased, you may download this material at http://booksupport.wiley.com. For more information
about Wiley products, visit www.wiley.com.

Library of Congress Cataloging-in-Publication Data:

Taulli, Tom, 1968-
    High-profit IPO strategies : finding breakout IPOs for investors and traders / Tom Taulli. — 3rd ed.
    p. cm. — (Bloomberg financial series)
    Rev. ed. of: Investing in IPOs. c2001.
    Includes bibliographical references and index.
    ISBN 978-1-118-35840-5 (cloth); ISBN 978-1-118-42033-1 (ebk);
    ISBN 978-1-118-43418-5 (ebk); ISBN 978-1-118-41697-6 (ebk)
    1. Going public (Securities). 2. Investments. I. Taulli, Tom, 1968- Investing in IPOs.
II. Title.
HG4028.S7T38 2013
332.63'2042—dc23

                        2012030210

Printed in the United States of America.

10 9 8 7 6 5 4 3 2 1

Contents

PART IV: OTHER IPO INVESTMENTS

Foreword

Most any small private company that has a vision to become a major influencer in its industry also has a vision to go public. The seeds of an initial public offering (IPO) are often sown as the company starts up, providing a framework that guides business evolution over the ensuing years. That was certainly the case with NetSuite when we launched in 1998, at the height of the Silicon Valley dot-com boom, with the vision of delivering a business management application over the Internet. An IPO was in our DNA from the start.

I met Tom Taulli as we enjoyed an Oakland Athletics baseball game shortly before we went public. At that game, which I'm sure the A's won (full disclosure: A's General Manager Billy Beane is on NetSuite's board), Tom told me about his forthcoming book to demystify the IPO process for individual investors. This Foreword, which I was honored to be asked to contribute, appears in the third edition of that groundbreaking book. Having read it, I would say it is not only incredibly useful to the individual investor, it is also a must-read for those CEOs facing their first trial in the public markets.

In 2007 when we decided the time was right to go public, we viewed the IPO as a way to satisfy three main objectives: as a marketing strategy to raise our profile and credibility among customers, prospects, and industry influencers; as a validation for our employees that their hard work was paying off; and as a way to raise capital to fuel further growth. Our IPO in December 2007 was remarkably successful. We'd set an offering price of $13 to $16 per share, but market demand drove the price to more than $26—a figure that was the largest jump in initial-to-final pricing since the Google IPO a few years earlier.

Some of our IPO ideas were considered trendsetting in 2007 but have since become far more prevalent (and of course, this book does a great job of explaining the ins and outs of these various choices). For instance, we conducted a true Dutch auction rather than a traditional IPO sale, and we believe that approach raised more cash for the company than a more common approach to the IPO would have. We raised $175.9 million, and though we didn't realize it at the time, that capital would prove useful when the financial crisis of 2008–09 unfolded. It was a key factor in our ability to grow the business during the global slowdown, even as companies in technology and other industries shrank or folded.

We also sold a very small percentage of the company—just 10 percent, far less than the norm at the time—to raise adequate capital while not diluting the company. And we decided to list on the NYSE rather than on the NASDAQ. We were one of the few technology start-ups listed on the NYSE at the time, and since then, we have been joined by many others, including LinkedIn and SolarWinds. In the final analysis, the goals we had for our IPO to enhance our customer success, employee pride, and cash on the balance sheet were met with flying colors.

Successfully executing an IPO—and meeting the demands for transparency and compliance that attend a public company—is a rite of passage that leverages the management skill and processes developed during the private years. The IPO is a major milestone for a successful company that fosters even greater discipline, focus, and leadership, and ultimately strengthens our great engine of capitalism. Conversely, history has shown that ill-prepared companies can stumble and fail at the IPO and in the harsh light of public scrutiny. Helping investors understand the risk and rewards of an IPO and apply their own due diligence is what this third edition of Tom Taulli's *High-Profit IPO Strategies* is all about.

Zach Nelson, CEO
NetSuite Inc. (NYSE: N)

Introduction

I've been involved in the initial public offering (IPO) market since the mid-1990s, which was certainly a great time to get involved. Netscape sparked the Internet revolution with its massive IPO on August 19, 1995. On its first day of trading, the stock soared from $14 to $57 and then ended the day at $58.25. The company sported a market value of $2.9 billion even though revenues were meager.

During this time, I got Internet fever and co-founded a company called WebIPO. It was an early player in the industry to allocate IPO shares to retail investors. All in all, it was a tremendous experience, but I also realized how difficult it was to break through the walls of Wall Street.

Of course, the IPO market today is much different from IPOs during the dot-com boom. It's rare to see an IPO double or triple on the first day of trading. In fact, the volume of deals is much lower today. Whereas the late 1990s may have had 500 to 600 a year, the number is now about 100 to 150.

But this is not necessarily a bad thing. The fact is that the IPO market provides a vetting process. That is, it makes it tough for a flaky company to hit the markets. Don't expect to see crazy deals like Pets.com.

The IPO market remains a great place to find tremendous investment opportunities. Even though the past decade has seen two recessions and a horrible financial crisis, there have been standout public offerings, such as Google and Salesforce.com.

Many of the top deals were not necessarily tech companies, either. Just look at the successful IPOs from Chipotle Mexican Grill and Buffalo Wild Wings.

The good news is that the IPO market will continue to be the place to catch companies that are trailblazing the next big thing. Without a doubt, the tech sector already has promising megatrends like cloud computing, mobile, social networking, and big data.

But we'll also see much progress in other categories like biotechnology, new forms of energy, and transportation. There may even be advances in space exploration. Consider that SpaceX launched a rocket that docked with the International Space Station in May 2012. The company's ultimate goal is to reduce the costs of space exploration by a factor of 10. Oh, and the company has plans to go public.

Now, as of this writing, there is still a lot of skepticism. The U.S. economy is sluggish and unemployment is too high. Europe is having severe troubles, and even China is experiencing a slowdown.

Yet such things will not blunt innovation. After all, Bill Gates started Microsoft in the mid-1970s, when the U.S. economy was mired in a terrible recession. It didn't matter much to him.

So in my book, I want to help make your IPO investing a success and catch the next big waves of innovation. To this end, there are four main parts. Part One covers the fundamentals, such as the IPO process and how to obtain shares. Next, we do a deep dive into strategies and research. This includes covering online resources like EDGAR and RetailRoadshow. We also look at how to interpret the S-1 document—spotting the risk factors and analyzing the financial statements.

There's even coverage of short selling. Unfortunately, there are still many lackluster IPOs, but you can short them to make a tidy profit.

Part Three covers the many sectors of the IPO market. These include technology, biotech, financial services, retailers, energy operators, and real estate investment trusts (REITs). We also look at how to invest in foreign companies. Let's face it—there are many growth opportunities in global markets.

The final part of the book looks at specialized transactions, such as spin-offs. There is also coverage of the emerging area of secondary markets. Essentially, these allow you to buy shares in pre-IPO companies.

Throughout the book, I cover a variety of short-term investment strategies. While they can be good for decent gains, I think these can miss the big picture, though. Getting the big gainers often means holding on to a stock for several years. Just imagine if you had sold Amazon.com or Microsoft in the early days. If so, you would have missed out on massive profits.

It's true that IPOs are unpredictable. But then again, buying the no-brainer blue-chip stocks can be risky, too. Just look at what happened to companies like Eastman Kodak and Lehman Brothers.

As with any effective investment strategy, the way to deal with risk is to diversify. You might, for example (depending on your risk profile), invest 5 percent of your net worth in IPOs. You can then allocate the rest of your funds to other asset classes, such as stocks, bonds, and perhaps a little bit of gold.

In fact, chances are that you have already participated in the IPO market and don't realize it. How is this possible? The reason is that mutual funds are the biggest purchasers of IPOs.

But again, if you want to get the big gains, you'll need to do some research and buy the stocks. And in this book, I give you all the information you need to get going.

So let's get started.

HIGH-PROFIT
IPO STRATEGIES

PART I

IPO Fundamentals

CHAPTER 1

Getting IPO Shares

The most common question I get from investors is: How do I get shares in a hot initial public offering (IPO)? After all, many IPOs have strong gains on the first day of trading. During the dot-com boom of the late 1990s, there were many that more than doubled. The environment got so crazy that Barbra Streisand offered free concert tickets to get allocations of hot IPOs.

But even as things have calmed down, there are still IPOs that surge. And yes, they get lots of headlines.

Unfortunately, it is extremely difficult to get shares at the offering price. Instead, often individual investors have no choice but to buy the stock once it starts trading, which can be risky. If anything, it is usually a good idea to wait a few days until the trading activity subsides.

For the most part, the investors who get IPO shares at the offering price are large players—like wealthy investors, endowments, mutual funds, and hedge funds. They have the ability to buy large chunks of stock. Plus, these investors may be more willing to do heavy trading with other investments. In a way, IPOs are a nice reward for top clients.

Seems unfair? Perhaps so. But it is legal, and the Securities and Exchange Commission (SEC) actually encourages it. This is from the agency's website at www.sec.gov:

> By its nature, investing in an IPO is a risky and speculative investment. Brokerage firms must consider if the IPO is appropriate for you in light of your income and net worth, investment objectives, other securities holdings, risk tolerance, and other factors. A firm may not sell to you IPO shares unless it has determined the investment is suitable for you.

Interestingly, though, even some large investors fail to get allocations of hot deals. The process can be hit-or-miss. In fact, it is often the case that a big

3

investor will get only a portion of the shares requested. This is actually a way for the underwriters to create a sense of scarcity. After all, if you got all the shares you wanted, might this indicate there is not much demand for the IPO?

Despite all this, there are still ways to get in on the action. Let's take a look.

Risk

Even if you can get shares in an IPO, this is no guarantee of getting profits. These types of deals are always risky. For example, on August 11, 2005, Refco went public, with the stock increasing 25 percent on its first day of trading. The company was a top broker for futures and options. It also had top-notch private equity investors, such as Thomas H. Lee Partners.

Unfortunately, Refco's CEO, Phillip R. Bennett, had been cooking the books for at least 10 years and failed to disclose as much as $430 million in debt. By October 17, the company was bankrupt and the stock was worthless.

True, this is an extreme case. But it does happen, although a more common event is a broken IPO. This is when the stock price falls on the first day of trading. This is often a bad sign and may mean further losses down the road as institutional investors try to bail out.

Yet there is still a lot of opportunity when getting shares in an IPO. So in the rest of the chapter, we'll look at some key strategies.

The Calendar

Before investing in IPOs, you need to track the calendar. This is a list of the upcoming IPOs. A good source is Renaissance Capital's IPO Home at www .renaissancecapital.com, shown in Figure 1.1. It will show the upcoming IPOs for the next month or so. This gives you time to check out who the underwriters are so as to perhaps get an allocation of shares, as well as to do research on the companies.

As you follow the calendar, you'll notice some things. First, there is seasonality to the IPO market. Generally there are no more IPOs during mid-December, and the market does not get started again until mid-January. The IPO market is also closed in August and does not get going again until mid-September.

Moreover, there will usually be five to 10 deals in a normal week. But when there is lots of instability in the market, there may be none. Keep in mind that during the fourth quarter of 2008—when the world was ensnared in the financial crisis—there was only one IPO.

FIGURE 1.1   Renaissance Capital IPO Calendar

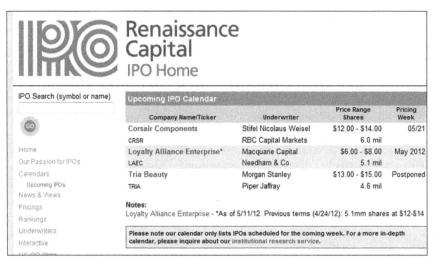

Source: Renaissance Capital, Greenwich, CT (www.renaissancecapital.com)

Some deals may be postponed. And yes, this is not a good sign. A company will usually blame "adverse market conditions," but the real reason is probably that investors are not interested in the deal. In many cases, a postponement will turn into a withdrawal of an offering.

Online Brokers

In the IPO market, there has been resistance to the changes in technology, and there are still many elements of the old boy network. However, the Internet has certainly made a huge impact.

A key was the emergence of Wit Capital.

In 1995, a beer company called Spring Street Brewery, a microbrewery that sells Belgian wheat beers, needed to raise money. Unfortunately, the company was too small to interest a Wall Street underwriter, and venture capitalists wanted to take too much control of the company.

So the founder of the company, Andrew Klein, decided to sell shares of the company directly to investors. One option was to sell directly to his growing base of customers—by putting a notice of the offering on the beer bottles.

Because Klein had considerable experience in finance (he was once a securities attorney at one of the most prestigious Wall Street firms, Cravath, Swaine & Moore), he decided to take another, more sophisticated, route. He organized the prospectus, made the necessary federal and blue-sky filings, and prepared to sell the offering over the Internet. He posted the prospectus online, and Spring Street raised $1.6 million from 3,500 investors. Overnight he became a celebrity, as the *Wall Street Journal*, the *New York Times*, CNBC, and many other media covered the pioneering IPO.

However, Klein did not stop with the Spring Street Brewery IPO. He recognized the need for a mechanism to buy and sell stock on the open market for companies such as Spring Street that are not on a regular stock exchange. So he created a trading system where buyers and sellers could make their transactions commission free.

The SEC stepped in and suspended trading, but to the surprise of many, within a few weeks, the SEC turned around and gave conditional approval of the online trading system. From there, Klein decided to build an online investment bank, called Wit Capital. It would be a place where individual investors had access to IPOs at the offering price and to venture capital investments. Before that, such services had been provided mostly to high-net-worth individuals and institutional investors.

But of course, a big driver for Wit Capital—as well as other IPO digital brokers—was the dot-com boom. Investors had a huge appetite for new issues, and the market exploded.

Yet after the market fell apart, so did many of the online brokerages. As a result, the main players in digital IPOs are the larger players, such as Fidelity, E*Trade, and Charles Schwab.

So it is worth checking out these firms and seeing what deals are available. But they all have eligibility requirements; take Fidelity (see Figure 1.2).

A customer must have a minimum of $100,000 in assets with the firm, or must have placed 36 or more stock, fixed-income, or option trades during the past 12 months. Also, there must be at least $2,000 in cash in the account.

Then there is the following process:

- *Alerts.* This is an e-mail system that will indicate when an IPO is available. There will also be e-mails for when offers are due, the effectiveness of the offering, the pricing, and the share allocation.
- *Q&A.* A customer must answer a variety of questions (which are based on securities regulations). Essentially, these are meant to flag a so-called restricted person, a customer who has some type of connection to the financial services industry that may forbid him or her from participating in the IPO.
- *Review the preliminary prospectus.* This is done by downloading the document.
- *Enter an indication of interest.* This is the maximum number of shares to buy in the offering. You will not be able to indicate a price since it

FIGURE 1.2 Fidelity.com IPOs

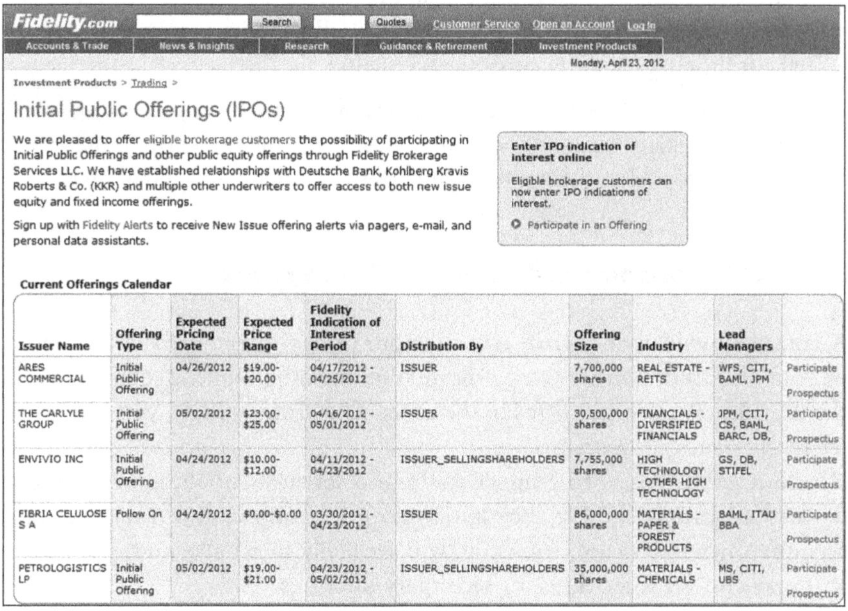

Fidelity.com Search Quotes Customer Service Open an Account Log In

Accounts & Trade | News & Insights | Research | Guidance & Retirement | Investment Products

Monday, April 23, 2012

Investment Products > Trading >

Initial Public Offerings (IPOs)

We are pleased to offer eligible brokerage customers the possibility of participating in Initial Public Offerings and other public equity offerings through Fidelity Brokerage Services LLC. We have established relationships with Deutsche Bank, Kohlberg Kravis Roberts & Co. (KKR) and multiple other underwriters to offer access to both new issue equity and fixed income offerings.

Sign up with Fidelity Alerts to receive New Issue offering alerts via pagers, e-mail, and personal data assistants.

Enter IPO indication of interest online

Eligible brokerage customers can now enter IPO indications of interest.

Participate in an Offering

Current Offerings Calendar

Issuer Name	Offering Type	Expected Pricing Date	Expected Price Range	Fidelity Indication of Interest Period	Distribution By	Offering Size	Industry	Lead Managers	
ARES COMMERCIAL	Initial Public Offering	04/26/2012	$19.00-$20.00	04/17/2012 - 04/25/2012	ISSUER	7,700,000 shares	REAL ESTATE - REITS	WFS, CITI, BAML, JPM	Participate Prospectus
THE CARLYLE GROUP	Initial Public Offering	05/02/2012	$23.00-$25.00	04/16/2012 - 05/01/2012	ISSUER	30,500,000 shares	FINANCIALS - DIVERSIFIED FINANCIALS	JPM, CITI, CS, BAML, BARC, DB,	Participate Prospectus
ENVIVIO INC	Initial Public Offering	04/24/2012	$10.00-$12.00	04/11/2012 - 04/23/2012	ISSUER_SELLINGSHAREHOLDERS	7,755,000 shares	HIGH TECHNOLOGY - OTHER HIGH TECHNOLOGY	GS, DB, STIFEL	Participate Prospectus
FIBRIA CELULOSE S A	Follow On	04/24/2012	$0.00-$0.00	03/30/2012 - 04/23/2012	ISSUER	86,000,000 shares	MATERIALS - PAPER & FOREST PRODUCTS	BAML, ITAU BBA	Participate Prospectus
PETROLOGISTICS LP	Initial Public Offering	05/02/2012	$19.00-$21.00	04/23/2012 - 05/02/2012	ISSUER_SELLINGSHAREHOLDERS	35,000,000 shares	MATERIALS - CHEMICALS	MS, CITI, UBS	Participate Prospectus

has yet to be determined. Instead, the deal will have a price range, such as $12 to $14.

Keep in mind that you may not get the amount of shares requested—or any shares. The offer is not binding.

- *Effectiveness.* On the day the deal is declared effective, you will get an e-mail to confirm your indication of interest. You can also withdraw the offer before the transaction is priced, which usually happens within 24 hours.
- *Allocation.* You will receive an e-mail showing the number of shares you have purchased. In the case of Fidelity, the allocation is based on a propriety system that evaluates a customer's relationship, such as the level of trading and other activities with the firm. According to the website at www.fidelity.com:

> The allocation methodology is done as fairly and equitably as possible. The size of a customer's indication of interest is not considered during allocation other than the fact that we will not allocate more than the customer requested. Therefore, you should only enter an indication of interest for the amount of shares you are interested in purchasing as entering a larger number will not help you receive additional shares and there is always the possibility that you could be allocated everything you ask for.

- *Check your account.* Make sure you received the allocation. Mistakes do happen. There will also be a link to the final prospectus.
- *Trading.* You can sell the shares at any time. But again, you may be penalized for flipping them. According to Fidelity:

> If customers sell within the first 15 calendar days from the start of trading in the secondary market, it will affect their ability to participate in new issue equity public offerings through Fidelity for a defined period of time.

Build Relationships with the Syndicate Firms

A company will usually have two or more underwriters. They manage the offering. But they also form a syndicate of many other brokerage firms to sell the deal. You'll find these firms in the prospectus. Interestingly, you will often see many boutique operators.

So a good idea is to contact them and learn about these firms. How do they allocate IPOs? Do they like to have a certain level of assets in your account? By building a relationship, you are likely to get allocations in IPOs. You may also get some deals for secondary offerings.

Dutch Auction

More and more, auctions are becoming a popular way for people and companies to do business on the web. It was the Nobel Prize–winning economist William Vickrey who developed the ingenious auction system. It's the same system that the U.S. Treasury uses to auction Treasury bills, notes, and bonds. Why not use it for IPOs?

Actually, a firm called WR Hambrecht + Co does have an auction system set up for IPOs. It is called, appropriately enough, OpenIPO. The founder of the firm is William R. Hambrecht, who is also the founder of the traditional investment bank Hambrecht & Quist. He started the firm because he wanted to "balance the interests of companies and investors." OpenIPO allocates IPOs to the highest bidders. However, the auction is private, and all winning bidders get the same price. Consider that top companies such as Google, Morningstar, and NetSuite have used the system.

Here's how it works: Suppose that XYZ wants to go public and has offered to sell one million shares. Its investment bankers have performed the necessary due diligence and have established a price range of $10 to $14.

Anyone can go to OpenIPO—rich or poor, individuals or institutions—to place a bid on the shares.

Let's say you want to bid for 1,000 shares of XYZ at a price of $14 a share. Before you can make the bid, you must first establish an online OpenIPO brokerage account for a minimum of $2,000. Keep in mind, though, that when bidding on an IPO you will need to have enough cash to cover the maximum IPO bid price. It is important also to take note of the fee schedule listed on the website. What's more, you cannot buy IPO shares on margin, and the minimum bid is for 100 shares, although there is no maximum. You can submit multiple bids, say 2,000 shares at $13 and 1,000 shares at $11, and so on. If you have second thoughts, you can withdraw any of the bids.

Let's say there is a lot of action for the XYZ IPO, and many bids come in (the auctions typically last between three and five weeks before an IPO is declared effective). The OpenIPO proprietary software processes these bids. It determines that at a price of $13 per share, 1.1 million shares will be purchased. This is known as the clearing price.

Since there are more shares demanded than have been offered for sale, XYZ has two choices. First, it can have the IPO at $13 per share, in which case you will get 91 percent of your bid. (This is calculated as 1.0 million divided by 1.1 million, or 0.91. As a result, you will get 910 shares, which is 91 percent of 1,000.) Or second, XYZ can decide to lower the price below the clearing price. Suppose it lowers the price to $12. At that price, there is demand for 1.3 million shares, which means a 77 percent ratio. Thus, you will get 770 shares (77 percent of 1,000).

There are certainly successful Dutch auction IPOs. Perhaps the most notable was the offering of Google, which was on August 19, 2004.

Actually, the company used a modified Dutch auction. That is, Google reserved the right to set the final price, not a computer.

So for the IPO, the company priced its shares at $85, which was at the bottom of the range of $85 to $95. But on the first day of trading, the stock closed at $100.34.

In a true Dutch auction, this first-day pop would probably not have happened since the demand would have equaled the supply of shares. But perhaps Google wanted to provide a nice return for its shareholders.

However, it would not have been smart for shareholders to take this quick profit. By October 2007, the shares would go over $700.

Despite the success, Dutch auction IPOs are fairly rare. The reason is likely that Wall Street investment banks prefer the traditional approach, which gives them more power over the process and often results in higher fees.

Buy on Secondary Markets

Secondary markets in IPOs have seen tremendous growth over the past few years. Two of the top operators are SharesPost and SecondMarket.

These firms have platforms that allow investors to purchase pre-IPO shares. This is done by purchasing stock from employees and venture capitalists. No doubt the hottest trading to date was in the shares of Facebook.

But there are some drawbacks. First, the fees can be high and it can easily take several months to pull off a transaction. Besides, the companies may never go public, making it difficult to get a return on the investment. In Chapter 22 we'll go into much more detail on secondary markets.

Private Placements

A secondary market involves buying shares from existing shareholders. In a private placement, you buy shares directly from the company. For the most part, the buyers tend to be venture capitalists and private equity investors.

But this is starting to change. Over the past few years, there have emerged some marketplaces for private placements. One is actually SharesPost.

In late 2011, the firm helped with the private placement of TrueCar, an online service to buy cars. The company raised $200 million in debt and equity.

In the process, investors received a document called a private placement memorandum (PPM). It is like an IPO prospectus but is usually not as in-depth. In the case of TrueCar, there was an online video of a presentation from the CEO.

A private placement will also usually involve one or more investment bankers. They will perform due diligence as well as put together the investor materials.

But to participate in private placements, an investor must be accredited. This means he or she must have made over $200,000 for the past two years (or more than $300,000 for married couples).

Even if you meet the criteria, you still may not get shares in a private placement. Keep in mind that the company will often want certain types of investors in its company—that is, those who have demonstrated a long-term focus.

IPO Mutual Funds

There are a variety of mutual funds, closed-end funds, and exchange-traded funds (ETFs) that focus on IPOs. Examples include the Global IPO Fund, Direxion Long/Short Global IPO Fund, First Trust U.S. IPO Index Fund, and GSV Capital Corp.

Because of their scale, they can get shares at the offering price. In fact, some even purchase shares in the secondary market. For example, GSV Capital has invested in pre-IPO shares of companies like Groupon, Twitter, and Facebook.

These funds also have the advantage of professional management. In Chapter 19, we'll take a closer look at IPO funds.

Directed Share Program

A directed share program (DSP) is when a company sets aside a certain number of shares for friends and family. These usually account for about 5 percent of the offering. So yes, if you know someone at a company that's going public, it's worth asking if there are shares available. A DSP must be disclosed in an IPO prospectus.

In many cases, DSP shares are not subject to the lockup (this forbids an investor from selling shares for a period of time, which is usually a six-month period after the offering). But companies are starting to change this.

In some situations, a company may have a DSP for employees, customers, and suppliers. This was the case for the General Motors IPO. Actually, with the Dunkin' Donuts offering, the company had a DSP for its franchisees.

But this type of program is not without its risks. For example, when Vonage had its IPO in 2006, it set up a DSP for customers to purchase at the offering price of $17.

Unfortunately, the stock price plunged, hitting $6 within a couple of months. As a result, many of the DSP investors failed to pay for the shares!

Follow-On Offerings

After a company has an IPO, it may have other offerings of stock. These are known as follow-on offerings, but many investors also call them "secondaries."

A follow-on offering is similar to the process of an IPO in many ways, such as with disclosures. In other words, there will be a new prospectus filing, and management will have a road show.

It is fairly common for a company to have a follow-on offering within six months to a year after the IPO. In many cases, it is a way for executives, venture capitalists, and private equity firms to sell off shares. It tends to be better to have a follow-on offering than for them to start dumping stock. Interestingly, though, a follow-on offering may require these holders to extend the lockup on the rest of their shares.

To generate demand in a follow-on offering, a company will price the shares below the market price—say by a few percentage points. Thus, buying follow-on shares can mean a nice short-term profit. But like getting an IPO, you need to establish a relationship with an underwriter. Or you might want to check out some top online brokers. Consider that Fidelity provides access to follow-on offerings.

Direct Public Offerings

A company using a direct public offering (DPO) does not use an underwriter. Instead, the company offers stock directly to the public. In many cases, these investors are customers or friends of the company. The company, in a sense, is leveraging its goodwill to do an IPO and avoiding the costs of hiring an underwriter.

Small companies seeking less than $5 million in capital usually pursue DPOs. Often, companies going the DPO route have had trouble getting financing from venture capitalists or underwriters.

Until 1995, DPOs were quite rare. In most cases, when a company did a DPO it sold its stock only to its established customers, known as an affinity group. Perhaps the best-known DPO was Ben & Jerry's selling its IPO stock at its ice cream stores. The offering was announced on the bowls of ice cream.

But not all companies have such loyal affinity groups. As a result, DPOs were scarce. Then the Internet arrived and offered companies a huge, cost-effective distribution channel to sell stock directly to investors.

The simplicity and low costs of putting up a web page make it enticing for companies to engage in securities fraud. And yes, there have already been numerous cases of DPO fraud.

One such case involved Interactive Products and Services, of Santa Cruz, California. The company raised $190,000 over the Internet from 150 investors. Unfortunately for those investors, the company was a complete sham, and the investors lost everything. Netcaller, the company's only product, was a figment of the founder's imagination, based on a rejected patent application. Interactive Products made false statements in its web prospectus, and the founder spent the money it raised on personal items such as clothing, stereo equipment, and groceries.

Interactive Products' Netcaller was described in its prospectus as a "hand-held cordless Internet appliance which enables the user to browse the World Wide Web, send and receive e-mail messages, have real-time communication through the Internet, and two-way voice communications using Internet telephone software."

Interactive Products actually placed extensive web banner ads, many of which stated: "The next Microsoft is offering its stock to the public over the Internet." When you hear such inflated claims for a product that is seemingly too good to be true, stay far away.

There are other concerns with DPOs, including lack of liquidity. There is usually no market for buying and selling shares in a DPO. One company, Real Goods Trading, did a DPO and allowed its investors to trade their Real Goods stock from its website. In such cases, the transaction is then cleared through an escrow agent. But even this approach does not guarantee a good price for your stock. According to the Real Goods website, there was very little trading activity.

To get more liquidity, a DPO will often try to list on a national exchange like the New York Stock Exchange or NASDAQ. No doubt this will create much more liquidity and exposure for the stock.

In some cases, it has happened. But as an investor, it is not a good idea to count on it. DPO companies tend to be niche operators that do not have the growth ramp required for a national listing.

Another chief concern with DPOs is the absence of an underwriter to chaperone the deal. This means that vital tasks such as due diligence, research, and deal structuring, which ordinarily fall to underwriters, are left largely unmonitored and without expert assistance.

IPOs to Avoid

Sometimes you will get offers for IPOs that may seem too good to be true. It's probably best to avoid these.

Here's a look:

- *Spam.* It has become a huge business, primarily because it is so easy and cost-effective to send simultaneous messages to millions of people. Some look very personalized, and others look as if they were sent to you accidentally. But keep in mind that spam is never accidental. It's a marketing tool, not objective information. Some spam will offer you the "opportunity" to buy into IPOs or investments. It's a good idea to stay away. It is common to see these kinds of messages, like "Get the next Facebook." Unfortunately, they are scams. Keep in mind that a Wall Street firm would never use spam to sell a deal. It would be illegal.
- *Unsolicited mail.* If you sign up for magazines or online journals, you are likely to be put on a variety of mailing lists. In order to promote their IPOs,

small companies will purchase these lists and send out very professional-looking, glossy marketing materials. In most cases, a company has hired a public relations (PR) firm that knows how to hide the negatives and hype the positives. These may actually be pump-and-dump offerings—when a company's officers issue large amounts of stock to brokers, creating the illusion that the stock has done a successful offering as the price soars. The brokers, in turn, will dump the stock on clients.

- *Cold calls.* Cold calls are a key part of the brokerage business. It's called "dialing for dollars." These brokers are playing a numbers game. The more calls they make, the more people they reach who may put their money into the supposedly hot investments they are selling. Cold calling is by far the most cost-effective means of marketing. To be successful, there needs to be only a 1 to 2 percent closure rate.

  In most instances, you simply don't want to buy what cold callers are selling. Remember this: If it were such a hot investment, they wouldn't be selling it unsolicited over the telephone.

  But cold callers can be very convincing. They spend hours every day making the same calls, using the same script. If you want to reduce the number of calls you receive, ask the broker to put you on the Do Not Call list, or write a letter to the compliance officer of the firm.

- *Crowd funding.* In 2012, the U.S. government passed legislation that made crowd funding legal. Essentially, this allows small companies to issue shares using the Internet. But keep in mind that these investments will likely not reach the IPO market for many years, if ever. In Chapter 22, we'll take a closer look at crowd funding.

Conclusion

While it may seem tempting to get IPO shares for the opening day, it can be risky. Even Facebook fell over 20 percent within a few days of its offering. A better approach—at least for long-term investors—is to wait a quarter or two before jumping in. The hype will subside and the stock will get seasoned in the market.

CHAPTER 2

IPO Basics

It's a common misconception that initial public offerings (IPOs) are a guaranteed road to riches. Although there are many IPOs that do extremely well—like Google, NetSuite, Salesforce.com, Starbucks, and Chipotle—the fact is that IPOs are like any other investment: there is always risk. Before considering IPO investment strategies, it's important for investors to understand what IPOs are and how they work.

Anyone reading this book probably knows that an initial public offering is the first sale of stock by a company to the public. It's when a company makes the transformation from being privately held to becoming publicly traded, complete with its own ticker symbol. However, there's probably a lot of other, more advanced IPO terminology that most people don't know. For example: What does it mean when an IPO goes "effective"? What is the registration statement? What is the "red herring"? What exactly do the underwriters do? These questions—plus a great deal more about investing in IPOs—are covered in this book.

This chapter takes a look at what motivates a company to launch an initial public offering as well as a look at the drawbacks. We will also meet the major players in the IPO process.

Why Do Companies Go Public?

There is no single answer to that question. It's a major decision that will surely change the character of a company and mean many sleepless nights for management. What's more, an IPO is very expensive. The company will need to hire attorneys, accountants, printers, and many other advisers described later in this chapter.

But first, let's look at the main reasons a company might decide to go public.

15

Prestige

An IPO is a major accomplishment. Wall Street will suddenly begin to take notice. Analysts will start following the company; so will the media. And hiring new employees will become easier, because publicly traded companies are generally perceived to be more stable than private companies.

Since a public company must meet rigorous compliance requirements as well as provide periodic financial reports, this helps to create more trust for investors, customers, and suppliers. This can certainly be an important competitive advantage, especially for those companies that focus on large customers. It's never easy for a private company to snag a contract with a mega player like IBM or Coca-Cola.

Yet an IPO may turn into a public relations (PR) nightmare. This happened with the public offering of BATS Global Markets, the number three stock exchange operator in the United States. The company attempted its IPO on its own platform and the IPO was supposed to be a showcase of its abilities. But on the day of the transaction, the BATS computers malfunctioned and the stock price plunged to 4 cents per share. The glitch even impacted the trading in the shares of Apple, which plunged by 9 percent. BATS had no choice but to cancel all trades and withdraw its IPO. The company's CEO wrote in an e-mail: "On Friday we were under the brightest spotlight imaginable, opening our own stock on our own exchange for the first time ever. It doesn't get much more public than that. It shouldn't have failed, but it did, and the timing couldn't have been worse."

Getting Rich

Staging an IPO is one of the best ways for company principals to get rich. An example is Mark Pincus, who founded a variety of Internet companies in Silicon Valley and was an early-stage investor in companies like Twitter and Facebook.

In 2007 he got an inspiration for a new-style online gaming company. At the time, he was having trouble beating other gamers and was certainly willing to pay money for extra help to win. Mark thought others would feel the same way. So he created Zynga, which produced hit games like FarmVille, CityVille, and Zynga Poker. He also was smart to focus on developing these titles on the fast-growing Facebook platform.

By 2011, the company had generated $1.1 billion in revenues and had 240 million average monthly active users across 175 countries. Zynga went public in December of that year and raised $1 billion. But before this, Mark had already sold $109 million of his stock. This type of transaction has become a big business over the past few years with the emergence of secondary marketplaces like SharesPost.

However, it's not just the founders who get rich; a company's employees can, too. In the case of the Facebook IPO, it minted over 1,000 millionaires. One was David Choe, who painted murals for the company. Instead of taking cash compensation, he got stock options. They ultimately became worth over $100 million.

Cash Infusion

An IPO will typically raise a lot of cash for a company. This money does not have to be paid back. It can be used to build new facilities, fund research and development, and float the acquisition of a new or expanded business. But in some cases, all or a portion of the cash from the public offering will not go to the company. Instead, it will be used to purchase existing holdings from executives and investors.

For the most part, an IPO will raise about $100 million to $200 million. But in some cases, the amounts can be staggering. Here's a list of the biggest IPOs in history:

Company	Date	Amount (in billions)
Visa	03/18/08	$17.8
ENEL SpA	11/01/99	$16.4
Facebook	05/18/12	$16.0
General Motors	11/17/10	$15.7
Deutsche Telekom	11/17/96	$13.0
AT&T Wireless Group	04/26/00	$10.6
Kraft Foods	06/12/01	$8.6
France Telecom	10/17/97	$7.2
Telstra	11/17/97	$5.6
Swisscom	10/04/98	$5.5
United Parcel Service	11/09/99	$5.4

Lower Cost of Capital

For the most part, the public markets offer the lowest cost of capital. A key reason is that there is a larger pool of investors. This means it is easier to find those who are interested in the opportunity. And because there is lots of volume in the stock, the transaction costs are low.

In fact, the cost of capital can be extremely low during bull markets. Just look at the dot-com bubble of the late 1990s. During this period, companies were able to raise hundreds of millions of dollars by issuing small amounts of stock since the valuations were extremely high.

Easier to Raise More Capital

Once a company becomes public, it is usually easier to raise additional capital— in terms of either more stock issuances or debt financing. Keep in mind that since the company has a trading record, it allows investors to make quicker investment decisions. Besides, it has already been issuing ongoing financial reports.

Some companies will actually put together a so-called shelf registration. This means that there can be a sale of stock at almost any time. So if there is a bullish move in the price, a company can get additional capital at a relatively low cost.

Stock as Currency

Publicly traded stock is almost like cash. As a result, a company can use it as payment for acquisitions. This can be attractive when the stock price is at a high valuation. In a sense, this can be a way to buy a company on a cheap basis.

However, there may still be restrictions. For example, the buyer may require that the current management team stay on board for a year or more until being allowed to sell the shares. This can be an effective way to create an incentive for the managers to continue to perform on behalf of the company— and generate more value.

Liquidity for Investors

Except in rare occasions, a company that goes public will usually have institutional investors, which may include private equity funds or venture capital firms. While they tend to hold on to their investments for the long term—say five to 10 years—they will ultimately want to sell their positions. Often, an IPO will generate the highest returns.

In some cases, institutional investors may have registration rights. This means they can basically force a company to go public. An example is the IPO of casino operator Caesars Entertainment. In February 2012, the company sold only 1.8 million shares or 1.4 percent of the outstanding shares. Why issue such a tiny amount? The main reason was that Caesars was trying to keep the stock price high by tightly limiting the supply of stock. It also allowed a variety of its investors—like Paulson & Co., Blackstone Group (NYSE:BX), and Goldman Sachs (NYSE:GS)—to sell their shares.

This is actually a rare scenario but could become common over the next few years. Consider that there was a massive boom in private equity buyouts from 2002 to 2007. So the investors are likely to find ways to cash out of these deals, which may mean more forced IPOs.

But investors need to be cautious. The trading activity can be extremely volatile. With Caesars, the stock soared 71 percent on its first day of trading to $15.31. But after a couple months, it was at $9.

Reasons Not to Go Public

An IPO is not the answer in every case. There are many reasons why a company might decide not to do an IPO. Here are some of them.

Expense

The biggest money pit that comes with an IPO is known as the underwriter's discount. This fee ranges from 2 percent to 7 percent of the amount raised in the offering. Beyond that, there are billable hours for attorneys and accountants. Printing costs (the paperwork is mind-boggling) and filing fees for both the federal government and the states in which the IPO will be offered push the bill even higher. In all, it is common for these out-of-pocket expenses to be $3 million to $5 million.

Managerial Distraction

The IPO process can last six months to a year. During this time, a CEO needs to find ways to make sure the transaction is completed but also focus on the growth of the business. If not, the prospects of the offering could be jeopardy. Just imagine if the revenues and profits start to fall off.

This is why it is important for a company to have a highly experienced management team. This means having a chief financial officer who has credibility with Wall Street as well as a chief operations officer who can manage the company when the CEO is not available.

Short-Term Focus

Wall Street analysts and investors always want to see consistent growth on a quarter-by-quarter business. But this is extremely difficult for a company to achieve. In some cases, it is impossible to avoid a bad quarter.

To deal with this, a company may take short-term measures to keep up with Wall Street's expectations. This may mean boosting prices or ramping up production. However, such actions may ultimately harm the company.

Loss of Control

Over time, the original founders of a company will experience a reduction in their percentage ownership. This process is known as dilution. The cause includes the issuance of more shares to investors, board members, and employees.

When a company goes public, there will be further dilution. It's common for a company to sell anywhere from 10 percent to 20 percent of the outstanding stock in an offering.

And the dilution will likely not stop. A company may issue more shares in a secondary offering as well as for acquisitions.

With a dwindling ownership position, the founders will be vulnerable to possible hostile takeovers. This involves an investment fund or firm that buys a large position in the company and then agitates for change, which may mean selling the company or even firing management. This is accomplished by using the proxy process, which involves the vote on critical matters like the board of directors.

To avoid the loss of control, some companies will adopt two classes of stock. One version will be for public shareholders, which will have one vote per share. The other class will be held by the founders and senior managers and may have 20 or more votes per share. Companies like Zynga, LinkedIn, Google, and Facebook have this type of share structure.

A company may also adopt antitakeover provisions, such as offering cheap shares to existing shareholders other than the hostile acquirer. These measures make it extremely difficult for a hostile takeover, although they are far from foolproof. If a bid is at an attractive price, it is often tough for a company to just say no.

Loss of Privacy

When a company initiates an IPO, it must comply with the myriad regulations meant to protect investors. A company must disclose all material information. For example, in the prospectus (which is the document given to those who want to invest in an IPO), a company must disclose its financial reports, business strategies, customers, executive compensation, and risk factors. Not much is left to the imagination.

And after a company becomes public, it must make available a variety of reports to its shareholders. These include three quarterly reports (10-Qs) and then an annual one (10-K). In between these filings, a company must report major events—such as a resignation or an acquisition—with the Form 8-K.

Not only do these disclosures require lots of time and money, but they may also provide useful information to competitors, such as key contracts, business strategies, and revenue/profit levels. Because of this, some companies, like Google, LinkedIn, and Facebook, have waited as long as possible before going public.

Consider that the ongoing expenses of being a public company can easily be $2 million to $3 million per year. Thus, if a company has only $100 million in revenues, this means a material reduction in the margins.

Stock Restrictions

Even though senior management, board members, and venture capitalists (VCs) have an opportunity to sell shares, there may still be restrictions. For example, there is usually a lockup provision, which forbids any selling for a period after an IPO (the term is generally six months).

Even after this expires, there are other restrictions. For example, key shareholders will usually need to meet the requirements of Rule 144. This imposes restrictions on the volume of stock that can be sold on a monthly or quarterly basis.

Then there is the issue of insider information. Because insiders have access to nonpublic information, they may be subject to civil and even criminal sanctions if they trade on it. As a result, they will generally sell their stock when major information has already been released to the public. In fact, a company may impose a so-called blackout period surrounding earnings announcements.

Insiders must also comply with the short swing rule. This means that an insider must give back to the company any profits made from the purchase and sale of the company's stock within a six-month period. The reason is to focus insiders on holding stock for the long haul. It may also help to minimize the possibility of trading on insider information.

Shareholder Litigation

If there are material misstatements in the Form S-1 filing by which a company registers its securities with the Securities and Exchange Commission (SEC), or with the ongoing financial disclosures, a company's directors and senior officers will be liable. The main trigger for litigation is usually a big drop in the stock price. This is common with IPOs since they are generally newer companies that may have unproven business models.

There are a variety of law firms that specialize in shareholder suits. While most companies will have insurance for their top ranks, a lawsuit will still be a drain on management's time.

In 1995, Congress passed legislation to help reduce this type of litigation, but it has not had much of an impact.

Sarbanes-Oxley

In the aftermath of the Enron implosion in late 2001, President George Bush and Congress put together legislation to improve the regulation of public companies. The process accelerated when WorldCom went bust in 2002 because of an accounting scandal.

The result was the passage of the Sarbanes-Oxley Act (SOX). It turned out to be a landmark bill and has had a wide-ranging impact on IPOs. If anything, it has made it much tougher for companies to go public.

Here are some of the main elements of SOX:

- *Certifications.* The CEO and CFO must sign the quarterly and annual reports. Thus, if these documents are proved to be inaccurate or fraudulent, they are personally liable. The penalties include fines up to $1 million and prison sentences of up to 10 years. If the violations are deemed "willful," the fines have a maximum of $5 million and the prison term is up to 20 years.
- *Clawbacks.* If there is a restatement of the financial statements, the CEO and CFO may have to forfeit bonuses received or the profits from stock sales. This is the case even if there is no proof of knowledge of any problems.
- *Auditor regulations.* There are a variety of rules that help to reduce the possibilities of conflicts of interest. They include audit approval requirements, periodic partner rotations, and the prohibition of certain consulting services for the client.
- *Company loans.* These are forbidden for corporate officers.
- *More disclosures.* The financials must report on areas like off-balance-sheet transactions and other complex details for companies.
- *Section 404 auditor's attestation.* This requires assessments from auditors on a company's internal controls. It essentially looks at the security and accuracy of the financial reporting. Section 404 is rigorous and can require millions in ongoing consulting expenses.
- *Board of directors.* A majority must be independent (that is, not part of the management team). There is an exception for controlled companies (that is, where the founder has voting control).

JOBS Act

In 2012, President Barack Obama and Congress passed the Jumpstart Our Business Startups (JOBS) Act. The focus was to make it easier for small companies to raise capital, which should lead to more job creation. There was also rollback on some of the provisions of SOX.

Here are the takeaways:

- *Emerging growth company.* This is defined as a company with less than $1 billion in revenues. For these operators, only two years of audited statements will be required. In fact, there will be no need for a 404 auditor's attestation report, either.
- *Executive compensation.* A company will also be permitted to provide less disclosure about executive compensation.
- *Shareholder limit.* The old rule was that if a company had over 500 shareholders, it would have to become a reporting company, which means it would have to start filing 10-Qs, 10-Ks, and 8-Ks. But with the JOBS Act, the limit has been increased to 2,000 shareholders. What's more, this does not include employees.

Cast of Characters

In addition to the company senior managers and board members, many other parties take part in an IPO. Here are some of the major ones.

Angel Investors and Venture Capitalists

Before the IPO process can be put into motion, a company needs to attract financial support. The first step is for the company to seek capital from friends, family, and angels. Angels are the private investors who fund startups, many being entrepreneurs who have amassed fortunes by taking their own companies public and now invest in other ventures.

After this, a company will need to get much larger amounts of capital. The source is usually a venture capital (VC) fund. A VC will generally invest in groups. The early rounds of financing may be $5 million to $10 million. The later rounds could be over $100 million. Most of the money will go into the company's coffers. But as the company grows, the founders may get some of the money as a bonus.

VCs usually bring more than money to the table. They will usually help recruit executive talent as well as assist with obtaining customers. Because of this, it is a good idea to focus on IPOs that have VC backing. It is a validation of the company.

Strategic Investors

Large corporations will often invest in pre-IPO companies. Some of them may even have their own venture capital arms, such as Intel or SAP.

These companies are known as strategic investors. Actually, they may not necessarily be concerned about the rate of return on their investments but usually have other considerations. In the fast-changing high-tech world, it is often difficult for large companies to innovate quickly. Investing in start-ups—companies that are known to be terrifically innovative—can be one solution for a large company. Smaller start-up companies have an advantage, since they do not have to deal with what can be a stifling bureaucracy and can focus on one product.

For some types of industries, strategic investors can be crucial. One example is biotechnology. These types of companies need huge amounts of capital. Plus, they require a large distribution platform to commercialize their drugs.

Auditor

The purpose of an auditor in the IPO process is to vouch for the accuracy of a company's financial statements. An auditor's analysis ensures that the company's accounting practices are consistent with generally accepted accounting principles (GAAP). The auditor is required to be independent of the company in order to avoid any conflict of interest.

Auditors will also help the IPO candidate draft the financial reports in compliance with SEC requirements and will issue a so-called comfort letter that the underwriter uses for due diligence.

Having an experienced, well-regarded auditor is very important. If the audit is mismanaged, the IPO may be delayed by SEC questions about the financial data.

Attorneys

Conducting an IPO requires a team of attorneys to deal with the many complex regulations for proper state and federal compliance and disclosure. Talented legal counsel is absolutely essential to any IPO. If counsel makes mistakes, the IPO could be a disaster.

The role of the attorneys is to review existing contracts, amend the articles of incorporation and bylaws, develop stock incentive plans, readjust the capital structure, and so on. They will help deal with the officials at the SEC, review the registration documents, and provide advice on what management can and cannot say to the public.

In some cases, a company will, out of loyalty, use the attorneys it has dealt with since inception. Although this will ensure that the attorneys are very familiar with the company's practices, it may also be problematic if counsel does not have the necessary IPO experience.

Financial Printer

IPOs generate a blizzard of paperwork. A prospectus, for example, can easily be 300 to 400 pages long. Depending on the size of the offering, a company may have to send out thousands of prospectuses across the United States and throughout the world. The printing must typically be done on very short notice—in many cases within 24 hours. What's more, there must be no typos—the document must be flawless, as the SEC requires.

There are only a handful of financial printers that specialize in IPOs and are familiar with the myriad of SEC rules regarding filing formats, such as paper, type size and font, colors, and so on. In other words, having your neighborhood copier company do the printing would be a big mistake.

Interestingly enough, when *Wired* magazine attempted to go public in 1996, there was so much disagreement between the company and its underwriter (Goldman Sachs) regarding the font style that it should have been a warning sign that the offering was in trouble.

Believe it or not, such seemingly insignificant things can wreck a deal.

Public Relations Firms

Public relations firms are crucial in stock offerings. After all, PR is a powerful tool for attracting investors. There are many companies going public these days, all competing for the attention of the press and investors. Without good PR, an IPO can easily be lost in the crowd.

However, as with most things financial, the SEC has certain guidelines regarding public relations. The company cannot disclose anything that varies from the contents of the prospectus. If this rule is violated, the company could suffer serious consequences—such as the SEC terminating the offering. PR firms that specialize in IPO marketing know the rules and know how to get the message out to the right brokers, investors, institutions, analysts, and market makers.

Unfortunately, some companies use PR to cloud the facts. This type of misleading information is sometimes found in obscure offerings from unknown companies. Therefore, it is wise for investors to be skeptical about information contained in the press releases. After all, some of the facts are bound to be glossed over in the spin. It's better to focus on the facts contained in the prospectus.

Transfer Agent/Registrar

The role of the transfer agent is to maintain shareholder information. For example, the transfer agent will hold the name, address, Social Security number, and number of shares purchased for each shareholder. In an IPO it is the transfer agent who handles the physical delivery of stock certificates to those who have indicated interest in purchasing shares. When the stock begins trading, the transfer agent will handle the transfer of stock certificates in every buy-sell transaction.

The registrar, in turn, ensures that the correct number of shares is exchanged when there is a buy-sell transaction. The registrar will also keep records of destroyed, canceled, or lost stock certificates.

The company doing the IPO will typically hire an outside firm, such as a bank, to act as the transfer agent. In most cases, this firm will act as both the transfer agent and the registrar.

Underwriters

Underwriters play a pivotal role in executing a successful initial public offering. The managing underwriters are the investment bankers who run the IPO show. They determine the price of the offering; help draft the prospectus and other filing documents; conduct due diligence; and, most important, find investors for the offering.

In many cases, the underwriter will continue to provide services even after the IPO is completed. For example, the underwriter might advise the newly public company on matters such as mergers and acquisitions or debt offerings.

The managing underwriters will also assemble a group of syndicate underwriters. It is the syndicate that helps sell the IPO's stock to the public. The main reason for a syndicate is to share liability; that is, if there is a shareholders' lawsuit, the liability can be dispersed.

It's hard to exaggerate the importance of an underwriter. Having the right one in place can mean the difference between a successful IPO and a failed offering. So before you invest in any IPO, it makes sense to investigate the underwriter. Interestingly, the underwriting business is the prime source of revenue for securities firms. For more information on types of underwriters, see Appendix A.

Conclusion

On one hand, there are many clear advantages for a company to go public. Perhaps the two most important are the cash raised from the offering and the credibility of being a public company.

On the other hand, the process can be long and expensive. A company will also need to have done much planning before pulling the trigger on an IPO. But this is really a benefit for the shareholders, because by the time a company goes public, it has gone through much vetting.

This chapter is meant as a general overview to give the reader a sense of the IPO world. The next section, Part Two, goes into greater detail on the IPO process. It is surprising that even many investment professionals do not understand some of the changing intricacies of IPOs. However, to be a successful IPO investor, it is imperative to know how the procedure works.

References

Cowan, Lynn, and Alexandra Berzon. 2012. "Caesars Surges in First Day of Trading." *Wall Street Journal*, February 9. http://goo.gl/Nhqdh.
Renaissance Capital: http://goo.gl/fGpEv.
Rooney, Ben. 2012. "BATS CEO Issues Apology for Glitch." *CNNMoney*, March 26. http://goo.gl/uvXa7.

CHAPTER 3

IPO Process

This chapter takes a look at the initial public offering (IPO) process from the moment when management decides to do an IPO to the time when shares are sold to the public. These are the basic steps that precede an initial public offering:

- The company selects underwriters to lead the deal.
- An organizational meeting is held.
- Due diligence is conducted.
- A letter of intent is signed.
- A registration statement is drafted and filed with the Securities and Exchange Commission (SEC).
- The road show begins the marketing.
- Investors are solicited.
- The company chooses a listed exchange or over-the-counter (OTC) market.
- The offering is finalized.

The IPO process is more complicated than many investors realize. Before examining each step, let's take a quick look at descriptions of the legislation that governs IPOs.

Laws That Impact IPOs

The two primary federal statutes that cover IPOs were legislated during the Great Depression after abuses in the stock market during the 1920s, and two other laws were enacted more recently. The Securities and Exchange Commission (SEC) enforces these laws:

- *Securities Act of 1933.* This "truth in securities" act requires that before any stock is sold to the general public, the securities must be registered with the SEC. The prospectus can contain no material misstatements. Such misstatements can lead the SEC to file civil sanctions against the company and its underwriters. The Justice Department can also use the Act to bring criminal charges.

- *Securities Exchange Act of 1934.* This requires that a registered public company make periodic disclosures. Furthermore, the act has sanctions for violations of unfair market practices, such as insider trading.
- *Sarbanes-Oxley Act and Jumpstart Our Business Startups (JOBS) Act.* These are recent laws that are covered in the prior chapter.

In addition to these federal laws, there are also state laws, called blue-sky laws, regulating IPOs. The name is derived from a nineteenth-century court case in which the judge compared a stock offering to someone selling the blue sky. These laws are important because they dictate the logistics of the IPO process.

Steps of the IPO Process

The IPO process is the same for all companies. Keep in mind that it is based on explicit rules from the federal government. They are meant to help ensure that a company is in compliance with the necessary disclosures.

So let's take a look at the key steps:

Pre-IPO Preparation

The IPO process can take anywhere from six to 12 months. To help shorten this process, a company will take steps to make itself "public company ready." In fact, it will essentially operate as if it were public. This means it will:

- Have a strong senior management team.
- Have top-notch financial, legal, and information technology systems in place.
- Report results on a quarterly basis.
- Have a majority of board members who are independent and who have public company experience.

Some companies will even have investor conferences so that mutual funds, hedge funds, and other major investors will get to know the story of the company. In some cases, a company will sell shares to these types of investors in private transactions.

The Bake Off

The first major step in the IPO process is what is called the "bake off." This is when a company interviews underwriters to lead the deal. A company will have one or two managing underwriters.

For a hot deal, the process can be intense. Underwriters will often court companies even before the bake off.

One example was Amazon.com. To get the deal, an analyst for an underwriter, Bill Gurley, put together his IPO proposal in the form of a book!

While such touches are noteworthy, a company wants a proven underwriter. To this end, the company looks for those underwriters that have lots of credibility with investors and strong track records in the company's industry. Another key is having well-respected analysts.

Top Underwriters in 2011 in Terms of Overall Deal Value	
Morgan Stanley	$9.7 billion
Bank of America Merrill Lynch	$8.3 billion
Goldman Sachs	$6.0 billion
JPMorgan	$3.8 billion
Citi	$3.2 billion
Barclays Capital	$1.2 billion
Credit Suisse	$967 million
Deutsche Bank Securities	$746 million
Raymond James	$601 million
UBS Investment Bank	$597 million
Jefferies & Co.	$348 million

Organizational Meeting

After a company selects the underwriters, the next step is the organizational meeting. The goal is to come up with a timetable for the IPO process as well as to cover the key issues, such as the presentation of the financial information and any corporate cleanup needed.

The company is also prohibited from making any public statements about its intent to go public for 30 days before the filing of the registration statement. Doing so could be a violation known as "gun jumping" and result in delaying the IPO. The SEC will then impose a cooling-off period and may even ban the underwriters from being part of the deal.

Due Diligence

Drafting the registration statement is a time-consuming task. A key part of the process is conducting an extensive due diligence. The process is important for the underwriters since they could be liable for any misstatements or omissions in the registration statement. But at the same time, the process is useful in putting together the necessary documents so that they meet the requirements of the SEC.

Here are some of the main areas of due diligence:

• Industry research.
• Background checks on senior officers and directors.
• Calls with suppliers and customers.
• Evaluating any pending or potential lawsuits.
• Analysis of corporate documents like the bylaws, shareholder agreements, board minutes, and material contracts.
• Compensation plans.
• Analysis of intellectual property, such as patents and copyrights.

The due diligence process will involve the request of documents as well as in-depth interviews with employees of the company. There will also be interviews with outside service providers, such as the auditor.

Letter of Intent

A letter of intent is an understanding between the company and the underwriter. It sets forth the tentative terms of the relationship, like the percentage of ownership, minimum/maximum amount of money to be raised, counsel for the underwriter, counsel for the company, compensation for the underwriter, and so on. The letter of intent also establishes a range for the offering price of the issue. For example, the price range may be $14 to $18, but over time this price may be adjusted. Since it is likely to take several months to get approval for the offering, it is virtually impossible to determine an exact price for the stock. Much can happen in today's volatile equity markets.

A letter of intent is little more than an agreement to agree. It is not a binding contract. A final agreement is not usually signed until the day before or the morning of the offering. The company's responsibility to pay all of the fees for professional services, however, is binding after the letter of intent is signed. Though cancellations are rare, the collapse of an IPO can leave the company with debilitating expenses.

The final underwriting agreement is identical to the letter of intent except for the addition of the final stock price and number of shares to be issued. There will also need to be an agreement among underwriters. This document expresses the number of shares to be allocated among the co-managers and syndicate members and enumerates the compensation breakdown.

Deciding the price of the issue is one of the most complex tasks of an underwriter. The firm will look at factors such as the valuations of prior IPOs in the same sector and the company's stature within its industry. If a company has a proprietary technology or tremendous market share, there may be a premium to the valuation, such as was the case for the Facebook IPO. But ultimately, the pricing tends to be more of an art than a science.

The stock must not be priced too high, which could deter investors. In fact, offerings are typically underpriced to encourage investor participation. When the stock is offered, the price will often make a big jump on the first day. It's not uncommon to see the stock price soar 30 to 40 percent immediately.

At one time it was considered an embarrassment to have such a major price increase on the first day, because it meant that the company could have raised much more money, but it's now becoming standard practice to witness these huge jumps.

For the most part, it is very risky to purchase an IPO on the first day of its offering. There tends to be a frenzy of trading activity and price fluctuation; rationality can go out the window as investors bid on a limited number of shares. It's often safer for individual investors to wait several months and let the dust settle before buying their shares.

Drafting and Filing the Registration Statement

After completing the due diligence process and signing the letter of intent, the company, attorneys, and underwriters will begin the drafting of the registration statement. While the format is standardized, it often involves extensive debate and analysis.

The registration statement has two parts: (1) the prospectus and (2) supporting documents, which include summaries of the expenses, insurance for officers and directors, the underwriting agreement, and so on. The most important document is the prospectus, which we cover in more detail in Chapter 5.

The company will file its registration electronically with the SEC. If it qualifies as an emerging growth company, the filing will not be made public in the EDGAR system until there has been a review (the same goes for foreign companies that list on a U.S. exchange). This makes it possible for a company to work out key issues with the SEC, such as accounting treatments, without causing bad public relations (PR).

The SEC will have comments for the registration statement, which will be sent back to the company. The back-and-forth process can easily take three months or more. It depends on the workload at the SEC. When times are booming, there are often delays.

A company can also publish a press release about the filing of the registration statement. But it is fairly bare-bones, with some basic information about the offering like the names of the underwriters as well as a short description of the company.

The Road Show

Also known as the dog-and-pony show, the road show allows a company to generate interest from brokerage firms and institutions for the IPO. For approximately one to two weeks, the senior managers visit financial centers, such as New York, San Francisco, and Los Angeles, to give presentations. During the typical breakfast and a slide show, the audience can ask the managers questions.

The general public is not allowed to attend road shows. But there is a recording available at RetailRoadshow (www.retailroadshow.com). We'll look at this site in more detail in Chapter 4.

Securing Investors

Before the SEC gives its approval, it is not uncommon for the preliminary prospectus to be distributed to potential investors to generate interest. At this stage, the preliminary prospectus is known as a red herring. The reason is that traditional documents had a disclaimer in red letters. It says:

> The information in this prospectus is not complete and may be changed. We may not sell these securities until the registration statement filed with the Securities and Exchange Commission is effective. This prospectus is not an offer to sell these securities and we are not soliciting offers to buy these securities in any state where the offer or sale is not permitted.

Yes, this is lawyer mumbo jumbo. However, it is important for investors to note the disclaimer and realize that the information in the prospectus is not yet final and the offering not yet approved. For example, the number of shares and the final price have yet to be determined.

Members of the underwriting syndicate use the red herring to begin locating investors for the offering. However, before a broker can even talk to a client about an IPO, the broker must provide the red herring for review (this can be done by sending a web link). It is the only information that can be provided. If the investor is interested, he or she will sign an indication of interest. This does not constitute a sale, because the price has not yet been established. It is not until the day of the offering that the sale becomes final. Any broker asking for money before the day of the offering is in violation of securities laws.

A company may also have a "free writing prospectus." This document has extra material that goes beyond the red herring. Basically, it is a better way to create more interest in the offering. However, the SEC has strict requirements on what can be included.

Choosing a Market to List On

Before a company can issue shares to the public, it must decide in which market the shares will be listed and traded. In most cases, an IPO will choose between the New York Stock Exchange (NYSE) or NASDAQ. For smaller companies, the option may be a smaller platform like the OTC Bulletin Board (OTCBB) or the Pink Sheets.

Let's take a look at the different options.

NYSE Euronext

The origins of the NYSE Euronext go back to 1792 when 24 stockbrokers gathered on Wall Street to put together the rules for trading stocks and bonds. Since then, the exchange has become a global platform. There are now over 8,000 listed issues from more than 55 countries. In fact, its equities trading volume represents about a third of all such activity in the world. Though the NYSE Euronext has an advanced information technology system, the exchange still has a physical trading floor.

The listing requirements for an IPO are rigorous. This is a reason there were few dot-com offerings deals in the 1990s.

To be listed on the NYSE Euronext, the company must have 1.1 million shares outstanding and a market capitalization of at least $40 million. One of the exchange's financial criteria is the earnings test, which means a company must have aggregate pretax income for the prior three years of $10 million, and each year must have a minimum of $2 million in income. For the year of the IPO, the pretax income must be positive.

However, over the past few years, the NYSE Euronext has allowed earlier-stage companies to list. Some of the notable examples include LinkedIn, Pandora, Yelp, and Millennial Media.

NASDAQ

Launched over 40 years ago, NASDAQ started as one of the first electronic stock exchanges. The goal was to focus on the trading of smaller stocks, which were part of the over-the-counter (OTC) market. However, over time the NASDAQ became a major platform for larger companies.

Some of the most iconic IPOs got their start on the NASDAQ. Examples include Microsoft, Starbucks, Oracle, Apple, eBay, Cisco, and Google.

To list on the NASDAQ, a company must have a market capitalization of $45 million and 1.25 million shares outstanding. The company must also generate earnings of $11 million in the past three fiscal years and a minimum $2.2 million for the past two years.

OTC Bulletin Board

The OTC Bulletin Board (OTCBB) provides real-time quotes on stocks that are not listed on major exchanges like the NASDAQ or the NYSE. However, most brokerage firms subscribe to the service and allow investors to trade in the marketplace.

Some companies will say they are going public on the OTCBB, but this is not accurate. Instead, the company gets on the platform through a process called a "reverse merger." This is when a private company merges with an existing public company, which is basically a shell.

Some of these companies will even say they are going public on NASDAQ. This is false as well. If you see this, stay away from the company.

Companies on the OTCBB must be current with their financial reports with the SEC. Yet the fact is that there continue to be frauds periodically. However, the SEC has been increasing its efforts to combat this type of fraud.

OTC Pink

The OTC Pink is similar to the OTCBB. That is, it is an electronic platform for quoting prices on stocks. What's more, a company will start trading on the system through a reverse merger. But there are some important differences.

One is that there are no requirements for disclosing financials. As a result, it can be extremely risky to invest on the OTC Pink.

According to the SEC:

> With the exception of a few foreign issuers, the companies quoted in OTC Pink tend to be closely held, extremely small and/or thinly traded. Most do not meet the minimum listing requirements for trading on a national securities exchange, such as the New York Stock Exchange or the Nasdaq Stock Market. Many of these companies do not file periodic reports or audited financial statements with the SEC, making it very difficult for investors to find reliable, unbiased information about those companies. For all of these reasons, companies quoted in OTC Pink can be among the most risky investments.

Finalization of the Offering

Within 48 hours before an IPO, the underwriters will send an "acceleration request" to the SEC. This means that the agency will quickly make the registration statement "effective." That is, the underwriters will be able to sell shares to the public.

On the evening before the IPO will begin trading, the underwriters and the company's management will engage in negotiations on the final offering price. These negotiations can be contentious. Just a $1 change can result in a difference of millions of dollars. There may also still be negotiations on the compensation for the underwriters.

But after the final price is agreed upon, the underwriters will sign the letter of intent and then put together the final prospectus. They will then allocate the shares to the investors, who will confirm the purchases.

For the company's management, the day of the IPO will be a whirlwind of activity. The CEO will ring the bell of the NYSE Euronext or open the NASDAQ. There will usually be a variety of interviews, such as with CNBC, Reuters, and Bloomberg TV.

The closing of the IPO will happen within four business days. At this time, the auditor and counsel will render their final opinions and the certificates will be sent to the original investors. The net proceeds of the IPO will then be wired to the company.

After 40 days, the quiet period will end. At this point, the analysts of the underwriters can start publishing research reports on the company. Interestingly, this often results in a jump in the stock price.

Conclusion

As you can see, the IPO process is a lengthy one. The main reason is the extensive securities regulations. Because shares are being issued to the general public, it is essential that there be sufficient disclosure and safeguards.

It is important for investors to focus on IPOs on the NYSE and NASDAQ. They have rigorous standards, which have been effective in preventing fraud.

PART II

IPOs for Investors

CHAPTER 4

Finding the Best IPO Information

The first step in any smart investment decision is research. But the reality is that many individuals don't spend nearly enough time investigating the soundness of their potential investments. Instead, they act on rumors or rely on tips from their hairstylist or other questionable so-called experts. Sure, it is possible to get lucky with this type of advice; the stock might soar—but relying on luck is risky.

So the first lesson for any investor is: Don't buy any initial public offering (IPO) strictly on rumors. After all, if you're going to spend $1,000 to $5,000 or even more on a stock, isn't it a good idea to investigate the company?

At the other end of the spectrum there are investors engaging in "analysis paralysis." They think that in order to win on Wall Street you need to have the most complex, state-of-the-art investment strategies. You need to use esoteric investment vehicles, such as derivatives, and calculate extensive mathematical formulas. Thankfully, you can make a lot of money without engaging in these mental gymnastics. It has been shown time after time that good investing has everything to do with common sense—as long as it is based on a foundation of sound facts. In other words, it took a gut instinct when investing in the early stages of breakout companies like Starbucks, Cisco Systems, and Chipotle.

As recently as a few years ago it was difficult to get reliable research on companies. You had to purchase expensive subscription services. But all that has changed. Today, the Internet and social media have resulted in an explosion of helpful resources—much of them free.

This chapter is designed to help you find the information you need about upcoming IPOs, see what the analysts are saying about their chances, and track their performance.

Information to Get Your Feet Wet

There are a lot of great places to read about the comings and goings of IPOs. These publications and websites will help you to learn about the industry and to feel comfortable with the terminology. We describe more advanced IPO investment tools later in this chapter.

The *Wall Street Journal*

This is the daily bible for IPO investors—and just about every other type of investor, too. There are routinely a variety of articles on specific IPOs, plus stories on current trends in the IPO market. The "Heard on the Street" column will occasionally cover hot IPOs, and you will see frequent IPO stories from the *Wall Street Journal* staff writers Randall Smith and Lynn Cowen.

The print version of the *Wall Street Journal* costs $413.40 per year; the online edition is $207.48 per year ($501.80 if you are a subscriber to the printed and online version). The website has the same information as the printed version. In fact, in many cases, the online articles are longer and more up-to-date.

You can also set up your own "Personal Journal." This tool allows you to create a customized section of the *Journal* that will search for articles based on key words and phrases, such as "IPO." It's a very simple yet powerful tool to track IPOs. There is also a portfolio feature, with which you can track stocks. One strategy is to create a hypothetical portfolio of IPOs and track their performance over time. It's a great way to learn about IPOs without actually risking your assets.

Reuters, Bloomberg and the Deal Pipeline (www.thedeal.com)

These websites also have valuable up-to-date information on IPOs. Some of the top reporters to follow are Olaf Domis, Olivia Oran, Douglas MacMillan, Brian Womack, and Lee Spears.

IPO Playbook

This is my blog, which is part of InvestorPlace (www.investorplace.com). I have daily coverage on IPOs and even CEO interviews. You'll also have a look at upcoming deals, detailed analysis on companies, and how-to guides.

Google News

Google News (news.google.com) aggregates thousands of publications across the world. You can set up filters that will e-mail alerts on articles that contain certain terms, such as "IPO" or "initial public offering."

IPO Home

IPO Home is the website of Renaissance Capital (www.renaissancecapital .com), which is a provider of IPO research for institutions. The firm also has its own mutual fund, called the Global IPO Fund.

IPO Home is a great resource for IPO information, and it's free. Some of the features are an IPO calendar, recent pricings, company profiles, breaking news, rankings, and statistics.

RetailRoadshow

RetailRoadshow (www.retailroadshow.com) is a great resource. Essentially, it has videos of the upcoming road shows. The videos are usually 30 to 40 minutes long. Unfortunately, though, there are no videos of the question-and-answer sessions.

Plus, the video player is kind of awkward. For example, the rewind feature takes you to the prior slide in the presentation, which can make things difficult for watching.

Since the video is actually the first presentation for the IPO, the CEO may be a bit raw. Keep in mind that is not uncommon for the content to change somewhat (especially in light of the investor questions).

The presentation will usually be chock-full of helpful slides, which makes it easier to get a sense of the company. For the first half, the CEO will usually cover key areas like the market opportunity, the business model, the team, and case studies. Then the CFO will describe the financial model. In fact, there will also be a projected model, which will show the expected margins. This is extremely helpful in evaluating the company. If the margins are likely to remain low, then the IPO probably should be avoided.

In-Depth IPO Information

Here are some of the best places to do in-depth research on specific companies and upcoming IPOs. If you're serious about investing in IPOs, you should familiarize yourself with one or several of these resources. As you'll see, all of these databases and ratings services are online, which allows constant updating and real-time information.

Most importantly, the following analysts are independent.

IPOBoutique.com

The firm provides investment ratings on every IPO. There are also alerts for any changes. An annual subscription runs $995.

The operator of the site is Scott Sweet, who claims that he has been investing in IPOs since he was 15.

Before starting his research service, he managed his own hedge fund. To get information on upcoming IPOs, he and his staff have multiple accounts with many of the top underwriters in the United States.

IPODesktop.com

The site e-mails its research reports on Thursday the week before the IPO. This gives investors enough time to evaluate whether to buy or avoid the offering. IPODesktop.com also gives opinions about whether to buy an IPO in the aftermarket.

Francis Gaskins, who runs the website, has followed the IPO market since the 1990s. He is routinely quoted in media venues like CNBC and the *Wall Street Journal.*

Gaskins focuses on sequential revenue trends for the past four to six quarters and looks at the momentum in gross margins. There are also valuation comparisons to recent IPOs in the same sector. His motto is: "Knowing a good thing before anyone else sees it."

A subscription is priced at $9.99 per month.

IPOCentral.com

The site, which is a part of Dun & Bradstreet, provides information on pricings and upcoming IPOs (this information is free). There is a subscription service to obtain details on each company. However, they are really not for investors. They are focused for salespeople who want to get leads for companies that may be potential customers! In other words, there is no investment analysis or ratings.

IPO Financial Network

The IPO Financial Network offers IPO research and analysis. The core service has an annual subscription of $40. With it, you will get predictions of the first-day trading gains or losses as well as an "IPO Pick of the Week."

The head of IPO Financial is David Menlow, who has been following the IPO market for more than the past two decades.

The site is at www.ipofinancial.com.

IPOMonitor.com

This site is a database of IPO information, which is fully searchable. For example, you can query based on industry, geography, and underwriters. There are also extensive reports on IPO performance.

The subscription fee is $29 per month (www.ipomonitor.com).

EDGAR Resources

The first place I visit to investigate any IPO is EDGAR, which stands for Electronic Data Gathering Analysis and Retrieval. This huge online database of financial filings was developed by the Securities and Exchange Commission (SEC).

Any company that files a registration statement for an S-1 offering must present an electronic version of the filing, which is placed in the EDGAR database. In other words, by going to the EDGAR site, you can get the full version of any company's prospectus. And as we will see in the next chapter, it is in the prospectus that you will find much of the necessary information to help you make investment decisions.

In Chapter 5, we take a look at how to use EDGAR and understand its often archaic processes. But there are also premium services that help make things easier. These include EDGAR-Online.com and Morningstar Document Research at www.10kwizard.com.

Other IPO Information Resources

There are many general-purpose websites, social networks and blogs that provide useful information on IPOs. Here's a look at some of the standouts:

Twitter and Stocktwits

Check out Twitter feeds for the company going public. You'll often get a sense of the buzz for the deal. Another helpful source is Stocktwits.com.

Discussion Groups

These can be very worthwhile for investors who want expert answers to questions. But you should also be skeptical of what you read on message boards—there is no real way of knowing who is posting a message. True, it could be from someone who understands the investment. But the respondent may also be a former investor who has an ax to grind or the CEO who wants to pump up the stock.

Disregard messages like "This stock will go up 600 percent in two months" or "This stock will definitely go bust."

In fact, a variety of phony IPOs have been orchestrated by using discussion groups. Be skeptical of information that seems too good to be true.

Industry Publications

These can be extremely helpful when researching IPOs. There are many specialized trade websites for industries like biotech, energy, and technology. For example, if you are thinking about buying stock in a company in the social networking space, a good idea would be to look at sites like Techcrunch, Pandodaily.com, and Venturebeat.com.

Company Websites

If you want information on a specific company, why not go right to the source? Looking at the website of the company can be a tremendous resource. You will see press releases, bios on the management, a customer/partner list, testimonials, case studies, and a lot of other detailed content. But as you might suspect, this isn't the place to look for unbiased, hard-hitting data. Expect to find mostly public relations–approved news.

Your Broker

A final source of information on IPOs is your stockbroker. Many brokerage firms have access to research that is not accessible to the general public. And if you're lucky, your broker may have heard the buzz on the Street regarding an upcoming IPO and be willing to share information with you.

But be wary. Brokerage research—which is also known as sell-side research—may not be the best. Keep in mind that often the firm will be involved in the underwriting of the company's IPO. While there have been reforms aimed at making it more unbiased, investors should still look at alternative sources as well as do their own analysis. In Chapter 10, we'll look into more detail on sell-side research.

Conclusion

I'm a bit biased, but my IPOPlaybook.com is a way to get up-to-date information and analysis on IPOs. In addition, IPO Home is an excellent resource. But more than anything, make sure you get the S-1 filing first at EDGAR. This is the key document to base your investment decisions on. Finally, it is also a good idea to look at the road show on RetailRoadshow. It's a way to get a sense of the CEO and the main focus of the company.

CHAPTER 5

Making Sense of the Prospectus

Most of the specifics you need to evaluate an initial public offering (IPO) are contained in the prospectus. The company is required by law to disclose all material information—the good, the bad, and oftentimes the ugly. It's all in there.

And it can be overwhelming. Keep in mind that the prospectus can easily be hundreds of pages. You'll also find in-depth disclosures on complicated accounting principles as well as legal matters, such as for patents.

Because of all this, professional investors do not read the whole prospectus (which is also referred to as the S-1). There's simply not enough time to do this. Like any financial document, the key is understanding the relevant parts. The good news is that a prospectus must conform to rigorous format standards. This makes it even easier to scan the document.

At the same time, the Securities and Exchange Commission (SEC) has also adopted plain-English rules for drafting prospectuses. These rules require that the cover pages, the summary, and the risk factors sections be easy to understand, for obvious reasons. Basically, the issuer must comply with these three rules:

1. Short sentences with concrete, everyday language
2. Active, rather than passive, voice
3. Bulleted lists for complex information, absolutely no legal jargon, and no multiple negatives.

To help promote plain-English rules, the SEC vows that it will delay approval for registration statements and prospectuses that do not comply. This happy development makes it much easier to analyze an IPO prospectus.

Getting a Copy of the Prospectus

There are several ways to get a copy of the prospectus. One way is to go to the SEC's EDGAR database, which is at www.sec.gov. You will do the following three steps:

1. Click the "Search for Company Filings" link.
2. Click the "Company or fund name" link.
3. Enter the name of the company. Make sure you spell it right; unfortunately, EDGAR's searching technology is a bit archaic and you'll get no results from the query if you misspell it.

You will then see a page like the one in Figure 5.1.

These are the most recent SEC filings for Facebook.

On February 1, 2012, the company filed an S-1. After this, the company filed a variety of S-1/A forms. These are disclosures that are based on the amendments from the SEC. You'll typically see eight to 10 of these before a company files its final prospectus, which is denoted as Form 424B4. After this, the company will start to file ongoing reports like 8-Ks, 10-Ks, and 10-Qs.

Besides EDGAR, there are a variety of premium services to access IPO filings. One is Morningstar Document Research at www.10kwizard.com. The service has helpful features like financial ratios, documents on foreign companies, downloads to Excel, redline changes (from document to document), alerts, and sophisticated searching capabilities. However, the service is not cheap. It is based on annual subscriptions that range from $779 to $1,339.

So while EDGAR is not as robust, it is usually enough for many investors.

Main Sections

As you continue reading prospectuses, the process will get easier and faster. But like anything else, it takes practice. As you read through this chapter, it's a good idea to have a sample prospectus in front of you to look at as the pertinent sections are described here.

A prospectus usually has between 20 and 30 sections. These 24 sections are the most common ones investors should expect to see:

1. Prospectus Summary
2. Risk Factors
3. Letter from Our Founder
4. Special Note Regarding Forward-Looking Statements

5. Market Data and User Metrics
6. Use of Proceeds
7. Dividend Policy
8. Capitalization
9. Dilution
10. Selected Consolidated Financial Data
11. Management's Discussion and Analysis of Financial Condition and Results of Operations
12. Business
13. Management

FIGURE 5.1   SEC EDGAR Filings for Facebook

U.S. Securities and Exchange Commission

Home | Latest Filings | Previous Page

EDGAR Search Results

Search the Next-Generation EDGAR System

SEC Home » Search the Next-Generation EDGAR System » Company Search » *Current Page*

Facebook Inc CIK#: 0001326801 (see all company filings)
SIC: 7370 - SERVICES-COMPUTER PROGRAMMING, DATA PROCESSING, ETC.
State location: CA
(Assistant Director Office: 3)
Get insider transactions for this issuer.

Business Address: 1601 WILLOW ROAD / MENLO PARK CA 94025 / 650-618-7714
Mailing Address: 1601 WILLOW ROAD / MENLO PARK CA 94025

Filter Results: Filing Type: | Prior to: (YYYYMMDD) | Ownership? ☉ include ◉ exclude ☉ only | Limit Results Per Page 40 Entries | Search | Show All

Items 1 - 24 RSS Feed

Filings	Format	Description	Filed/Effective	File/Film Number
S-8	Documents	Securities to be offered to employees in employee benefit plans / Acc-no: 0001193125-12-241917 (33 Act) Size: 710 KB	2012-05-21	333-181566 12859534
424B4	Documents	Prospectus [Rule 424(b)(4)] / Acc-no: 0001193125-12-240111 (33 Act) Size: 7 MB	2012-05-18	333-179287 12855943
CT ORDER	Documents	Confidential treatment order / Acc-no: 9999999997-12-009764 (33 Act) Size: 10 KB	2012-05-18	333-179287 12853970
EFFECT	Documents	Notice of Effectiveness / Acc-no: 9999999995-12-001584 (33 Act) Size: 1 KB	2012-05-17 16:01:00	333-179287 12853793
S-1/A	Documents	[Amend]General form for registration of securities under the Securities Act of 1933 / Acc-no: 0001193125-12-235588 (33 Act) Size: 6 MB	2012-05-16	333-179287 12847255
S-1/A	Documents	[Amend]General form for registration of securities under the Securities Act of 1933 / Acc-no: 0001193125-12-232582 (33 Act) Size: 6 MB	2012-05-15	333-179287 12840860
CERTNAS	Documents	[Paper]Certification by the National Association of Securities Dealers Automated Quotation approving securities for listing / Acc-no: 9999999997-12-009505 (34 Act) Size: 1 KB	2012-05-14	001-35551 12027125
8-A12B	Documents	Registration of securities [Section 12(b)] / Acc-no: 0001193125-12-230161 (34 Act) Size: 14 KB	2012-05-14	001-35551 12837020
FWP	Documents	Filing under Securities Act Rules 163/433 of free writing prospectuses / Acc-no: 0001193125-12-222498 (34 Act) Size: 21 KB	2012-05-09	333-179287 12826822
S-1/A	Documents	[Amend]General form for registration of securities under the Securities Act of 1933 / Acc-no: 0001193125-12-222368 (33 Act) Size: 6 MB	2012-05-09	333-179287 12826586
S-1/A	Documents	[Amend]General form for registration of securities under the Securities Act of 1933 / Acc-no: 0001193125-12-208192 (33 Act) Size: 6 MB	2012-05-03	333-179287 12809344
S-1/A	Documents	[Amend]General form for registration of securities under the Securities Act of 1933 / Acc-no: 0001193125-12-175673 (33 Act) Size: 6 MB	2012-04-23	333-179287 12773060
S-1/A	Documents	[Amend]General form for registration of securities under the Securities Act of 1933 / Acc-no: 0001193125-12-134663 (33 Act) Size: 5 MB	2012-03-27	333-179287 12717970
S-1/A	Documents	[Amend]General form for registration of securities under the Securities Act of 1933 / Acc-no: 0001193125-12-101422 (33 Act) Size: 7 MB	2012-03-07	333-179287 12674993
S-1/A	Documents	[Amend]General form for registration of securities under the Securities Act of 1933 / Acc-no: 0001193125-12-046715 (33 Act) Size: 4 MB	2012-02-08	333-179287 12582350
S-1	Documents	General form for registration of securities under the Securities Act of 1933 / Acc-no: 0001193125-12-034517 (33 Act) Size: 6 MB	2012-02-01	333-179287 12563103
NO ACT	Documents	[Paper]No Action Letter / Acc-no: 9999999997-08-043090 (34 Act) Size: 1 KB	2008-10-14	021-76945 08058683
REGDEX/A	Documents	[Amend][Paper]Notice of Sale of Securities [Regulation D and Section 4(6) of the Securities Act of 1933], item 06 / Acc-no: 9999999997-06-030858 (34 Act) Size: 1 KB	2006-07-10	021-76945 06042267
REGDEX	Documents	[Paper]Notice of Sale of Securities [Regulation D and Section 4(6) of the Securities Act of 1933], item 06 / Acc-no: 9999999997-06-019912 (34 Act) Size: 1 KB	2006-05-08	021-76945 06035743

14. Executive Compensation
15. Certain Relationships and Related-Person Transactions
16. Principal and Selling Stockholders
17. Description of Capital Stock
18. Shares Eligible for Future Sale
19. Material United States Federal Income Tax Consequences to Non-U.S.
    Holders of Our Class A Common Stock
20. Underwriting
21. Legal Matters
22. Experts
23. Where You Can Find More Information
24. Index to Consolidated Financial Statements

The remainder of this chapter explains the portions of the prospectus that
IPO investors need to understand and to focus on.

Front Matter

The first section of the prospectus is called the front page. And yes, it all fits
on one page. This is where you'll find some basic reference information on the
company. Figure 5.2 shows the front page for Zynga Inc.

As you can see, the company is based in San Francisco. You'll also see
names and addresses of the company's lawyers.

It's really not much information. Instead, the next page, shown in Figure 5.3,
is more important.

This page shows that Zynga plans to offer 100 million shares of Class
A common stock. The price range is $8.50 to $10.00 per share, which may
change. If it is boosted, then that is a clear sign of strong demand for the
offering. Of course, a drop in the price range is very ominous; in fact, it may
mean that the IPO may not even get done.

In most cases, a company will have only one class of stock. But Zynga
is different. It actually has three classes: A, B, and C. All shares are identical
except for the voting rights. Essentially, this is known as a dual-share structure
and is meant to keep voting control with the founders.

In most cases, all the capital from the offering will go to the company.
This is known as a primary offering. But sometimes the company's founders,
directors, and investors will sell their shares as well. This is called a secondary offering, which actually gets confusing because this is also the name used
when a company has a sale of its shares after its IPO.

If you see an IPO in which the founders and officers are selling 30 percent or more of the amount being offered, it may mean that they are bailing

FIGURE 5.2   Zynga Front Page

out; in other words, these individuals may not believe in the long-term viability of their company but want to get as much cash as possible on the day of the offering. This should be a red flag for IPO investors.

You can find the names and amounts for the secondary offering in the section called "Principal and Selling Stockholders."

The front matter will also state where the shares will be listed, usually the New York Stock Exchange or NASDAQ.

The lead underwriters are also listed. The main one is always on the top-left.

The underwriters also get the right to purchase additional shares, which is known as the green shoe. This is meant to help better manage the supply and demand of the shares once the stock begins trading.

You'll also see the following disclaimer:

> The Securities and Exchange Commission and state securities regulators have not approved or disapproved these securities or determined if this prospectus is truthful or complete.

FIGURE 5.3 Zynga Stock Offer Plan

100,000,000 Shares

zynga

Class A Common Stock

ynga Inc. is offering 100,000,000 shares of its Class A common stock. This is our initial public offering, and no public market currently exists for our Class A common stock. We nticipate that the initial public offering price will be between $8.50 and $10.00 per share.

ollowing this offering, we will have three classes of authorized common stock, Class A common stock, Class B common stock and Class C common stock. The rights of the holders f each class will be identical, except with respect to voting and conversion. Each share of Class A common stock will be entitled to one vote per share. Each share of Class B ommon stock will be entitled to seven votes per share. Each share of Class C common stock will be entitled to 70 votes per share. Each share of the Class B common stock and lass C common stock will be convertible at any time into one share of Class A common stock. Outstanding shares of Class B common stock will represent approximately 72.5% of e voting power of our outstanding capital stock following this offering, and outstanding shares of Class C common stock will represent approximately 25.7% of the voting power f our outstanding capital stock following this offering. Mark Pincus, our founder and Chief Executive Officer, holds shares of Class B common stock and all of the shares of lass C common stock and will control approximately 36.2% of the total voting power of our outstanding capital stock immediately following this offering.

e have applied to list our Class A common stock on the NASDAQ Global Select Market under the symbol "ZNGA."

nvesting in our Class A common stock involves risks. See "Risk Factors" beginning on page 14.

PRICE $ A SHARE

	Price to Public	Underwriting Discounts and Commissions	Proceeds to Zynga
er Share	$	$	$
otal	$	$	$

ertain of our stockholders have granted the underwriters the right to purchase up to an additional 15,000,000 shares of Class A common stock to cover over-allotments. We will ot receive any proceeds from the sale of shares by the selling stockholders.

he Securities and Exchange Commission and state securities regulators have not approved or disapproved these securities or determined if this prospectus is truthful or complete. ny representation to the contrary is a criminal offense.

he underwriters expect to deliver the shares of Class A common stock to purchasers on , 2011.

IORGAN STANLEY *GOLDMAN, SACHS & CO.*

BofA MERRILL LYNCH *BARCLAYS CAPITAL* *J.P. MORGAN*

ALLEN & COMPANY LLC

, 2011

In other words, the SEC will not advise whether the offering is a good or bad investment; it is not in the business of recommending stocks. It is up to you to decide whether the investment has potential. The SEC simply maintains that the company has complied with the securities laws, such as disclosing the necessary information in the right format.

Graphic Material

In some prospectuses, there will be a variety of graphics. Keep in mind that the SEC does not want these to be promotional. It is part of the goal of trying to protect investors.

But these graphics can be a good way to get a sense of the firm. With Zynga, one graphic shows that the company's games are for all platforms—PCs, mobile devices, and tablets (see Figure 5.4). Another graphic (Figure 5.5) provides a good rundown on the metrics of the business.

FIGURE 5.4 Zynga Graphic—Platforms

Qualification Requirements

In some prospectuses, but not all, you'll see a section just before the Prospectus Summary that's entitled "Qualification Requirements."

Investors beware. Qualification requirements mean that a state or the SEC deems the offering to be highly risky and that only high-net-worth individuals may participate. Such a restriction can have a severely negative impact on an offering.

FIGURE 5.5   Zynga Graphic—Metrics of Business

Prospectus Summary

Make sure you read this section. All in all, it is a quick way to get a good sense of the overall company.

Some of the key points I look for are the following.

Core Focus

Does the company have a core focus that you understand? If not, then stay away. Some businesses are truly complicated and may have unproven business models.

Basically, you want a good elevator pitch. This means a vision that can be said during, well, an elevator ride.

Zynga's is actually quite good:

> We founded Zynga in 2007 with the vision that play—like search, share and shop—would become one of the core activities on the Internet. As a pioneer of online social games, we have made them accessible, social and fun. We are excited that games have grown to become the second most popular online activity in the United States by time spent, even surpassing email. We have a lot of hard work, innovation and growth ahead of us to create a future where social games are a daily habit for nearly everyone.

Growth Metrics

Get a feel for the main ways to gauge a company's progress. It could actually be more than just looking at the financials. For example, Zynga highlights some interesting metrics that showed how users love playing its social games:

- An average of 227 million monthly active users in 175 countries.
- $2 billion in cumulative bookings since its inception in 2007.
- Largest player audience on Facebook, with more users than the next eight social game developers combined.
- Strong portfolio of games like CityVille, FarmVille, Mafia Wars, Words with Friends, and Zynga Poker.

Business Model

It should be clear how the company generates revenues. Zynga pioneered a free-to-play approach. However, game players pay a fee to get an edge, such as pay real cash for things like extra energy or a digital item like a pick.

Market Size and Growth

The Prospectus Summary section will usually have useful information on the areas of market size and growth. Often, these are references to third-party market researchers. Some companies will hire an organization to do this work. In such cases, the research is probably not as valuable.

Zynga provides several sources of research. One is about the market for social networking. The company points to a report from International Data Corporation (IDC) estimating that the population of users will go from 1.1 billion globally in 2011 to 1.6 billion by 2014. In other words, there is still a large number of potential users for Zynga's games.

The company also references a report from In-Stat regarding the market for in-game virtual goods. It forecasts that the size of that market will double to $7.3 billion by 2014.

Place of Incorporation

The Summary section will also state where the company has been incorporated. In most cases, this is in Delaware. The main reason is that Delaware has a long history with corporate law, and the courts tend to act quickly. The judges also are usually pro-management.

But sometimes a company may incorporate in an offshore setting, such as in the Caymans. The reason may be to pay lower taxes, but it also could mean a ploy for avoiding liability exposure.

Risk Factors

The fact that a prospectus lists risks doesn't, in itself, mean that the IPO is a bad investment. In fact, a prospectus that fails to list any risks would probably never receive SEC approval. After all, by nature investments are never entirely free from uncertainty. Chapter 9 goes into greater detail on some of the more significant risk factors investors should watch for. Here are some of them in brief:

- *Need for more financing.* Some types of companies—such as in the biotech industry—need huge amounts of capital. The IPO often does not raise enough money for the company to continue operating.
- *Going concern.* When a company's auditor believes that it may go bust within a year or so, this is called going concern risk.
- *Small market potential.* Though a company may have a great product, the size of the opportunity may be small. To continue to grow, it will need to expand into new categories, which is never easy.
- *Legal proceedings.* Lawsuits are difficult to quantify. What's more, lawsuits can drain resources and divert the attention of management away from business operations.
- *Inexperienced management team.* Running a public company requires an experienced management team. Managers who are not qualified will often cause major problems for the company.
- *Competition.* This is always an issue for a company. But some industries have especially fierce competition. For example, when Groupon went public, there were over 1,000 rival services.

- *Reliance on the government.* This is common for certain types of industries like health care and renewable energy. But government support can be very fickle.
- *Product concentration.* Relying on a single product is risky. If the customer base dries up or the product becomes outdated, the impact can be substantial.
- *Limited history of profitable operations.* It's common for unprofitable companies to go public. The main reason is that management is focused on growth. But there are some companies that—because of the business model or the competition—may never reach profitability.

Letter from Our Founder

Although not common, some companies will have a letter from the founder. This sets forth the overall vision of the company and also provides some insight into the culture. Some notable ones include Google and Groupon.

Google

The co-founders—Sergey Brin and Larry Page—were clear about their vision of the company. It was to "provide a great service to the world—instantly delivering relevant information on any topic. Serving our end users is at the heart of what we do and remains our number one priority." To do this, Brin and Page said that they would look at the long term when making decisions, even if it meant lower profitability. In fact, they even said they would not provide any quarterly guidance for investors.

Groupon

The co-founder and CEO, Andrew Mason, is not a typical CEO. Consider that he actually had a video of himself on YouTube doing yoga—in his underwear.

But Mason proved to be skilled in pioneering a new industry, called daily deals. It was a unique way to allow local merchants to sell vouchers to allow customers to get cut-rate deals. As a result, Groupon grew at hyperspeed.

Mason's letter certainly reflected his goofiness. In it, he said: "Life is too short to be a boring company."

But there was a part of the letter that concerned the SEC. It had the title "We don't measure ourselves in conventional ways." Well, the SEC usually likes conventional approaches to accounting.

In that section, Mason talked about a unique way of calculating profit called adjusted consolidated segment operating income (adjusted CSOI). It essentially excluded marketing costs, which were substantial.

The SEC required that the letter be modified to provide more details about the metric as well as the statement: "While we track this management metric internally to gauge our performance, we encourage you to base your investment decision on whatever metrics make you comfortable."

Market Data and User Metrics

This section is often found with technology companies—and it usually provides extremely helpful information. Zynga stated that it sees its target market as being for "global entertainment." Based on research from IDC, IBISWorld, and Screen Digest, the market was over $1 trillion in 2011.

Even more interesting information came in the "user metrics" section. Here the company showed how it tracks its progress in daily active users, monthly active users, and monthly unique users.

Another key metric was "virtual items created every second." It is a key way to measure the level of passion and engagement for Zynga's games.

Use of Proceeds

As the name implies, the Use of Proceeds section indicates what a company intends to do with the money it raises in the IPO. In many cases, this section is vague. This is how Zynga expressed it:

> As of the date of this prospectus, we cannot specify with certainty all of the particular uses for the net proceeds to us of this offering. However, we currently intend to use the net proceeds to us from this offering primarily for general corporate purposes, including working capital, game development, marketing activities and capital expenditures.

However, investors should look for certain things. For example, you will often see an estimation of how long the company will survive on the infusion of IPO capital. In most cases, it is more than one year—but keep in mind that this is only a guess. Many things can happen to a company, good and bad. If more than 50 percent of the proceeds from an IPO are earmarked for outstanding debts, chances are that the company has dismal growth prospects. Besides, investors want to buy shares in a company that expects to grow, not just pay off liabilities.

This was a big issue with a variety of companies that were backed by private equity firms. Keep in mind that the core strategy of private equity firms is to use huge amounts of debt to buy companies and then eventually take them public again. But between 2010 and 2011 investors resisted this move. And for those IPOs that were able to get off the ground, there were some lackluster performers, like Hospital Corporation of America (HCA).

Dividend Policy

For the most part, companies that do IPOs don't pay dividends. The reason is that most of them will invest the IPO capital back into their operations in order to accelerate growth.

But there are some industries that do pay dividends. Real estate investment trusts (REITs), for example, are required by law to distribute at least 95 percent of their annual taxable income to shareholders in the form of dividends. Other industries that pay dividends include banks, insurance companies, and energy operators.

On occasion, you will see a major dividend distribution when the IPO is initiated. This is always a one-time event with the purpose of providing liquidity for the owners of the company, who, in most cases, founded the business years ago and are using the opportunity to cash in. It is understood that the company founders should reap the benefit of their efforts and vision, but sometimes that compensation can go too far.

Capitalization

This is a complicated section, but it does have helpful information. It provides a breakdown of all the shares outstanding as well as those securities that will turn into shares when holders of warrants and stock options exercise their rights.

For IPO investors, you can find the total shares that will be available when all of the warrants and options are exercised. This is a better gauge of the value of the company than current shares outstanding are. You will take this number and multiply it by the stock price, which will give you a market capitalization value that is on a fully diluted basis.

Dilution

Dilution is the difference between what existing shareholders (founders) and new shareholders (investors) will pay for shares. The existing shareholders usually pay a much lower price for the stock than IPO investors do. Dilution is common in all IPOs. However, sometimes it can be excessive.

This was the case with the Vringo IPO (the company is a developer of ring tones). According to the prospectus:

> The initial offering price of our units is substantially higher than the net tangible book value per share of our common stock immediately after this offering. Therefore, if you purchase our units in this offering, you will incur an immediate dilution of $3.51 (or 70%) in net tangible book value per share from the price you paid, based upon the initial public offering price of $4.60 per unit.

Selected Consolidated Financial Data

Here there will be various charts that show the income statement and balance sheet data broken down by quarters. All in all, it is an effective way to get a sense of the overall trends.

However, keep in mind that some of the quarterly data can be misleading. For example, a bad quarter may be the result of a cyclical factor and not an indication of the deterioration of the company. So if you are looking at fourth-quarter results, compare them to the fourth quarter of the prior year instead of to other quarters.

Management's Discussion and Analysis of Financial Condition and Results of Operations

The Management's Discussion and Analysis (MD&A) section is definitely a must-read. Keep in mind that the Securities and Exchange Commission spends much time on this section because of its importance.

In the MD&A, you get information on areas like:

- A brief history of the key developments of the company, such as new products and acquisitions.
- Dependence on customers and products.

- Plans for investment.
- Explanation of the business.
- Key financial and operating metrics.

Actually, there will be details about the key factors that will impact the performance of the company. Zynga listed the importance of creating new games, the dependence on a small percentage of customers who pay for virtual goods, the high costs of game development and recruitment of engineers, and the heavy dependence on Facebook.

Finally, you will see detailed analysis of the main cost centers for the company.

Business

This is an expanded version of the Prospectus Summary. In a way, it is the company's full-blown business plan. If you want to get more detail on a particular part of the company, such as its marketing approach or product line, this is the place to find it.

Two other sections that are worth looking at are "Competition" and "Litigation."

Management

This section lists the senior managers of the company and the board members. Each will be described in a one- to two-paragraph resume. As much as possible, look for a team that has prior experience in running public companies.

For the most part, Zynga has a top-notch team. Founder Mark Pincus has created several social and consumer Internet companies since the mid-1990s. He was also the chairman of Support.com, which was a public company. In terms of education, Pincus got an MBA from the Harvard Business School. By the time of the IPO, he was 45.

Other key executives include:

- Owen Van Natta, executive vice president and chief business officer: former executive at MySpace, Playlist, and Facebook.
- John Schappert, chief operating officer: former executive at Electronic Arts and Microsoft.
- David Wehner, chief financial officer: former executive at Allen & Company, an investment bank focused on media and technology.

- Cadir Lee, executive vice president and chief technology officer: former executive at Support.com.
- Reginald Davis, senior vice president and general counsel: former associate general counsel at Yahoo! and a partner for 10 years at Hancock Rothert & Bunshoft LLP (now part of Duane Morris LLP).

Here's the board:

- Brad Feld: a managing director at Foundry Group, a venture capital (VC) firm.
- William "Bing" Gordon: a partner at Kleiner Perkins Caufield & Byers, a venture capital firm and a co-founder of Electronic Arts.
- Reid Hoffman: a partner at Greylock Partners and a co-founder of LinkedIn.
- Jeffrey Katzenberg: CEO of DreamWorks Animation SKG and former executive at Disney.
- Stanley Meresman: a former venture partner with Technology Crossover Ventures.

Executive Compensation

This section provides extensive disclosure of the compensation of the executive officers and directors. There will also be details on perquisites. For example, Zynga provided Pincus with security services, as he was actually the target of a female stalker.

It is not easy to determine what is a sound compensation structure. For the most part, the market for senior executives is extremely intense, especially for those who have experience with public companies.

What's more, a big bulk of an executive's compensation is noncash. That is, it will be based on stock incentives, such as options. If the stock price increases, the payday can be huge. Consider that eBay's Meg Whitman became a billionaire because of her options.

When looking at the compensation section, there are some key themes to look for:

- *Performance.* As much as possible, look for compensation that is tied to meeting certain milestones, such as growth in revenues or profits. There are actually bonus structures that are really just guaranteed payouts! Clearly, this is a sign of a poor compensation structure.

- *Over-the-top option grants.* If you see grant levels of 10 million options or more, then this is a warning sign. Just a $1 increase in the stock price will translate into a $10 million windfall for the executive.
- *Corporate jet, country club, and helicopter.* It's fine if an executive has these toys, but make sure he or she reimburses the company.
- *Layoffs.* If these happened in the past and there were still executive bonuses, then this is an indication that management is not much concerned for the employees. It could mean that the company has poor morale.

There may also be sign-on bonuses, which can be large. It is not uncommon for a top executive—especially the CEO—to get $5 million or more. On its face, it seems obscene, but it may be reasonable. When a top executive moves from one firm to another, he or she is usually giving up wealth that was built up with options but will have to be forfeited when moving over to the new firm.

Certain Relationships and Related-Person Transactions

A related-person transaction occurs when an executive or board member has some type of extra business relationship with the company. This may mean a prior loan or a consulting arrangement. Even more troubling is when the company is doing business with another firm owned by a senior manager. Thus, the company may not get the best deal, which could hurt shareholder value.

There may even be examples of nepotism. That is, executives may hire family members. This is actually quite common in China and other countries. While it is not necessarily wrong, it may mean that there are unneeded expenditures on salaries and equity compensation.

Principal and Selling Stockholders

This section lists the major equity holders in the company. Look to see if these are well-known private equity firms or venture capital funds. If so, this should bode well for the IPO.

Zynga had top-tier VC firms like Kleiner Perkins, Institutional Venture Partners, Union Square Ventures, Foundry Venture capital, Avalon Ventures, and DST Global. There were also top-notch angel investors like Reid Hoffman.

Description of Capital Stock

Here you will find in-depth analysis of the types of stock in the company. There will usually be two types: common and preferred.

Common stock is the most basic type of ownership in a company and is represented by a physical certificate. Common stock will have certain rights, such as to vote on matters like acquisitions. And assuming there is board approval, there will be cash dividends paid. In most cases, it is common stock that is issued in an IPO.

As we saw earlier in this chapter, there may be different classes of common stock. This is to allow more voting power for the founders and executives.

These shares may also be subject to antitakeover provisions. This makes it tough for a third party to engage in a hostile takeover.

Preferred stock is known as a hybrid security because it has aspects of a bond and a stock. In terms of a bond, there is usually an automatic cash payment and there will be priority in a bankruptcy. Consider that common shareholders are last in line in this event (which means they usually wind up with nothing in a bankruptcy).

Preferred stock usually goes to VCs and private equity firms. But once a company goes public, these securities are often converted into common stock.

Shares Eligible for Future Sale

Six months after a successful IPO, you may see the stock suddenly fall, say 10 or 20 percent, for no apparent reason. The cause of such a sell-off may be that the lockup period has expired and company insiders are cashing in some of their stakes.

A lockup provision, disclosed in this section of the prospectus, gives control of a company's stock to the underwriters for a limited period of time. Essentially, venture capitalists, founders, and senior executives are restricted from selling their stock for about 120 to 180 days to prevent major selling pressure.

When the lockup period expires, however, the holders of the stock may want to start selling, especially if the stock has increased a great deal in price and appears to be overvalued. Investors should be aware of the lockup expiration date and realize that they may see some shares changing hands and some price movement at that time.

Index to Consolidated Financial Statements

This section of the prospectus includes the full financial statements of the company: the balance sheet, income statement, and statement of cash flows. In the next three chapters, we will take an in-depth look at each, and will also look at financial ratio analysis.

Miscellaneous Sections

At the end of the Form S-1, you will see sections like "Underwriting," "Legal Matters," and "Experts." Usually these sections provide information that is not of much concern for investors.

Conclusion

Congratulations to the reader. You have just made your way through the most important parts of an IPO prospectus. Remember: The prospectus is an investor's best friend. It contains most of the information you need to make your investment decision.

CHAPTER 6

Balance Sheet

When it comes to analyzing an initial public offering (IPO), the financials will be critical. The prospectus will actually have various sections that repeat the financials as well as provide in-depth explanations; one is called the Management's Discussion and Analysis (MD&A) section. No doubt, to make a good evaluation of the stock, you will need a good foundation in understanding the core elements: the balance sheet, income statement, and statement of cash flows.

In this chapter, we take a look at the balance sheet. To understand it, we'll use Buffalo Wild Wings Inc. as an example. The company got its start in 1982 near Ohio State University and then 10 years later began an aggressive expansion with a franchise strategy.

In November 2003, the company went public by raising $51 million. At the time, the company operated 227 restaurants in 28 states. The key menu items included Buffalo, New York–style chicken wings spun in one of 12 signature sauces.

The IPO would go on to generate a return of 645 percent for its investors.

Some Fundamentals

Before diving into the balance sheet, it is first important to look at some of the critical concepts of accounting. These actually go back to the fourteenth century. As European economies began to grow and capitalism started to flourish, there was a need to track financial transactions. If not, it would be nearly impossible to make business decisions. Besides, accounting helped companies avoid fraudulent schemes like embezzlements.

Many of the key principles of accounting came from Luca Pacioli, who devised the system known as double-entry bookkeeping. It's really a simple approach. That is, every transaction should balance. For example, if a company makes a purchase of equipment, it should increase the asset section. But it will also reduce the cash balance. Doing this ensures much consistency to financial reports.

Since then, accounting principles have evolved. As for the United States, a key point was the formation of the Securities and Exchange Commission (SEC) during the 1930s. After all, it enforced the disclosure of financials. Before then, the rules were fairly loosey-goosey, which resulted in many fraudulent enterprises that helped lead to the crash of 1929 and the Great Depression.

Another important development was the creation of generally accepted accounting principles (GAAP). Keep in mind that all IPO filings must conform to the standards, which can be complex and sometimes vague. But again, they have been crucial in helping investors evaluate investments.

GAAP is an evolving set of principles based on the work of a variety of organizations. These include the American Institute of Certified Public Accountants (AICPA), the Financial Accounting Standards Board (FASB), the Public Company Accounting Oversight Board (PCAOB), and, yes, the SEC.

Despite all the complexity, there are some core principles to keep in mind.

Historical Costs

The principle of historical costs means that when a company purchases an asset, it is valued at what was paid for it. It's really that simple. The reason is that it would be too subjective to create a model to place a true value for the asset.

But the historical cost principle can still cause distortions in the financials. After all, suppose Facebook bought property in Palo Alto for $5 million. But a few years later, it has doubled in value. Well, the value of the property on the books must still be $5 million. There are no exceptions.

Because of this, some investors will try to estimate the private market value of a company's assets.

Accrual Accounting

This involves two key principles. First, a company must recognize revenues when they are earned, not when cash is received. For example, let's say Facebook gets an order for $1 million in advertising. In this situation, the company will report this as revenue, even though payment may not come until a month or more has passed.

Second, a company must recognize expenses when they are incurred, not when it makes a cash payment. So, continuing with our example, let's suppose that Facebook purchases $200,000 worth of office supplies. It will have to report this as a current expense regardless of when it pays for the supplies.

Why do all this? It is to conform to yet another concept: the matching principle. This means that a company needs to report all expenses that relate to the relevant revenue. This gives a truer picture of the financial position.

Balance Sheet Overview

The balance sheet includes a company's assets, liabilities, and equity. No doubt investors want to see a strong balance sheet, which usually means growing assets and minimal liabilities. Yet this is not essential. For the most part, IPOs are small companies that usually do not have large asset bases. In fact, the key assets may be severely undervalued or not even reported—such as a patent portfolio or a brand.

A balance sheet is essentially a snapshot of a company's financial position at a specific point in time. As you can see with the Buffalo Wild Wings balance sheet, the statement is as of a certain day for a three-year period.

Buffalo Wild Wings Balance Sheet
December 30, 2001, December 29, 2002, and September 28, 2003
(Dollar amounts in thousands)

Assets	December 30, 2001	December 29, 2002	September 28, 2003
Current Assets			
Cash and cash equivalents	$7,388	$4,652	$6,564
Accounts receivable	696	637	715
Accounts receivable—other	2,375	4,309	1,340
Inventory	651	784	907
Income tax receivable	0	1,008	0
Prepaid expenses	539	533	1,272
Deferred income taxes	820	733	734
Total current assets	12,469	12,656	11,532
Property and equipment, net	26,485	34,874	39,661
Restricted cash	424	1,369	1,675

(Continued)

Assets	December 30, 2001	December 29, 2002	September 28, 2003
Marketing fund receivables	263	370	0
Other assets	666	713	692
Goodwill	664	759	759
Total assets	40,971	50,741	54,319
Liabilities and Stockholders' Equity			
Current Liabilities			
Unearned franchise fees	1,009	1,043	1,602
Accounts payable	2,920	3,301	1,602
Accrued income taxes	947	0	591
Accrued compensation and benefits	2,865	4,133	4,027
Accrued expenses	2,239	2,299	2,507
Current portion of long-term debt	189	205	217
Current portion of deferred lease credits	217	229	489
Current portion of obligations under capital leases	2,617	3,617	4,099
Total current liabilities	13,003	14,827	15,134
Marketing fund payables	577	1,739	1,675
Accrued income taxes	111	0	0
Deferred income taxes	1,330	3,328	3,403
Long-term debt, net of current portion	697	502	338
Deferred lease credits, net of current portion	3,321	4,958	5,317
Obligations under capital leases, net of current portion	4,678	5,036	5,209
Total liabilities	23,717	30,390	31,076
Preferred stock	10,331	11,788	12,992
Common stock	1,842	1,862	2,413
Retained earnings	5,081	6,701	7,838
Total common stockholders' equity	6,923	8,563	10,251
Total liabilities and stockholders' equity	40,971	50,741	54,319

You'll also notice that the full numbers are not reported. Instead, they are in thousands. So in the "Cash" item for 2003, the figure of $6,564 is really $6,564,000. This is to make it easier for investors to read the statement and is common for financial statements.

Another convention is that when a number is in parentheses this indicates a negative amount.

What's more, as you read the items on the balance sheet, some of them may be vague descriptions. But the good news is that there should be footnotes to the statement that explain things.

The Assets

An asset is what a company owns, and these are put into certain categories. What's more, they are listed in order of their liquidity. That is, cash and the assets that can be easily converted into cash are listed first.

Actually, the most liquid assets are put into a large category called current assets. These are items that should be easy to convert into cash within a year. The main current assets include cash and cash equivalents, marketable securities, accounts receivable, and inventory.

Cash and Cash Equivalents

This category includes the cash in checking accounts, savings accounts, and petty cash (which are for small emergencies). For an IPO, it is typical to have under $100 million in cash. But in some cases, the amounts can be substantial. For example, Facebook had over $3 billion in its bank account. All in all, it was a sign that the company was a huge cash generator and had little problem raising capital—which are always good signs for investors.

As for Buffalo Wild Wings, its cash balance was reasonable. Essentially, it looked like management was taking a fairly steady approach to growth, without jeopardizing its liquidity.

Marketable Securities

Cash and cash equivalents have extremely low yields. So to better returns, a company will often invest large amounts of excess cash in marketable securities. These include commercial paper, Treasury bills, and certificates of deposit (CDs).

But these are not necessarily fail-safe. Keep in mind that from 2000 to 2007 high-yielding marketable securities emerged that were based on complex investment vehicles, like derivatives. Unfortunately, during the financial crisis, these securities became illiquid and some companies incurred substantial losses.

As a result, the SEC now requires disclosures on the risks of marketable securities. In light of the financial crisis, the trend is to focus on highly conservative investments.

Accounts Receivable

In many cases, it can take 30 days or more to receive cash from a sale to a customer. If payment is made earlier, there may even be a discount on the purchase.

The amount of cash owed on the sale is an asset called an account receivable. The asset is usually fairly liquid, and some companies even use accounts receivable for financing. That is, they may sell these assets to a third party to get cash more quickly. However, if you see this practice, be careful. This type of financing, called factoring, can be expensive. It may also be a sign that a company is having trouble with its cash flows.

Also be concerned if you see notes receivable. These are more formal arrangements with customers, which may include interest penalties and collateral to back up the obligation. In some cases, notes receivable are used when a customer is having trouble paying its accounts receivable. In other words, it means that the customer base may be weak.

Even more worrisome are long-term receivables. These are customer contracts that are likely to not be collected for at least a year.

But some types of companies have low levels of receivables, such as restaurants. The reason is that customers pay in cash or credit cards. But if a restaurant has franchises—like Buffalo Wild Wings has—there will usually be a large amount of receivables. These are cash payments, such as for royalties, that will eventually go to the parent company.

Allowance for Doubtful Accounts

Unfortunately, some customers will fail to pay their bills. And it's fairly normal.

To deal with this, a company will have an estimate for these nonpayments, which is called an allowance for doubtful accounts. To find this figure, you will probably need to do a word search on the S-1 form, but it is worth it.

The reason is that the metric can be an easy way for companies to manipulate their financials. For example, suppose a company booked sales of $50 million for the year and had an allowance for doubtful accounts of $1 million. This means the company will report net sales of $49 million.

But let's suppose the estimate was too optimistic and there were actually $3 million in nonpaying customers. The company will need to take charge and lower its revenues to $47 million. For Wall Street, this would be a big surprise and would likely mean a drop in the stock price.

So when analyzing the S-1, look to see if the company has been lowering the allowance for doubtful accounts. If so, it could be a telltale sign that there will be trouble ahead.

Another way to get a sense of the trends in the accounts receivable is to compute the days sales outstanding (DSO). It shows how long it takes to convert accounts receivable into cash. Here's the formula:

$$DSO = (Ending\ receivables/Credit\ revenue) \times Number\ of\ days\ in\ period$$

First, it is a good idea to compare this to DSOs of competitors. Is it higher than the industry average? If so, this could mean that the company is having trouble getting payments from customers.

Next, it is a good idea to compare the rate of growth in receivables to sales. If the accounts receivable are growing faster than sales, this is certainly ominous. It could indicate that the company is selling its products to dicey customers. Or it could be a sign of what is called "stuffing the channel." This means sending products to a company even though there has been no purchase order.

In any case, the quality of the revenues may be suspect, and the company may run into some major problems over the next year or so.

Inventory

Inventory comes in three forms:

1. *Raw materials.* These are the main commodities used to make the final product. For Buffalo Wild Wings, the main raw material is fresh chicken.

   The important things to watch about raw materials are the supply and demand trends in the commodities markets. Are there shortages? An oversupply? These can have a major impact on a company's profitability.

   In some cases, a company may engage in sophisticated strategies like hedging. This includes buying futures contracts on the commodities to help mitigate any rise in prices. But this strategy is far from foolproof and can be costly.

2. *Work in progress.* For the most part, this is for a manufacturing firm and represents inventory that has been modified but has yet to be turned into a product.
3. *Finished goods.* These are products ready to be shipped to customers.

Unfortunately, sometimes there is little demand. This often happens with apparel makers when there are changes in the seasons or consumer tastes. To deal with this, a company will need to write off the inventory, which will result in a loss. If you see this on a frequent basis, it is an indication that a company does not have a good sense of the market fundamentals. It may also be a sign of low quality.

In other words, inventory is a big cost. This is why it is critical to focus on those companies that know how to create efficient systems. A classic one is Dell.

In the first few years after its IPO, Dell had poor inventory systems. The result was that the stock was a laggard until the mid-1990s.

Like all its peers, Dell made substantial purchases of raw materials—like memory chips and microprocessors—that were based on forecasted demand. But it was extremely tough to gauge customer expenditures.

Dell realized it needed a better approach, so it pioneered the build-to-order process. That is, the company ordered components as purchase orders came in. It was not easy to create the infrastructure to pull this off, but it became a key differentiator as many other PC manufacturers went bust.

By having low levels of inventory, Dell had much more cash on hand. This made it easier to grow as well as to invest even more resources into its infrastructure. From 1994 to 1998 revenues went from $2 billion to $16 billion.

Thus, analyzing inventory is often critical. And there are some useful analytic tools to help out. One of the most common is the inventory turnover ratio, which is measured as follows:

Inventory turnover ratio = Cost of goods sold/Average inventory

Compare this company's metric against those of others in the industry and also track the trends. If it is falling at a steady rate, that should result in stronger profits and cash flows.

Taxes

In the Buffalo Wild Wings balance sheet, you will see several assets for taxes. These are for refunds or other monies owed by governments. While these are a source of cash, they are often ignored by investors since they are really not part of the core function of the business, and they are often quite volatile.

Prepaid Expenses

Prepaid expenses are known as "soft assets." These may have other names like "software development costs," "other assets," or "other noncurrent assets." To get an understanding of these items, you should take a look at the footnotes.

One thing to be wary of is capitalization of expenses. Yes, this is when a company turns a current expense into an asset. How? It is most common for marketing expenses. For example, a company will spend $10 million on a marketing campaign. However, the customers that result from this effort will likely generate ongoing revenues, so the temptation is to recognize only a part of the total amount of marketing expenditure as a current expense. This may make some sense and it means that profits will be higher, at least in the short run. But in the end, it is likely to be misleading and usually an artificial boost.

Property and Equipment

This includes plant and capital equipment. For a restaurant, this category is usually the biggest asset. And this is certainly the case with Buffalo Wild Wings, which had $39.6 million in property and equipment in 2003.

The balance sheet also has the word *net*. This means that the assets were added to the balance sheet at their original cost but have been reduced over time by depreciation. Depreciation is a way to account for the loss in value of an asset, such as by wear and tear and obsolescence.

Assets will fall into certain categories that have fixed time periods for depreciation. Computers, which go obsolete quickly, have a term of five years. A building, in contrast, depreciates over 30 years.

One common approach is for a company to use straight-line depreciation. This means that an equal amount of depreciation is taken for each year. For example, suppose that Buffalo Wild Wings buys a chicken processor for $1 million and its term of depreciation is 10 years. In this case, the company will take depreciation charges of $100,000 per year.

A company also has the option of using a variety of accelerated depreciation methods. That is, a company can take a higher percentage in the early years. This often depends on government policies that encourage investment in new capital equipment. In fact, after the financial crisis of 2008, the federal government offered several lucrative accelerated depreciation methods.

Depreciation can be a way for a company to manipulate its earnings results. For example, let's say it increases the term of its depreciation on the chicken processor to 20 years. With this, the depreciation charge is only $50,000 per year.

Restricted Cash

Do not include restricted cash in a company's cash balance. Restricted cash means any funds that cannot be spent—at least not for a while. It may be a part of a long-term venture or contract.

Goodwill

Goodwill is a way for a company to account for acquisitions (Buffalo Wild Wings acquired several restaurants over its history). It is calculated as the purchase price minus the net asset value of the target. To understand this concept, let's take an example: Suppose Buffalo Wild Wings buys a company for $10 million. But the acquired company's assets are $5 million and the debts are $1 million. This means the net asset value is $4 million. But to make everything balance out, Buffalo Wild Wings must add $6 million to the balance sheet, which is the goodwill.

Why is there a gap between the purchase price and the net asset value? There are a variety of reasons. In some cases, it may be that the buyer overpaid for the company. Or it could be that the target has certain intangible assets like a strong brand, customer list, or patents.

But a company must test the goodwill every year. If there is a decline in value—known as an impairment—then there will need to be a write-off. If you see that a company has a high percentage of its assets as goodwill, say 50 percent or more, then be cautious. It may have been too aggressive with its acquisitions, which ultimately could result in losses.

The Liabilities

Current liabilities are those that generally must be paid within one year. As for long-term liabilities, these usually take more than a year to pay off. But this can be much longer, say 10 years or even 20 years.

Keep in mind that a portion of long-term liabilities will turn into current liabilities each year. If there is a debt payment that is coming due, then this can inflate the current liabilities section. This could be a dangerous sign. Interestingly, though, it could be a reason for a company to go public: to raise enough cash to pay down its debt.

Here's a look at the main types of current liabilities:

- *Unearned fees.* This category is for prepayments for franchise fees. Buffalo Wild Wings cannot recognize these as revenues since they have yet to be

earned. To deal with this, they are instead classified as assets. But over time, these unearned fees will turn into revenues. Investors want to see growth in these types of assets since they are often a sign of future revenue growth.
- *Accruals.* These are expenses that have been incurred but payments are not due. Buffalo Wild Wings has accruals for taxes, compensation/benefits, and other expenses.
- *Accounts payable.* These are amounts that are owed to vendors and suppliers.

Next, the liabilities section will list types of longer-term debt. The main ones include:

- *Note.* This is a debt that will come due in one to 10 years.
- *Bond.* This is a type of debt that has a term of five to 20 years. A company will issue these to public investors, and the securities will be traded on an exchange.
- *Mortgage.* This is a debt for buildings and property.

Finally, a company will often have leases. If it is an operating lease—which means a company must return the property after the term is up—it is not listed on the balance sheet. Instead, you will find these items in the footnotes of the financials.

However, a company must put capital leases on the balance sheet. This is a lease that transfers ownership of the property to the payor. Because of all this, some companies are tempted to focus on operating leases so as to make the debt load seem lower. Yet leases can be a major obligation and they are worth noting.

Analyzing Debt

There are some helpful ratios to use in evaluating a company's debt. A common one is the current ratio, which is calculated as follows:

$$\text{Current ratio} = \text{Current assets}/\text{Current liabilities}$$

This provides a look at a company's liquidity. Look for a current ratio of 2:1 or higher. This should be sufficient to carry on a company's operations.

Then again, if a company is highly dependent on inventory, a better option would be the quick ratio:

$$\text{Quick ratio} = (\text{Current assets} - \text{Inventory})/\text{Current liabilities}$$

This assumes that the inventory cannot be sold. If the quick ratio is 1:1 or higher, it should be relatively safe.

But liquidity is not the only criterion for investors. It is also a good idea to see whether a company has dangerous levels of debt—which could mean future problems. One calculation is the debt-to-equity ratio:

$$\text{Debt-to-equity ratio} = \text{Total debt}/\text{Total equity}$$

If this ratio is 70 percent or higher, then the company may have issues with paying its bills at some point. Actually, to get a better sense of this, you can also look at the times interest earned ratio:

$$\text{Times interest earned ratio} = \text{Earnings before interest and taxes (EBIT)}/\text{Interest expense}$$

Think of EBIT as a form of cash flow. So by comparing it to the annual interest expense, you will see whether a company has a good amount of margin to pay its obligations. A good level is 6 or 7.

Keep in mind that lenders will use the times interest earned ratio in their debt agreements. If the ratio falls below a certain level, it could mean that the company is in default. In this situation, the lenders can actually force bankruptcy, which could wipe out the shareholders.

Finally, you can take a look at a company's working capital:

$$\text{Working capital} = \text{Current assets} - \text{Current liabilities}$$

For the most part, you want to see a positive number. This means that the company can pay off its bills and not need to rely on more financing.

Be especially wary if a company has a history of negative working capital. This indicates the business model may be flawed or that management is not efficient with its resources—or both.

In rare situations, it may not matter that a company has negative working capital. The reason is that a company may defer payments to its vendors until it is paid first by its customers. This is actually a key part of Amazon.com's business model.

Equity

Equity is a residual amount that is the result of the assets minus the total liabilities. It's always good to see a positive number—and one that has been increasing over the years. But for IPOs, this is not always the case. The main reason is that many early-stage companies have substantial losses. The hope is that the company will achieve profitability, which will eventually lead to positive equity.

There are three types of equity on the balance sheet:

1. *Preferred stockholders' equity.* This is stock that goes to professional investors like venture capitalists and private equity firms. The security has special features, such as higher voting rights, veto power on major transactions, and dividends.

   Buffalo Wild Wings raised $12.9 million from investors and it was all in the form of preferred stock. But the shares were also "mandatorily redeemable," a clause that forces the investors to convert the preferred stock to common stock when there is an IPO. This is fairly common.

2. *Common stockholders' equity.* This is common stock that is issued to investors and employees (such as through stock option plans). When a company goes public, usually all the equity will be in this form.

3. *Retained earnings.* This includes all the profits and losses of a company since inception. Buffalo Wild Wings showed a history of increasing retained earnings before the IPO. It was certainly a healthy sign.

Conclusion

For those without an accounting background, it can be tough to navigate the balance sheet (as well as the income statement and cash flow statement). But just keep in mind that it is about noticing trends. If you see spikes in areas like inventory or accounts receivable, you should be alerted. It is also important to get a sense of the changes in a company's debt. Increasing debt could portend problems for the stock.

CHAPTER 7

Income Statement

Investors will spend much of their time analyzing the income statement, which shows whether a company is making money. When it comes to valuation, the key metric is earnings. And hopefully they will continue to grow and grow.

In this chapter, we'll delve into the key parts of the income statement. To do this, we'll use the S-1 filing of Annie's. Back in the late 1980s, Annie Withey started the company because she wanted to make food with real ingredients, not chemicals. At first, she marketed packaged organic macaroni cheese she had created.

Yet the company did not grow quickly. So in 2004, Withey hired John Foraker as CEO, who had an extensive career in the food business. It turned

Annie's Income Statement

	2009	2010	2011
Net sales	$93,643	$96,015	$117,616
Cost of sales	64,855	63,083	71,804
Gross profit	28,788	32,932	45,812
Selling, general, and administrative	25,693	25,323	30,674
Income from operations	3,095	7,609	15,138
Interest expense	(1,279)	(1,207)	(885)
Other income (expense), net	(289)	21	155
Income before provision for (benefit from) income taxes	1,527	6,423	14,408
Income from continuing operations	1,471	6,023	20,155
Loss from discontinued operations	(579)		
Loss from sale of discontinued operations	(1,865)		
Net income (loss)	(973)	6,023	20,155
Total basic net income (loss) per share	(0.07)	0.38	1.29
Total diluted net income (loss) per share	(0.10)	0.20	0.50

out to be a smart choice, as he expanded the product line to other categories like snack crackers, fruit snacks, and graham crackers.

In 2012, Annie's pulled off its initial public offering (IPO). In fact, the stock was up nearly 90 percent on its first day of trading.

In the S-1, the income statement actually had two main parts. First one covered the prior three years:

Then there was another section of the income statement, which covered the last nine months of 2010 and of 2011. This is because the company had not reported its fourth quarter yet. It is fairly common for a company to look at the most recent three months, six months, or nine months of the year, depending on when the IPO comes to market.

	Nine Months Ended December 31, 2010	Nine Months Ended December 31, 2011
Net sales	$81,021	$98,320
Cost of sales	50,269	60,034
Gross profit	30,752	38,286
Selling, general, and administrative	20,957	25,206
Income from operations	9,795	13,080
Interest expense	(881)	(66)
Other income (expense), net	128	(428)
Income before provision for (benefit from) income taxes	9,042	12,586
Income from continuing operations	(5,964)	4,926
Loss from discontinued operations	15,006	7,660
Loss from sale of discontinued operations		
Net income (loss)	15,006	7,660
Total basic net income (loss) per share	0.96	0.50
Total diluted net income (loss) per share	0.38	0.24

Management's Discussion and Analysis of Financial Condition and Results of Operations

Reading the Management's Discussion and Analysis (MD&A) section will provide much help in understanding a company's income statement. Essentially, management is required to accurately provide the main drivers of the business. For example, the MD&A section of Annie's points out that the company has seen substantial revenue growth because of increased penetration of mainstream grocery stores and larger discounters like Target and Costco. Other factors include product innovation as well as strong consumer demand for natural and organic food.

Sales

Sales or revenues are the money a company gets from customers. Another name is the top line since this category is at the top of the income statement.

A company like Annie's may have an item called "net sales." This is total sales that are reduced by certain items. For Annie's, these items are estimated product returns, spoils, slotting, and sales and promotion incentives.

As much as possible, you want to see a company that is growing its sales at a strong rate, such as in the double digits. If not, it could be tough for an IPO to get much traction in the aftermarket.

Annie's has certainly shown that it can have sustained sales growth. For the last nine months of 2011, sales increased by 21 percent. This is a rapid rate for a consumer products company.

In some cases, a company will have several revenue streams. It is important to look at how much each represents, which should be indicated on the income statement. For example, suppose a company has been getting 80 percent of its revenue from its product and the rest from services. Yet over the past year the services part increased by 5 percent. If this continues, it could be a problem for the company. Why? The reason is that service revenue tends to have lower margins. In other words, the product/service mix can have a major impact on a company's profitability.

Finally, some IPOs may not even have revenues. These are usually IPOs for biotech and renewable energy companies. They often have a long process for launching their products, but once they come on the market, the growth can be huge.

Revenue Recognition

Revenue may seem like an easy concept, but it can cause lots of confusion with a company's accounting. This is especially the case with companies that are innovating new business models.

For example, Zynga sells virtual items to its customers for its social games. These include things like energy boosts or weapons. Yes, gamers are willing to pay for these items. Consider that Zynga generated $1.1 billion in 2011.

When the company filed to go public, there were no other companies with similar models. So it had to create its own approach to revenue recognition. What did it do? For the most part, Zynga does not recognize all the revenue when a user makes a purchase. Instead, the company will recognize it over "estimated average playing period of paying players for the applicable game."

Consider that while in registration, Zynga actually shortened the estimated length of game play. The result was that doing so actually increased revenues and profits for the company!

This is not illegal or unethical. Accounting is far from clear-cut and is subject to much interpretation. But always be careful when a company has a new business model and has been willing to make changes in assumptions. This is especially the case when the changes lead to the improvement of the financial results.

Facebook also had some unique issues with revenue recognition, but the company did not make any changes in assumptions. It took a fairly conservative approach to its accounting. Because of this, the company had little trouble getting the registration through the Securities and Exchange Commission (SEC).

When looking at revenue recognition policies, there are some areas that raise red flags. They include:

- *"Bill and hold."* This is when a company will issue an invoice to a customer but keep the products in the warehouse. Yes, this means recognizing revenues early, which will make growth look stronger than it really is. But ultimately, a company can continue this for only a short period of time—that is, until customers simply will not accept the goods.

  In the meantime, a company will incur much higher inventory and carrying costs.
- *Acquisitions.* There is much leeway with the accounting for such transactions. For example, a company may be able to write down the assets of the target.

  While this is normal, the amounts may be excessively high. Why? The reason is that in the future the company can write up the asset values, which will generate higher profits.

  If you see an unusual jump in revenue after several acquisitions, then be wary.
- *Complete contract method.* This is revenue recognition for companies that have large, multiyear contracts. With this accounting method, it is possible to recognize a large part of the revenues up front. The problem is that these types of contracts can be risky. What if they are not completed on time and there are penalties? What if the customer cancels the engagement?
- *Vendor financing.* This is when a company provides financing for its customers. This is not necessarily a bad thing. If anything, it can be a lucrative business; the financing fees are usually fairly high.

But vendor financing is a sign that the customers may be shaky. While they are likely to pay when the economy is fine, things can be horrible during a recession.

So in a way, vendor financing could be a way to artificially boost revenues.

Cost of Sales

Cost of sales or cost of goods sold (COGS) includes all the expenses that are directly related to a company's sales. For Annie's, these are ingredients in the manufacture of products, contract manufacturing fees, packaging costs, and inbound freight charges.

The guidelines for what is included in COGS are a bit fuzzy and what to include is up to the discretion of management. Because of this, they can exclude certain items that will reduce the overall expense, which could be misleading. But it is not easy for an investor to detect this.

Gross Profit

This is revenue minus cost of sales. All in all, investors like to focus on this. The main reason is that it gives them a sense of whether a company's business model is inherently profitable

To analyze this, investors will look at the gross profit margin, which is:

$$\text{Gross profit margin} = \text{Gross profit/Sales}$$

Investors want to see this increase steadily over time. It may not necessarily make big jumps, though. Instead, its increase will usually be in terms of basis points. That is, each 1 percent equals 100 basis points.

For instance, a 10 basis points increase in the gross margins may be a big improvement and get investors excited. It is a sign that a company's business model has leverage and economies of scale.

There are several levers for improving margins. One is the ability to raise prices, which is often the case for branded products. In fact, Annie's has been able to do this with its product line.

Another key is finding ways to control costs. And yes, Annie's has taken steps in this area, too. The company has been able to manage volatility in commodity prices, improve its supply chain, and institute productivity improvements.

In general, you want a gross margin above 50 percent. This gives more comfort for a company to expand.

But the gross profit margin is also dependent on the industry. Keep in mind that companies like Walmart have extremely low margins. But then again, they generate huge volumes, which translate into substantial profits.

Selling, General, and Administrative Expenses

Selling, general, and administrative (SG&A) expenses is a catchall category for a company's overhead expenses. These costs will generally be the same regardless of the amount of revenue, at least for the short run.

Annie's lists the following: marketing and advertising expenses; freight and warehousing; wages; related payroll and employee benefit expenses, including stock-based compensation; commissions to outside sales representatives; legal and professional fees; travel expenses; other facility-related costs, such as rent and depreciation; and consulting expenses. However, marketing and advertising were the largest part.

You want to see a company that has maintained discipline with SG&A. And this has generally been the case with Annie's. Consider that the company has found ways to lower its freight and warehousing costs.

But for a growth company, it is okay to have some increases in SG&A, as these are really investments in a company's future. However, some companies may reduce SG&A to artificially increase their profits to attract IPO investors. This is often a sign that management is more concerned about playing accounting games.

Charges

From time to time, a company will take a charge against earnings, such as for unsalable inventory or the disposal of a division. Since charges tend to be infrequent events, a company will not include them in its operating earnings. For the most part, this is reasonable.

The issue is when these charges seem to happen every year. It is a bad reflection on the company since it is probably having trouble with its core business. For example, if a company is frequently writing down inventory, it could be a sign that it is not developing products that consumers want. Or it could mean that the industry is undergoing major changes. For example, the digital camera industry has seen steep declines in sales because smartphones, like the iPhone, have camera features.

Annie's had a one-time charge in 2009, but that charge had little impact on the overall growth rate.

Earnings

There are various measures for a company's earnings. But investors will generally focus on net income. They will also convert this into earnings per share (EPS), which is:

$$\text{Earnings per share} = \text{Net income/Shares outstanding}$$

Some investors will use diluted earnings per share. This assumes that all options and warrants will be exercised, which will add to the share count. For IPO companies, this is a good idea. In many cases, these securities will be exercised over time.

With the earnings per share, you can then calculate a company's price-to-earnings (P/E) ratio, which is:

$$\text{P/E} = \text{Stock price/EPS}$$

It's a simple metric but is widely followed. It is an easy way to get a sense of a company's valuation.

So, if the P/E ratio is 25 or higher, the valuation will look fairly expensive. Then again, some IPOs will have multiples above 100! Or the earnings may be negative and, as a result, there will be no P/E ratio (this is common for IPOs).

A flaw in the P/E ratio is that it looks only to the past—that is, the earnings for the past 12 months. To deal with this, some investors will instead use a forward P/E. This is based on the forecasted EPS for the next year. If a company is expected to grow its earnings at a rapid clip, then the ratio will look much more reasonable.

An investor may also look at the price-earnings/growth (PEG) ratio. This compares a company's P/E ratio to its growth in earnings. It is calculated as follows:

$$\text{PEG} = \text{P/E ratio/Growth rate}$$

Investors want these to be consistent. For example, if a P/E is 50 and the earnings growth rate is also 50, then the valuation would not be considered overvalued. If anything, it may be cheap. Keep in mind that growth companies tend to trade at a premium valuation. The reason is that it is not easy to find these opportunities.

But if the P/E is 50 but the growth rate is 25, then this could be a big problem. Unless the company ramps up its growth rate—which is never easy—the stock price could be vulnerable.

Okay, what if a company has no earnings? One approach is to use the price-to-sales (P/S) ratio. This compares a company's market capitalization to its annual sales. The market cap is the stock price times the number of shares outstanding.

The P/S ratio is not perfect, especially if sales are inflated. But it can provide a general sense of the overall valuation.

Yet even when using this metric, a company may still look overvalued. Again, just like the P/E ratio, it is important to look at the sales growth rate. So if a P/S ratio is high, say at 20 times, it may be fairly reasonable if the company is growing its sales at a hefty rate, say 50 percent or more.

Pro Forma Earnings

It is typical to see pro forma earnings in a company's S-1. These are ways of measuring profits by adding or excluding certain items.

But be careful. They can provide a misleading look at a company's profits.

First, pro forma earnings are not based on generally accepted accounting principles (GAAP). Instead, they are really just the creation of a company's management team. As a result, there is a temptation to come up with a metric that shows strong performance.

Next, since ways of measuring pro forma earnings vary from company to company, it makes it nearly impossible to make comparisons. Keep in mind that some companies will even change their own metric from time to time.

Despite all this, there is one number used in pro forma earnings that is worth considering: earnings before interest, depreciation, and amortization (EBITDA). This is a widely followed metric, and it is based on GAAP and audited financials.

For the most part, EBITDA is a rough measure for a company's cash flow. For example, depreciation is a noncash item. So excluding it does provide a better picture of how much cash is coming into the company.

However, when it comes to analyzing a company, it is still preferable to focus on metrics like net income or operating cash flows. They are hard to manipulate, and all companies must meet rigorous standards.

Taxes

Taxes can get complicated and, yes, boring. But they can provide some insight into a company's future. The item to focus on is deferred taxes. If a company has been reducing this account, this could be an indication that it does not expect to report profits in the future. After all, there will be no taxes due if there are no profits, right?

Common-Size Financials

A key to analyzing financials is getting a sense of the trends. This is not easy when comparing year-over-year or quarter-over-quarter numbers on an income statement. To help out, you'll find the common-size financials in the S-1. This shows each item in the income statement as a percentage of the revenues. Here's what it looks like for Annie's:

Annie's Income Statement

	2009	2010	2011	Nine Months Ended December 31, 2010	Nine Months Ended December 31, 2011
Net sales	100%	100%	100%	100%	100%
Cost of sales	69.3	65.7	61.0	62.0	61.1
Gross profit	30.7	34.3	39.0	38.0	38.9
Selling, general, and administrative	27.4	26.4	26.1	25.9	25.6
Income from operations	3.3	7.9	12.9	12.1	13.3
Interest expense	(1.4)	(1.3)	(0.8)	(1.1)	(0.1)
Other income (expense), net	(0.3)	0.0	0.1	0.2	(0.4)
Income before provision for (benefit from) income taxes	1.6	6.7	12.2	11.2	12.8
Net income from continuing operations	1.6	6.3	17.1	18.5	7.8
Loss from discontinued operations	(0.6)				
Loss on sale of discontinued operations	(2.0)				
Net income (loss)	(1.0)	6.3	17.1	18.5	7.8

Taking a look at this, you can see that gross margins have been declining over time. While this is worrisome, it is common when companies are in the early stages of growth. They need to make substantial investments in systems and purchases. But with Annie's, it looks like the drop is stabilizing.

Conclusion

When looking at the income statement, first get a sense of the revenues. Are they accelerating? Has the company shown a history of growth? For IPOs, it is critically important to show momentum.

But of course, you need to look deeper. Make sure that the quality of sales is strong, and that inventory and accounts receivable are not growing at a faster rate than sales.

You also want to track the gross margins and look for those companies that are showing increases. This is a sign that there is leverage in the business model and that future profits are likely to be strong.

CHAPTER 8

Statement of Cash Flows

While Wall Street tends to focus primarily on the income statement, it is a good idea to give some time to analyzing the statement of cash flows. As seen with the financial crisis of 2008, it is critically important to understand a company's liquidity position. Ironically, it is possible for a company to show a profit and yet run out of cash! What's more, the income statement is subject to much more manipulation because of changes in accounting treatments and assumptions.

Consider that an initial public offering (IPO) can also be misleading for a company's cash position. After all, an offering will mean a large amount of cash that will be deposited in the corporate treasury. All in all, it can help deal with any liquidity issues. Despite this, it is still important to take a look at the statement of cash flows.

Background

As seen in the preceding chapter, earnings before interest, taxes, depreciation, and amortization (EBITDA) are often used as a proxy for cash flow. But EBITDA is a simplistic calculation and really does not give the full picture. The statement of cash flows is a much better approach. In fact, it has three sections.

To get an understanding of these statements, we'll take a look at the statement of cash flows for Facebook. Started in a dorm room in 2004, the company has turned into an Internet powerhouse. In 2011, the company generated $1.5 billion in operating cash flows.

Facebook Statement of Cash Flows (in Millions)

	2009	2010	2011	Three Months Ended March 31, 2011	Three Months Ended March 31, 2012
Cash Flows from Operating Activities					
Net income	$229	$606	$1,000	$233	$205
Adjustments to Reconcile Net Income to Net Cash Provided by Operating Activities					
Depreciation and amortization	78	139	323	51	110
Loss on write-off of assets	1	3	4	1	1
Share-based compensation	27	20	217	7	103
Tax benefit from share-based award activity	50	115	433	69	54
Excess tax benefit from share-based award activity	(51)	(115)	(433)	(69)	(54)
Changes in Assets and Liabilities					
Accounts receivable	(112)	(209)	(174)	27	65
Prepaid expenses and other current assets	(30)	(38)	(31)	(26)	(28)
Other assets	(59)	17	(32)	(10)	(32)
Accounts payable	(7)	12	6	(3)	(3)
Platform partners payable		75	96	24	7
Accrued expenses and other current liabilities	27	20	38	6	2
Deferred revenue and deposits	1	37	49	17	3
Other liabilities	1	16	53	18	8
Net cash provided by operating activities	155	698	1,549	345	441
Cash Flows from Investing Activities					
Purchases of property and equipment	(33)	(293)	(606)	(153)	(453)
Purchases of marketable securities			(3,025)		(876)
Maturities of marketable securities			516		567
Sales of marketable securities			113		69
Investments in nonmarketable equity securities			(3)		(1)

	2009	2010	2011	Three Months Ended March 31, 2011	Three Months Ended March 31, 2012
Acquisitions of business, net of cash acquired, and purchases of intangible and other assets	3	(22)	(24)	(1)	(25)
Change in restricted cash and deposits	(32)	(9)	6	1	(1)
Net cash used in investing activities	(62)	(324)	(3,023)	(153)	(720)
Cash Flows from Financing Activities					
Net proceeds from issuance of convertible preferred stock	200				
Net proceeds from issuance of common stock		500	998	998	
Proceeds from exercise of stock options	9	6	28	9	5
Proceeds from (repayment of) long-term debt		250	(250)	(250)	
Proceeds from sale and lease-back transactions	31		170	1	62
Principal payments on capital lease obligations	(48)	(90)	(181)	(29)	(71)
Excess tax benefit from share-based award activity	51	115	433	69	54
Net cash provided by financing activities	243	781	1,198	798	50
Effect of exchange rate changes on cash and cash equivalents		(3)	3	1	(1)
Net increase (decrease) in cash and cash equivalents	336	1,152	(273)	991	(230)
Cash and cash equivalents at beginning of period	633	1,785	1,512	2,776	1,282

Now let's take a look at each of the sections.

Cash Flows from Operating Activities

This shows the cash flows from the core business. It starts with the net income, which then has a variety of adjustments. There is an increase for depreciation and amortization because these are noncash charges. This is also the case with share-based compensation.

Another big item is accounts receivable. If there is an increase, this reduces the cash. The reason is that customers have yet to make a payment. Investors will see if there is a trend of higher accounts receivable, which may be a sign that the company is too aggressive with its selling efforts.

Inventory is another critical element of cash flows. If it is increasing, then it is a drain on cash. Again, this could be a sign that the company is having trouble selling its products.

Cash Flows from Investing Activities

This is often confusing for investors. The word *investing* refers to when a company makes purchases of capital assets (also known as capital expenditures or capex). These have a life beyond more than a year, such as plant and equipment, and any purchase will reduce the cash flows. But if a company sells an asset, this will increase the cash flows.

Facebook has had to make large purchases of property and equipment to allow it to continue its growth. In other words, increases in capex can actually be a positive sign that the future is bright for the company.

The company has also made large purchases of marketable securities. This is because Facebook has raised big rounds of capital and wanted to put the money into higher-yielding securities.

What's more, you'll notice that Facebook has used cash fairly sparingly with its acquisitions. Instead, it appears that the company tends to use stock as currency for its deal making.

Cash Flows from Financing Activities

This shows the cash flows from issuing or buying back stock or debt. This is usually a positive number for pre-IPO companies because they tend to raise lots of capital. And yes, this has been the case with Facebook.

Focus on Operating Cash Flows

Of the three cash flows, this is usually the best one for investors. Operating cash flows show how the underlying business is performing. Consider that a company can hide problems by raising large amounts of capital, which will show up in the financing section.

If a company cannot consistently generate positive operating cash flows, it is a sign that the business model is flawed. This was the problem with many of the companies that went public during the dot-com era of the late 1990s.

There are some metrics to help with analysis, such as the operating cash flow margin:

$$\text{Operating cash flow margin} = \text{Operating cash flows/Sales}$$

If you see this increasing over time, it shows that a company is leveraging its platform, such as with economies of scale and pricing power.

Then there is the quality of earnings ratio:

$$\text{Quality of earnings ratio} = \text{Operating cash flows/Net income}$$

This is widely followed because it shows possible manipulation—that is, if the ratio is 0.50 or lower. This means that the net income is much higher than the operating cash flows. This is a red flag because they should be roughly the same. In other words, could the higher amount for net income be the result of manipulation?

Actually, you would have detected this disconnect between net income and cash flows for some of history's biggest corporate frauds, like Enron.

Then there is cash flow efficiency. It is as follows:

$$\text{Cash flow efficiency} = (\text{Current assets} - \text{Cash and marketable securities})/(\text{Current liabilities} - \text{Short-term debt})$$

Be careful if cash flow efficiency is below 1.0. For the most part, this would indicate that a company has been putting its cash into accounts receivable and inventory. Thus, the cash management is poor, and as a result there may be a need to seek out even more capital from investors.

Free Cash Flow

Free cash flow is the operating cash flows minus the capital expenditures. It's an important metric since it gives a better idea of the overall inflows and outflows of cash. As seen with Facebook, the capex can have major items.

If so, it is good to see if a company can still have positive free cash flow. It's a major sign that the company has a powerful business model and will probably not need to raise outside cash. Keep in mind that some of history's best IPOs have generated large free cash flows, such as eBay and Google.

Stock Options

These are common for pre-IPO companies, especially in technology and biotech. They are an effective tool in attracting and motivating top-notch employees. But they also mean less cash is spent on salaries and bonuses.

Interestingly, stock options can be a form of cash flow. How? An option will have an exercise price, which is what an employee will pay to purchase the stock. This amount is paid directly to the company.

However, the exercise price is often low because the options were granted in the early days of the company. So even though the option exercise will result in an influx of cash, it will be dilutive to existing shareholders. It's as if the company has issued a lot of stock at an extremely low valuation.

Thus, options have a real cost. To this end, the accounting profession has a variety of rules to deal with this. The result is that there is a reduction in a company's net income.

Factoring

Factoring is a common practice in corporate America. It is when a company sells its accounts receivable. While it means getting cash more quickly, it can be costly. A company usually must pay a high fee for this.

An increase in these types of transactions should alert investors. It could be a sign that a company is having cash problems.

Footnotes

You'll find these at the end of the statement of cash flows as well as at the end of the balance sheet and the income statement. They can get a bit convoluted, but it is worth scanning them, as footnotes can be a good place for management to hide important details.

One type of footnote will cover accounting principles, such as for recognizing revenues or expenses. Look to see if these have changed over time or if they are different from similar companies. Adjustments in time periods can be major red flags, especially for depreciation.

Another type of footnote will provide more detail about an item in the financials. For example, it can disclose the features of a debt, such as the interest rate and maturity. There will also be disclosures about leases, which can be serious obligations.

Fraud and Misrepresentation

All in all, it is fairly rare to see outright fraud with IPOs. This is definitely the case with offerings from top exchanges like NASDAQ and the New York Stock Exchange (NYSE). Laws like Sarbanes-Oxley have also been a big help. What's more, public companies have their books audited by independent firms.

Despite this, there are still some frauds that get pulled off. One of the most notorious was Refco. Within two months of its IPO, the company reported that the CEO had failed to disclose $430 million in debt. The company had to file for bankruptcy.

However, it is more common for the management of a public company to become too aggressive with its accounting. This may mean stretching out the term on depreciation or recognizing a large amount of sales early. These are not necessarily illegal but they could verge on being unethical.

Often, a company will be forced to restate its earnings. This means the financial statements need to be recalculated—and in most cases, it involves reducing the sales or profits. When this happens, Wall Street gets jittery and a company will often lose credibility. This happened with Groupon, which had to restate its first report as a public company. The stock lost over 50 percent within a couple of months.

So, when analyzing the financials, it is a good idea to look for the following red flags:

- Sales are growing much faster than profits, say by 25 percent or more.
- There is an expected drop in free cash flow. It is definitely worrisome if free cash flow goes negative and yet a company is still reporting positive earnings. This disconnect could mean that a company is engaging in manipulation of its books.
- Be wary if a company engages in many acquisitions. It can be a way to exaggerate profits. Besides, it is never easy to buy quality companies at attractive prices as well as to integrate them. Some of corporate America's biggest implosions were from companies that were too aggressive with acquisitions, such as Tyco International. From 1999 to 2002, Tyco purchased over 700 companies.

- Avoid companies with aggressive accounting methods like bill and hold.
- Accounts receivable are growing much faster than sales, such as by 25 percent or more. It could mean that management is stuffing the channel.
- Operating cash flows are mostly below net income, such as by half or more.
- Inventory is growing faster than sales, perhaps by 20 percent or more. Granted, it could be that a company is gearing up for a boost in sales, such as before the Christmas season. But it could also mean that it is having trouble selling its goods.
- A company unexpectedly drops its allowance for doubtful accounts. It may be a way to artificially increase sales. A notorious example is New Century. In 2006, the company lowered its loss estimates on its mortgage portfolio, even though the real estate industry was imploding. The company would soon go bust.

Conclusion

Of all the financial statements, the statement of cash flows gets the least attention from investors. But this is a big mistake. The statement of cash flows provides extremely useful information, such as on capital expenditures and activities like acquisitions. You can also see if a company has been using factoring, which may mean there are issues with the underlying business model.

CHAPTER 9

Risk Factors

At the height of the dot-com boom, Stephen Waldis founded Synchronoss Technologies and was able to raise $25 million in venture capital. He thought that mobile phones would essentially become handheld computers and started to create a platform to help telecom operators to handle functions like billing, provisioning, and activations. Though it took longer than he thought it would, Waldis was able to build a strong company and would eventually benefit from the iPhone revolution.

In 2007, he set out to take the company public. It helped that Waldis had already put in place the necessary infrastructure, such as financial systems. He also had a top-notch senior management team, which proved critical in the grueling initial public offering (IPO) process.

When Waldis started things off with the drafting of the S-1 filing, it was certainly a tedious process. "We spent the first two weeks thinking about all the reasons an investor would not want to participate in the IPO," he said.

It sounds counterintuitive, but it is a legal requirement. That is, an S-1 needs a section that lists the downsides for investors.

For the most part, many of these are really worst-case scenarios and are legal boilerplate. But there are some that investors should keep an eye on: management issues, the need for more financing, legal problems, competition, and lack of a sustainable business model.

Inexperienced Management Team

When Michael Dell was only 23, he took his company public. His age was certainly a big concern for investors, despite the company's fast growth rate.

After all, many other PC operators had gone bust. But Dell proved that he had the skills to lead the company to dominance.

But this is really an exception. For the most part, it is extremely tough for a young CEO to handle the pressures of an IPO and keep up the growth momentum.

An example is theglobe.com (www.theglobe.com), which was a provider of free websites to consumers. Todd Krizelman and Stephen Paternot started the company in the fall of 1994 while they were students at Cornell University. Krizelman earned a bachelor's degree in biology and Paternot earned degrees in business and computer science.

The company went public in November 1998, at which time both founders were 24 years old and co-CEOs of the company. The stock shot up from $9 to $63.50, and the IPO raised $31 million. But after much turmoil and difficulty executing the business model—as well as intense competition from rivals like Yahoo!—the stock plunged to below $1 within a couple of years.

Need for More Financing

Some types of companies need huge amounts of capital. This is especially the case with biotech operators. But there are also some technology infrastructure companies that are capital intensive.

If these companies fall short of expectations, the result can be devastating on the stock price. Look at Clearwire. The company's mission was to build a next-generation network to provide wireless broadband. The company was the mastermind of Craig McCaw, who had a track record of successfully building large-scale companies. These included McCaw Cellular, which was sold to AT&T for $11.5 billion in 1994, as well as Nextel, which he merged with Sprint in a $36 billion deal.

In March 2007, McCaw took Clearwire public and raised roughly $600 million. The stock price was $25.

However, the prospectus indicated that it was likely that the company would need much more capital. The risk factors section said: "We do not expect to satisfy all of our long-term capital and spectrum acquisition needs through this offering. We believe our cash and short-term investments afford us adequate liquidity for at least the next 12 months, although we may raise additional capital during this period if acceptable terms are available."

Unfortunately, the subscriber numbers for Clearwire were too optimistic and the U.S. economy got hit by the financial crisis, which made it extremely difficult to raise more capital. By March 2009, the shares had fallen to about $3.

Legal Proceedings

Another risk factor worth investigating is serious litigation pending against the company. The greatest problem with litigation is that it is difficult to quantify. After all, it is almost impossible to know how a jury will decide a case, or how much it will award a company in damages. What's more, a protracted lawsuit can divert a company's attention and resources away from its focus.

One area to be wary about is any threat to a company's trademark. No doubt companies will spend huge sums to create a brand, which may make it extremely valuable. But in some cases, there may be a dispute over the trademark. Who really owns it?

This was the question with the WWF trademark. For years it was the brand for the World Wildlife Foundation, but then it became the symbol of the World Wrestling Federation. In 1994, the two organizations entered into an agreement to deal with the situation.

However, by the time the World Wrestling Foundation went public in October 1999, the World Wildlife Foundation had brought suit, claiming violations of the original agreement. Despite negotiations, there was no resolution. So in 2002, the World Wrestling Foundation changed its name to World Wrestling Entertainment (WWE). It was a costly process, as the company had to change the logos on its existing properties. There was also a need to launch a new marketing campaign.

Another worrisome type of litigation is a patent dispute. This has become much more common over the years. It appears that a key reason Google spent $12.5 billion for Motorola was to obtain its patents. Then there was America Online (AOL), which sold its patents for $1.1 billion to Microsoft in early 2012.

Tech companies will often patent seemingly minor concepts. Consider that Apple did this with its "slide to unlock" feature for its iPhone and iPad.

The avalanche of patent applications has put tremendous strain on the U.S. Patent and Trademark Office. The fear is that the federal agency will often grant a patent with not much analysis. As a result, it could mean more confusion in the marketplace and courtrooms.

The patent disputes can be a big problem for smaller tech companies, which do not have the resources to take on a giant. This happened with Vonage. The company was a pioneer of a disruptive technology called voice over Internet Protocol (VoIP), which leveraged the Internet to provide low-cost phone calls. It was definitely a big threat to incumbent telecom operators like Verizon, Sprint, and AT&T. To blunt the progress, these companies filed suits against Vonage for patent infringement, which were then disclosed in the S-1.

Over the next few years, the company had to shell out huge sums for settlements. These included $120 million for Verizon, $80 million for Sprint, and $39 million to AT&T.

Market and Customer Base

An ideal candidate for IPO investment is a company with a potentially large, fast-growing market. This sounds obvious, but not all IPO candidates are lucky enough or are designed to have diverse product offerings.

Product concentration can be a major problem for young businesses. A company may have only a few products, or sometimes just one. And if such a company's singular product hits a sales slump, it can lead to overall under-performance for the company and its stock.

Another problem is when a company relies on a small number of custom-ers. Even if they do not stop using the product, they may use their leverage to get better terms, which will reduce margins.

This was the predicament for LookSmart, which was an online search engine. In its S-1 for its IPO in 1999, the company stated the following risk factor: "We derive a significant amount of our revenues under an agree-ment with Microsoft Corporation, and after June 8, 2000, either party may terminate the agreement for any reason on six months' notice. For the six months ended June 30, 1999, revenues from Microsoft under this agreement accounted for 56.4 percent of our total revenues."

LookSmart was not able to diversify its revenues, and within three years Microsoft did not renew the relationship. At the time, the revenue concentra-tion was 65 percent, and the stock price plunged.

Going Concern

In most cases, when an auditor analyzes a company's books, there are no sur-prises. But sometimes there will be a so-called going-concern determination. Basically this means that the company is expected to run out of cash soon. Of course, with an IPO a company will get an infusion of cash, which often means there will then be no going-concern problem—at least for a while.

Back during the dot-com boom, it was common to see companies file to go public with going-concern disclosures. In light of new regulations like

Sarbanes-Oxley, this has been less common. But there are still examples, such as from small tech companies and biotech operators.

If you see a going-concern determination in a company's prospectus, it is probably a good idea to avoid the stock. Such companies typically continue to have financial problems.

For example, in February 2010 Vringo went public, raising only $9.2 million. The company, a provider of ring tones for mobile devices, had a boutique underwriter, Maxim Group.

At the time of the offering, Vringo had a mere $36,000 in revenue for the first nine months of 2009, and the accumulated losses were $18 million. Thus, it was no surprise that it had a going-concern determination from its auditor, KPMG LLP. Vringo stated: "All of our audited consolidated financial statements since inception have contained a statement by our auditors that raises substantial doubt about us being able to continue as a going concern unless we are able to raise additional capital."

The IPO was priced at $4.60, and within a couple months the stock price was at $1.25.

Competition

Competition is mentioned in every prospectus. It is the nature of business as we know it. In fact, the presence of competition can be positive, because it indicates that there is a market for the company's products or services.

However, sometimes competition can be extremely fierce, particularly in fast-paced industries like technology. In any case, it's a potential risk factor that investors need to be aware of. Reading the competition section of the prospectus can give investors a very good idea of the various players in the industry that are vying for market share. One good idea is to check out the rivals and see if they are real threats.

An example of how tough competition is can be seen with the IPO of Zeltiq Aesthetics (NASDAQ:ZLTQ). On its face, the company looked fairly unique. That is, it sold sophisticated machines that it claimed allowed physicians to reduce people's stubborn fat bulges. The technology relied on a natural process known as apoptosis, which uses cooling of fat molecules. The company had gone through the rigorous process of the Food and Drug Administration and also had patents on its innovations.

In late 2011, Zeltiq went public and its stock hit a high of $17.41 per share. But if investors read the risk factors, they would have seen that there was serious competition. What's more, the company was also having trouble differentiating its approach. Its advertising campaign, which was called "Let's Get Naked," had people running around in their underwear! It was not a clear marketing message.

When Zeltiq reported its quarterly earnings, the company posted an unexpected loss of $5.8 million, or 22 cents per share. It also indicated that the weakness would likely continue for the next couple of quarters. The culprit? Zeltiq indicated in its press release: "We observed a slower than normal end-of-year sales cycle due to a number of unanticipated product launches and trial offers that competed for physician capital equipment dollars. We expect these issues to work through the sales channel over time, and we have strengthened the focus and organization of our sales team to help neutralize these effects."

The stock plunged to $5 per share.

Dual-Share Structure

Henry Ford did not want to take his company public. Instead, he wanted his family to maintain absolute control. It was certainly an unusual decision for the emerging auto industry, which needed huge amounts of capital.

But nine years after Henry Ford died, his company did go public in 1956. It was actually the biggest IPO in history, as the company raised $643 million.

However, Henry Ford had put into place a dual-share structure. The Class A stock would be nonvoting and represent 95 percent of the equity. Then there was Class B stock, which had 100 percent of the voting rights.

The purpose of this was to avoid paying inheritance taxes. But in the end, it became a good structure for the Ford family to remain in control of the company after its IPO. In fact, it still serves this purpose today.

The dual-share structure has been fairly rare. Instead, it has mostly been media companies that have used this approach, such as the *New York Times* and the *Washington Post*. The main reason is to help protect editorial integrity.

Yet in 2004, Google announced it also would have a dual-share structure. In the company's S-1 filing, the founders, Sergey Brin and Larry Page, wrote a letter to shareholders that was called an "Owner's Manual." In it, they explained why they required voting control: they wanted the ability to take a long-term approach to investments and projects.

It caused a stir but was not enough to derail IPO investors. Since its offering, the stock has gone on to climb 500 percent.

But there are many who still believe that dual-share structures are a bad idea. These structures make it nearly impossible to throw out management.

This is particularly scary in today's dynamic world, where many CEOs do not seem to have strong leadership capabilities.

Besides, there are examples of CEOs who have built franchise companies without having the need for protections. This was certainly the case with Apple's CEO, Steve Jobs. Interestingly, he was kicked out of the company in 1985 but he learned valuable lessons from the experience. He went on to build Pixar and then returned to Apple, where he turned it into the world's most valuable company.

Despite all this, more Internet companies are adopting dual-share structures (for example, Facebook, Groupon, LinkedIn, and Zynga). While it's too early to tell about the impact, there are already some troubling signs.

This has been the case with Groupon. Since going public in late 2011, the company had a restatement of its earnings and a disappointing earnings report. During the IPO process, the company's CEO, Andrew Mason, wrote a memo that provided internal projections and thoughts about the competition. The language was also juicy: "The degree to which we're getting the sh-t kicked out of us in the press had finally crossed the threshold from 'annoying' to 'hilarious.'" The Securities and Exchange Commission (SEC) was not happy about this and the IPO was almost delayed.

Since its offering, Groupon's shares are off 50 percent.

CEO Dependence

No doubt the CEO is incredibly important. It should be no surprise that when there were departures at companies like Microsoft, Dell, and Starbucks, there was trouble for the stock price.

With some companies, the CEO is essentially the brand. One classic example is Martha Stewart Living Omnimedia. The founder and CEO, Martha Stewart, got her start in the 1970s as a caterer and then began to write best-selling books. From there she would make numerous appearances on TV shows like the *Oprah Winfrey Show* and *Larry King Live.*

These efforts would eventually turn into a media empire, with revenues that reached $180 million when her company went public in 1999. But the S-1 had an ominous risk factor: "The diminution or loss of the services of Martha Stewart, and any negative market or industry perception arising from that diminution or loss, would have a material adverse effect on our business."

And yes, this happened. In June 2003 the federal government indicted Stewart on charges related to an insider trading case and she was eventually convicted. She served a prison term of five months.

As should be no surprise, the impact was devastating on her company, which has not fully recovered.

Reliance on the Government

The U.S. federal government is a huge spender—and yes, a big source of revenues for thousands of companies. The problem is that the expenditures are often subject to change due to the turnover with elections, for example. The large budget deficits have also become a big issue.

But certain industries have little choice but to rely on government support. One is renewable energy. Because of the huge costs, there is often a need to get subsidies. However, during 2011 and 2012 there was a pullback in support, which had a detrimental impact on IPOs in the sector. Other countries, such as Germany and even China, were also reducing their expenses.

To get some of the deals off the ground, even venture capitalists (VCs) engaged in so-called insider purchases. This means that they actually bought more shares at the time of the IPO. This happened with the offering of Enphase Energy, a developer of solutions for the solar industry. With little demand for the IPO, the company raised only $54 million and the stock was priced at $6. The company's VCs—including Third Point, Madrone Partners, Kleiner Perkins Caufield & Byers, RockPort Capital, and Bay Partners—bought 2.5 million shares in the deal.

The company actually doubled its revenues in 2011 to $149 million. But IPO investors were concerned that there would be a fall-off, at least during the short term.

Another industry that usually has a major reliance on government spending is health care. Take a look at CardioNet, a developer of mobile monitoring systems for outpatient care. The company was growing quickly and the future looked promising.

But the S-1 warned: "We receive reimbursement for our services from commercial payors and from Medicare Part B carriers where the services are performed on behalf of the Centers for Medicare and Medicaid Services, or CMS."

Despite the risk, CardioNet was able to pull off its IPO in March 2008 at $18 per share and then had a secondary offering at $26.50 in August. But in the spring of 2009, the stock plunged. The reason was that the federal government began to pull back on its reimbursements for the company's devices.

Unproven Business Model

Often IPOs will have new business models. In some cases, they can be revolutionary, as seen with eBay. In the mid-1990s, eBay realized that there was untapped demand for online auctions, and the company turned into an Internet giant.

But sometimes the new business models may fail. Often, it is a matter of being too early. All in all, consumers are just not ready for the new approach.

One example of this was Drkoop.com. The site was a provider of useful medical content for consumers. Yet in the company's S-1, there was the following risk factor: "Consumers and the health care industry may not accept our product offerings." The company openly admitted that up to that point, consumers had relied on health care professionals as their main source of health care information. Of course, Drkoop.com thought this would change. What's more, the company bet that other companies would want to advertise on Drkoop .com, which had plans to provide e-commerce opportunities to consumers.

The company went public in June 1999. The offering price was $9 per share and reached a high of $45.75. Unfortunately, Drkoop.com was unable to attract enough revenues, continued to suffer losses, and began to run out of money. The stock would eventually fall below $1 per share.

It would not be until a few years later—as seen with companies like WebMD—that consumers would finally use the Internet as a source of medical information.

In other cases, a company may actually have a product that is seeing lots of demand but it pursues a strategy that is uneconomical. For example, Pets.com quickly became a high-growth seller of pet food and supplies in 1999 and 2000. The problem was that it was extremely expensive to build the brand, which was focused on its cute sock puppet. Keep in mind that the company had a commercial for the Super Bowl.

Another problem was that Pets.com provided free shipping. No doubt this was a nice perk for consumers, but was prohibitively expensive for the company.

Pets.com went public in February 2000 at $11 a share. Within a year, the company had to file for Chapter 11 bankruptcy.

Limited History of Profitable Operations

It takes time to build profitable operations. In its early stages, a company will spend a lot of money developing its infrastructure, products, and market share. But over time, the company should be able to reach critical mass and achieve profitability. In fact, raising capital through an IPO should help accelerate the process.

Many high-tech companies, for example, have big losses in their early years. This was the case with Priceline.com, which spent millions building its infrastructure and customer base. Once this was complete, though, the company became a dominant player in the online travel sector and had the wherewithal to survive the dot-com bust. As of now, the company's market capitalization is $36 billion.

So just because a company is unprofitable in the short term does not mean the IPO will fail. Rather, the key factor is that the expected future growth rate should be high and the margins will be strong enough to get to profitability.

But be wary of those companies that describe long-term losses—over 10 years or more. This is a strong indication that the business will never be profitable.

SkyMall (SKYM), a provider of catalogs for airline passengers, is an example of an IPO with long-term losses. Before going public, the company had impressive revenue growth. From 1991 to 1995, sales grew from $5.4 million to $43.1 million, while sales per passenger increased from $0.038 to $0.084. Despite this growth, the company was unable to generate any profits. The gross margins were small because of high distribution and printing costs and low markups. Actually, the company had accumulated losses of $32.4 million.

SkyMall went public in December 1996. The amount raised was $16 million, and the offering price was $8 per share. But the company could not get to profitability and the stock plunged.

Small Market Potential

To be sustainable and to keep the interest of public investors, a company needs to address a huge market opportunity. The rule of thumb is that the potential market must be at least $1 billion per year. If less, it could be tough to grow the company.

Interestingly, though, there are some companies that have gone public even though the market size was fairly small. An example is IntraLinks. Founded in 1996, the company was a developer web-based tools that allowed investment bankers to manage their transactions.

There was certainly a need in the market for such tools, and IntraLinks built a comprehensive solution. The problem was that the market was relatively small.

Despite this, IntraLinks wanted to go public. In fact, it had two failed attempts because there was not enough investor demand. But in August 2010, the company was able to launch its IPO. The stock was priced at $13 and then hit $30 within less than a year.

But the company was not able to keep up the momentum, and the revenues hit a wall. It also announced that a major customer was cutting back on its business. The stock plunged to $3.

Cyclical Businesses

A cyclical business is one that is highly sensitive to the economy. That is, when the economy is growing quickly, revenues will spike, but sales will plunge when there is a recession. For the most part, cyclical businesses focus on commodities or the sale of expensive capital or consumer goods.

Keep in mind that it is common for cyclical businesses to go public when the economy is thriving. It is an opportune time to raise lots of capital and pay back private equity firms.

But it can be the wrong time for public investors to buy shares.

Conclusion

Now, do not let the risk factors scare you. Even the best companies have major issues. Rather, focus on some key factors that could limit a company's growth, such as problems with the business model or a small target market. When you see such things, you could be setting yourself up for a bad investment.

CHAPTER 10

IPO Investment Strategies

All great investors have their unique approaches. Warren Buffett, for example, looks for stocks that have strong brand names, substantial market share, and top-notch managements. Interestingly, he does not buy initial public offerings (IPOs)!

But other great investors may not necessarily spend much time with the fundamentals. Paul Tudor Jones focuses heavily on reading charts. And yes, he's also a billionaire.

For the most part, there are no surefire approaches to investing. But there are some core strategies that should help—and can be applied across industries.

Neighborhood Investing

In some cases, a great IPO might be happening right in your own backyard. Local companies make tempting investment opportunities because you'll have firsthand knowledge about the business and easy access to research. Perhaps you're even a customer who knows the management personally.

At the very least, close proximity to a company that's going public allows you the opportunity to visit the company's operations and make a firsthand evaluation of its environment. When you visit its offices, learn as much as you can about its products and staff. For instance:

• Do the employees look busy and content?
• Are the facilities organized and clean?

- Is the product good quality? Would you use it?
- What is the buzz in the local community?

So it's a good idea to talk to the employees. Get their feedback on what they like about their company. You may even get easier access to shares in the offering if you get to know some of the people who work there. Visiting the company personally won't provide all the answers you need to invest in an IPO, but it will give you a head start.

Another great source of information on regional companies is the local newspaper. You will typically find in-depth business and feature coverage of local companies, and you should even look at the classified ads to see if the company is hiring.

Perhaps one of the best examples of backyard investing is Walmart. The company is now the world's largest retailer and has made millionaires of thousands of residents of its hometown, Bentonville, Arkansas. Another example is Home Depot, which went public in 1984 with only 31 stores. Of course, this company, too, made many people millionaires in its hometown, Atlanta.

Invest in What You Know

It's a good idea to invest in the industries that you understand best. If you have insight into the mobile app business—perhaps because you're a coder—then chances are you have as much insight into industry trends and performance as the analysts. And you're in a great position to more easily determine the upside of companies in that field. In other words, you should consider your own profession and how it will help you invest in IPOs.

You can also use your knowledge as a consumer. If you are an avid book buyer, chances are that you wish you had invested in Amazon.com. If you want to invest in a restaurant IPO, make sure that you dine at that chain. If you are considering an investment in an Internet company, make sure you spend time on its website.

Use the knowledge you've gained over the years to spot the IPOs with the most potential. Although this is only one of many screens, it's one that everyone can start with.

Study Mutual Fund Holdings

As we discuss in Chapter 19, a variety of mutual funds buy large amounts of IPO shares. One simple strategy for individual investors is to examine the top holdings of such funds. You can find these from the EDGAR filings or the mutual fund's website.

If particular IPOs are good enough for portfolio managers, they might make sense in your personal portfolio, too. There's no telling what ideas you can glean from some of the experts. However, this doesn't exonerate you from engaging in the usual research on the IPOs you discover. After all, even portfolio managers sometimes pick lemons.

Strong Backers

Success attracts success. What top programmer or executive would not want to work for a company like Google or Microsoft during its heyday? In today's highly competitive world, perhaps the most important aspect is a company's people.

When looking at an IPO, spend time looking at the management team. This means reading the bios in the S-1. But you should also do outside research. A basic search on Google should bring up some articles on the key people. What is their philosophy? What were the setbacks? What were some of the important decisions made? Do they have a compelling vision for their company?

Another validator for an IPO is when a company has backing from venture capitalists (VCs). Are they top-tier players like Accel Partners, Benchmark Capital, Kleiner Perkins Caufield & Byers, and Sequoia Capital? These firms have a long history of spotting successful companies like eBay, Cisco, Oracle, and Salesforce.com.

Finally, it is important that an IPO have top-notch underwriters. It is even more impressive if two or three are on the same deal. For example, if Goldman Sachs and Morgan Stanley are the managing underwriters, it's a clear sign that a company has breakout potential.

Analyst Coverage

Sell-side analysts work for brokerages and investment banks. They will write periodic reports on companies, which include earnings forecasts and even price targets.

But there is a potential conflict of interest. That is, an analyst's employer generally makes lots of money from underwriting IPOs. So there is much incentive to make the research reports bullish. Besides, this will encourage more trading in the stock, which will lead to more commissions.

During the 1990s, there were many abuses with research. For example, analysts would often be involved in the selection of IPO candidates and might even get incentive compensation if a client was snagged. Unfortunately, there were cases where analysts had bullish reports on a company even though they believed the prospects were terrible.

When the dot-com bubble burst, the Securities and Exchange Commission (SEC) took action to clean things up. This was done with a massive legal settlement with the largest investment banks in the United States. The total fine was a whopping $1.4 billion.

The SEC also instituted various reforms:

- Analyst compensation could not be based on investment banking revenue. Rather, it would need to be tied to the quality and accuracy of the research.
- Investment banks could not direct which companies an analyst would cover.
- Analysts could not solicit investment banking clients.
- There would be more disclosures on an analyst's personal holdings.

Despite all this, sell-side research tends to be on the bullish side. But this can actually present an effective investment strategy. Keep in mind that sell-side analysts cannot publish any research reports until 40 days after the IPO (this is when the quiet period expires). After this, the stock will usually jump because of the "buy" ratings. It could mean a quick 2 percent to 5 percent jump in the stock.

But sometimes that research will give lukewarm support. If so, be cautious. If anything, it may be an opportunity to short the stock. This happened when the quiet period expired for Groupon. The analysts' reports had several ratings like "neutral" to "sector perform." Essentially, the general consensus was that the shares were overvalued because of the competition as well as difficulties with the underlying business model. Within a few months, the stock lost about half its value.

There are actually independent research analysts for IPOs, which can be a great source of helpful information. However, there are not many. The main reason is that it is tough to sell this kind of research. But in Chapter 4, you can find some of the top independent research services.

IPO Rules of Thumb

For IPOs, there are some traditional rules of thumb. One is that an IPO should not fall in price on the first day. If so, it is known as a "broken" deal. It's really a bad sign since it shows investors have a certain lack of confidence in the deal. Also, the loss can be something that investors may not forget for a while.

A broken IPO often means that there is a general lack of interest. Interestingly, though, the underwriters are allowed to make so-called stabilizing bids. These are purchases to help keep the stock from falling below the IPO price. In fact, this happened with the Facebook IPO. The problem is that underwriters can take these actions for only one month. No doubt traders will pounce once the support is gone.

Another rule of thumb is that a company should not miss its first quarter earnings estimate. When a company goes public, it will provide guidance to Wall Street about the next quarter's earnings and revenues. But if it cannot meet these forecasts, that is a terrible sign. Does the company have a good handle on its business? Is there serious deterioration?

Buy on the Opening or Wait for the Lockup to Expire?

If you are allocated IPO stock at the offering price and it is a hot issue, then it makes sense to participate. A hot issue is an IPO that increases in value immediately upon the effective date of the offering. So, investors holding stock at the opening price have made money immediately.

To spot a hot IPO, look for the following three factors:

1. Several days before the IPO, the underwriter increases the price range and the number of shares for the offering.
2. Brokers indicate that there are no more shares available.
3. You've seen and heard a good deal of buzz in the press about the IPO.

Buying an IPO at the offering price can mean a very quick profit for investors if they sell their shares quickly. When investors do this, it is known as flipping. Underwriters, however, do not look kindly on flipping, because it causes price volatility. In fact, they sometimes penalize investors who flip by not offering them shares in a future IPO.

If you are not allocated shares at the opening price of an IPO, the smartest thing to do is to wait. In many cases, after its initial rise an IPO will come back to its offering price at some point in its trading life—or even trade below it. The main reason for this is that when a company goes public, there is tremendous excitement. As a result of the hype, the stock will usually jump a great deal. In some cases, a company's shares can double in price.

Unfortunately, there is no scientific formula for buying into an IPO. But here is one sensible approach: Wait six months from the effective date before you buy your shares. This is about the time that the lockup period expires (as explained in Chapter 5), which means that the officers and founders of the company will be selling shares. This puts undue pressure on the stock, so you may have an opportunity to buy it at a very good price.

Buying on Margin

Buying on margin is when you purchase a stock with money that's borrowed from a broker. It should be noted that buying IPOs on margin only magnifies the risk that comes with the investment.

In fact, one of the reasons for the famous stock market crash of 1929 was the widespread use of margin (which at the time was unlimited and unregulated). It wiped out many wealthy investors of the day. Although margin accounts have been fairly lucrative during bull markets, they become very dangerous in bear markets.

For the most part, the interest rates on margin loans are very competitive (and much better than most credit cards). But keep in mind that this interest can slowly eat away at your portfolio.

Let's take an example of how margin trading works: Suppose you have a $100,000 portfolio of stocks. You can borrow another $100,000 on margin and buy 10,000 shares of the XYZ IPO at $10 each. In five months, if the stock skyrockets to $20, you will have made another $100,000.

But let's suppose the stock falls to $2 per share. Your portfolio of XYZ is now worth $20,000. However, all brokerage firms have a minimum maintenance margin of 25 percent to 30 percent of the original amount borrowed—in this case $25,000 to $30,000. Since the current value of the portfolio is below the minimum maintenance margin, you will receive a margin call. This means the broker will require you to put up more cash or securities to increase the portfolio to meet the minimum maintenance margin, or the stock in the portfolio will be sold off.

This is not to say you should avoid margin trading. It can actually be an effective tool to leverage your portfolio and improve your gains. But as with any investment approach, make sure you understand the risks and do not put your portfolio in jeopardy.

Options

Within a couple of weeks, options will trade on an IPO as long as the company meets several rules from the Chicago Board Options Exchange (CBOE). For example, at least seven million shares must be owned by those other than the insiders of the company and there must be a minimum of 2,000 stockholders.

Once options start to trade, the volatility can be high, especially for the first six months or so. The main reason is that there is little trading history. In fact, this makes it almost impossible to do technical analysis on these options.

Yet options trading can be an effective tool for IPO investors and there are some interesting strategies to consider. But before diving in, let's look at the basics.

An option is a contract that comes in two forms. First, there is a call option, which gives the buyer the right to purchase 100 shares at a fixed price for a period of time (usually three months). A put option, in turn, gives the investor the right to sell 100 shares at a fixed price for a period of time.

The contract will have two parties. There is the writer of the option, who is the person who creates the option. The buyer will then pay money for it.

If one of the parties defaults (does not exercise the option), there is nothing to worry about. The exchange has something called the Options Clearing Corporation (OCC), which will back up all the trades. This assurance helps to create liquidity in the market.

Let's take an example of an options trade: Suppose XYZ has gone public at $10 and after a few weeks the stock is now at $22. You think that the stock price will continue to increase over the next quarter. So you purchase a call option on the stock that has a strike price of $21. This means you can buy the stock for the next three months at this price.

The price of the option will be at a fraction to the stock price. In our example, it is $3. Thus, to buy the option, you will pay $300 ($3 times 100 shares). This is called the premium.

A premium has two types of values. First, there is intrinsic value. This is when the stock price is higher than the strike price (for a call option). In our example, the intrinsic value is $1 ($22 stock price minus the $21 strike price), which means the option is in-the-money. If the stock price is lower than the strike price, the call option is considered out-of-the-money.

The remaining $2 of the premium is the time value. This is what investors are willing to pay for the bet that the intrinsic value in the option will increase. However, the more time that goes by, the less chance there is of this happening, so the more the time value falls.

Let's say you are correct and the stock price goes up $4 to $26. The intrinsic value also goes up $4 and is now $5; the premium is now $6, which includes $1 in time value. As you can see, you have doubled your investment. This is the fact even though the underlying stock increased by only 23 percent. Basically, options provide you with the ability to leverage your trades.

You do not have to wait until the option expires to take the profit. Instead, you can sell your option on the open market. Consider that many options are not exercised.

But leverage can be a negative if the trade goes bad. Suppose the stock falls to $21. By the time the option expires, you will have $0 value in the option. This means your entire investment of $300 will be wiped out.

While a call option is a bullish bet, you can take the other side of the trade with a put option. This allows you to sell 100 shares at a fixed price for a period of time (again, usually three months). Continuing with our example, suppose XYZ falls to $18. The premium will be $6. Again, you will have made 100 percent. But just as with a call, if the trade goes against you, you can easily lose all your initial investment.

To deal with the problems of the erosion of time value, investors may instead use Long-Term Equity Anticipation Securities (LEAPS). These are the same as regular options but will expire within one to three years.

While this may seem attractive, the premiums for LEAPS can be expensive. In other words, if you make a mistake on the trade, you can still lose a substantial amount.

So as you can see, options and LEAPS can be risky. This is why a brokerage firm will require that you set up a new type of account, which may require more cash. It may also prevent you from using certain types of options strategies.

To better understand options, it is helpful to do paper trading. This involves doing hypothetical trades, such as by using a spreadsheet or a website. After a while, you get a feel for how options strategies play out and the kinds of risks to expect.

Now, let's take a look at some options strategies that can help with investing in IPOs.

Covered Call

There are two parties to an option: the writer and the buyer. The writer creates the option and gets to keep the premium. If the option is a call and you own 100 shares of the underlying stock, then you have a covered call.

Here's an example: You bought shares of the XYZ IPO for $20 and they have gone to $30. You think the long term is bright and do not want to sell just yet. But you have a nagging worry that the stock may fall.

To get some additional income, you can write a call for 100 shares at $31. The premium on the option is $300, which you get to keep.

If the stock does not go above $31 or falls lower, you get to keep the premium. The stock can actually fall by $3 and you will still have not lost any ground on your trade.

But a covered call will limit your upside. Suppose that XYZ has a blow-out earnings report and the stock soars to $38. True, you will keep the $3 but you will forgo the additional $4 because this will benefit the buyer of the call option, who will likely exercise the contract and buy your shares for $31 each.

Also, you do not have to wait for an option to expire. That is, you can cancel out your trade by buying an identical option. If you already have a gain in the covered call, you can close out the transaction. You can then set up another covered call. This rolling activity is quite common for investors who want to generate additional income.

Some investors will have a so-called naked position when they write a call. This means that they do not own the underlying 100 shares.

However, this can be risky. If the stock is exercised, you will have to buy the 100 shares in the aftermarket and then deliver them to the call buyer. Continuing our example, suppose the stock price of XYZ goes to $50. You will need to purchase 100 shares for a total of $5,000. Of course, it was not worth the small $300 premium to risk this happening.

Think of it this way: your gain is limited but your losses are theoretically unlimited!

Straddle

In a straddle, you will purchase a put and a call that have the same strike price and expiration date. Why do this? It is for when a stock is poised for a big move—whether on the upside or the downside. IPO investors will use this strategy several days ahead of an earnings report. Because the company is new to analysts, the stock can experience extreme volatility.

Example: Let's say XYZ recently had its IPO and will report its earnings in two days. The company is in the red-hot social networking space. But analyst earnings forecasts for XYZ have wide ranges, which indicate little confidence on the outcome of the quarter.

The current stock price is $20. You purchase a call and a put with the same exercise price. The call has a premium of $3 and the put has a premium of $2. You pay $500 for both of the options.

So let's say the company reports better than expected earnings and the stock spikes to $7. The call will have a value of $8 and the value of the put will collapse.

For the most part, the cost of this trade can be expensive. To deal with this, some investors will focus on out-of-the-money options, which should be cheaper. But still, the strategy can be risky and should be used with some caution.

Credit Spreads

Credit spreads involve simultaneously buying and selling options. This means the investor will need to make a purchase but will also get to collect a premium. Netting this out, if the investor winds up with more cash, it is a net credit. If not, the trade is a debit spread.

Here are some common approaches.

Bear Call Spread

You will sell a call with a strike price that is the same as the market price. Then you will buy an out-of-the-money call. With this trade, you are betting that the stock will fall.

Example: XYZ is selling at $50. You sell a $50 call for $2 and buy a $52 call for $1. You have a net credit of $100, which is your maximum profit. That is, you keep the premium if the stock price stays at the current price or falls, as the calls will then expire worthless.

Bull Put Spreads

You think the recent IPO of XYZ will continue to see gains. To capitalize on this, you set up a bull put spread. You will sell a put near the current stock price and buy a put that is below the stock price. If the stock price rises above the strike prices, you will earn a profit, as the options will expire worthless.

For example, XYZ is currently trading at $50. You sell a $50 put for $2 and buy a $45 put for $1. The net is that you get a $100 credit. If the stock remains at $50 or increases, you get to keep this.

But if the stock falls below this level, you will have a limited loss. While the value of the put you sold will fall, the value of the put you bought will increase. The maximum loss will be $400.

Conclusion

Perhaps the best piece of advice to take away from this chapter, and this book, is to avoid getting caught up in the hype that often comes with an IPO. It is easy to be lured by the potential for huge gains. But patience is the key. Do your research, study the fundamentals, and wait for the hype to subside. In the end, you should get better value.

CHAPTER 11

Short Selling IPOs

A famous example of short selling takes us back to the debunked carpet-cleaning company ZZZZ Best, founded in November 1985. The founder of the company, Barry Minkow, was in his early twenties.

In 1987, the Feshbach brothers, investors who specialized in selling short, began to spot some peculiarities with the company. First, ZZZZ Best announced an extraordinary $8 million contract for carpet cleaning of two buildings in Sacramento. After some research, however, the Feshbach brothers determined that the largest carpet-cleaning contract to date was a mere $3.5 million awarded for cleaning the carpets at the MGM Grand and the Las Vegas Hilton. Therefore, the $8 million announcement from Minkow looked like a sham.

The Feshbach brothers took the false contract as a sign that the company was in trouble, so they aggressively shorted the stock—and in the end made a fortune.

ZZZZ Best filed for bankruptcy soon after, and Minkow was eventually sentenced to 25 years for securities fraud. It turned out that ZZZZ Best had no revenues at all but was instead a money-laundering scheme.

You don't have to uncover criminal fraud to short a stock; however, you should have a good reason to believe the stock price is about to drop in value. And the way to make money on these trades is with short selling.

How Short Selling Works

Short selling somehow seems wrong. Yet many of the world's top investors engage in the practice. This is especially the case with hedge fund managers like George Soros, John Paulson, David Einhorn, Bill Ackman, and Paul Tudor Jones.

Consider that some of history's most profitable trades were short positions. For example, Soros made $1 billion in a few days when he shorted the British pound in the early 1990s.

But the biggest short was from John Paulson. In 2007 and 2008, he made $6 billion by shorting complex instruments that focused on subprime mortgages.

Even though short selling has been mostly for sophisticated investors, the mechanics are fairly straightforward. Let's take a look: Suppose a company does an initial public offering (IPO) and the stock soars from $10 to $20 on the first day of trading. Also let's say that you have reason to believe that at that price the stock is highly overvalued and it will collapse.

To short the stock, you will first borrow 1,000 shares; you then sell all of them at $20 each, netting $20,000. This amount will be kept in an escrow account.

To unwind the trade, you will need to pay back the 1,000 shares that you borrowed. This is known as "covering your short position." If the share price is below $20, you will make a profit on the trade. That is, suppose the stock falls to $15. You buy the shares for $15,000 and return them to the lender. In the end, you made $5,000.

However, the maximum gain you can make is $20,000 if the stock falls to $0. True, this happens, but it is rare.

But you can potentially lose much more than $20,000. For example, perhaps the stock soars to $60,000. You will have to buy the shares at this price, which will result in a $40,000 loss. As you can see, short selling can be a risky strategy.

Mechanics

To engage in short selling, you need to establish both cash and margin accounts. You will have to fill out various forms and put down a minimum amount of cash, say $1,000 to $2,000.

You will also need to disclose if you are an officer of a public company or a major shareholder (that is, you own 10 percent or more of the outstanding shares). The reason is that it would be illegal to short that stock.

The margin account essentially allows you to borrow shares to short. The total positions may not exceed 50 percent of the amount of cash and assets in the account. Keep in mind that such margin requirements are regulated by the federal government and can get extremely complex. Also, your brokerage firm will usually have more extensive requirements so as to help minimize some of the loss exposure.

In the margin account, you will need to own stock in Street name, which means that the brokerage will retain the stock certificates. This is actually a smart approach, anyway. After all, if you lose the certificates, you will need to post a bond and wait at least a month to resolve the matter.

Moreover, a margin account will have a hypothecation clause. It sounds scary, but it is straightforward. It means that the broker can use the stock in your account to make loans of your shares. Yes, these are used by other short sellers to make transactions.

Finally, you will probably have to get a credit check when setting up a margin account. It's normal. But if you are denied for some reason, you have a right to get the credit report. Make sure there are no errors.

IPO Shorts

Shorting IPOs can be quite lucrative. It is not uncommon for newly public companies to quickly have troubles—such as a bad earnings report—and see a big plunge in the stock price.

But there are limitations. For example, it will take a few weeks to be able to short the stock. Why? A brokerage firm will need to have physical possession of the stock to allow the short selling.

What's more, large investors like hedge funds may also borrow large amounts of the securities to take short positions. In other words, it can be difficult for retail investors to get any stock.

Finally, there are some stocks that are not marginable. Basically, they trade on a market other than the New York Stock Exchange (NYSE) or the NASDAQ or may be penny stocks. A broker sees these shares as too speculative.

Margin Calls

Let's say you short the IPO of XYZ. But after about a week, the stock price actually increases by 10 percent. Your broker will issue you a margin call.

Now, do not panic. Margin calls are quite common. And you should have a few days to respond. But you will need to put up more cash or start lightening up your position.

Some short sellers would prefer to do the latter. They see a margin call as a sign that the original analysis on the short was off base.

Short Selling Increases Outstanding Shares

If a stock pays a dividend, you will actually have to pay it when you short the stock. For this reason, many short sellers avoid these types of stock.

Why must you pay the dividend? The reason is that short selling increases the outstanding shares of a company.

Here's an example: XYZ has 10 million shares outstanding. You think the stock will plunge and decide to short a million shares. You borrow the shares from Howard and then sell them on the market.

Yet Howard still owns his million shares. So, the stock that you have sold has increased the number of XYZ's shares to 11 million.

When the company pays its dividend, there will be a payment to Howard for his one million shares but not to you. But the person to whom you sold one million shares is still entitled to a payment. In other words, you will need to write a check for this.

Risks of Short Selling

Because short selling is often considered nefarious, there are many regulations on the practice. Some of these have added to the risks.

The main risks are the following:

- *Interest.* By having a margin account, you will need to pay interest on your balances. While the rates are usually not high, they can still eat into your returns. This is especially the case if you hold on to a short position for over six months.
- *Bull market.* This is horrible for short sellers. In a bull market, most stocks increase in value, regardless of the quality. Things are even worse when the market is in a bubble, such as during the dot-com frenzy. Granted, some short sellers were right that stocks like Webvan and Pets.com would go bust, but many took positions too early. Some of these investors even went broke because they could not pay off their margin calls.
- *Buy-in.* When you set up a margin account, you must agree to this. It means that the brokerage firm can require that you cover your short position at any time. This is often the case when it has sold a lot of stock and needs to get the certificates. Unfortunately, a brokerage firm will usually issue buy-ins to smaller clients first.
- *Short squeeze.* This can be extremely painful. If there is positive news, the stock will spike, but the gain may be exaggerated because short sellers will panic and cover their positions. Of course, this means even more buying of the shares. The result can be an upward spiral in the stock price.

To avoid a short squeeze, you might want to look at the short interest in the stock. This shows the total number of shares short in a company. You can then divide this by the float, which is the number of shares that are traded. If the result is over 10 percent, the stock could be vulnerable to a short squeeze.

- *Mergers and acquisitions.* True, these are not common after an IPO, but they are still a risk. After all, an acquisition is often at a premium to the current stock price, say 30 percent or 40 percent. No doubt this could mean a big loss if you have a short position. So avoid any company that is likely to be a buyout candidate.
- *Uptick rule.* This is a federal regulation that goes back to the Great Depression. Again, it was a way to fight back against the shorts. The widespread belief was that short sellers were the main culprit for the economic mess.

  The uptick rule means you can short a stock only when the price has increased on the previous trade. While this is not necessarily a risk per se, it is yet another frustration that investors must deal with.

Taxes

Taxes can get complicated for short sales. In fact, it is worth getting a qualified tax adviser to help out.

For example, suppose you buy shares of the IPO of XYZ and the stock price surges by 50 percent. You are a bit worried there may be a pullback, so you short the stock. The effect is that you lock in your gain. If the stock falls, your long position will fall but your short position will offset the loss.

It is called "shorting against the box." But the problem is that the Internal Revenue Service (IRS) may consider this a "constructive" sale and you might owe taxes on the gains.

Something else: It is impossible to get a long-term capital gain on a short sale transaction. The reason is that the IRS considers that you own the shares for a brief period of time—that is, when you cover your short. This means you are subject to short-term capital gains or ordinary tax rates, which are generally higher than long-term capital gains rates.

Finding IPOs to Short

Throughout this book, we have taken a look at the types of factors that make an IPO less attractive, such as declining margins, more competition, and slowing growth. Of course, these can be excellent factors when evaluating a short sale candidate.

So here are some other general things to keep an eye on:

- A business model that has a long history of not producing profits.
- Aggressive accounting (see Chapter 9).

- A broken IPO (shows weak demand and lots of skepticism from investors).
- Missing the first quarter's earnings estimate as a public company.
- Substantial selling by the company's officers and founders—50 percent or more of their positions.
- Small underwriters.
- Going-concern audit determination.

Conclusion

Keep in mind that short selling is an advanced technique. So before doing it, start with small positions, which are a good way to learn about the risks.

It is usually a good idea to get out of a position early. The interest costs on your margin account can add up. There may even be a short squeeze. Thus, you may not want to keep a short position open beyond six months or so.

PART III

IPO Sectors

CHAPTER 12

Tech IPOs

The first thing that usually pops into people's minds when they think of initial public offerings (IPOs) is high-tech companies. Some of history's best stock gains have come from companies like Apple, Microsoft, Oracle, Google, and Cisco. There are cases in which regular investors have made hundreds of thousands or even millions of dollars from such stocks.

Of course, tech IPOs can be risky. Consider that many of the dot-com offerings wound up falling to zero. And going forward, there will certainly be other bubbles. It's the nature of the tech industry.

But for investors, the long haul should provide huge investment opportunities for IPOs. The world economy is going through an epoch of change comparable to the industrial revolution. But instead of wealth being generated by coal, iron, steel, oil, and railroads, the new economy is founded on things on a smaller scale: software, microchips, smartphones, and social networking.

The Cloud

Marc Benioff has had a storied career in technology. In the 1980s, he worked with Steve Jobs at Apple as a computer programmer. He then moved over to Oracle and became one of its top employees.

But he wanted to start his own company. So in March 1999, he rented a San Francisco apartment and set forth on the mission to achieve the "End of Software." The result was a pioneering company called Salesforce.com.

In his book *Behind the Cloud*, he wrote:

> I started salesforce.com . . . with the goal of making enterprise software as easy to use as a Web site like Amazon.com. That idea—to deliver business

131

applications as a service over the Internet—would change the way businesses use sophisticated software application and, ultimately, change the way the software business worked.

This type of technology would become known as the "cloud" and would make Salesforce.com into one of the best IPOs of the past decade. In June 2004, the company issued 10 million shares at $11 each. On its first day of trading, the stock hit $17.20. By 2012, investors got a return of over 845 percent.

The performance was no fluke. Other cloud companies that have come public have also seen top results, like SuccessFactors, NetSuite, and Concur.

Until about 2007 to 2008, the cloud market was still mostly for early adopters. Many companies simply believed that it was too risky to have data and applications outside their own walls. What about security? What if the cloud operator's system went down?

Along the way, there were certainly occasional problems. For example, in 2009 Salesforce.com had a major outage. Yet the company worked quickly to solve it and even set up Trust.salesforce.com. In real time it showed the uptime of all of Salesforce.com's services. It became a standard in the industry.

As time went by, the cloud gained greater acceptance. Even Fortune 500 companies started using the technology.

And it looks like the growth is still in its early stages. Gartner predicts that the cloud market is expected to grow from $10 billion in 2010 to $22.7 billion in 2015.

The primary way cloud companies charge for software is through subscriptions. They may be month-to-month purchases as well as arrangements that are based on the user count or the data usage. Often a cloud company will require a customer to pay a year's worth of subscription or more. Usually these contracts are noncancelable for the term (which can range from one to three years). This helps to improve cash flows as well as predictability of the revenue stream.

But under generally accepted accounting principles (GAAP), a cloud company is not allowed to recognize all of this revenue up front. Rather, it can recognize only the fees that relate to each quarter. So if there are fees beyond this, the cloud operator must classify them as deferred revenues.

Because of this, revenues tend to be understated for cloud companies. So for investors, it is important to look at deferred revenues to get a better idea of the overall business.

Keep in mind that not all revenues will be subscription-based. After all, a cloud operator will likely get fees for implementing and integrating software as well as training. If this revenue is 30 percent or more of the total, then that is actually a sign that the software is not easy to use and has a long sales cycle. It could mean there will be slower growth and a muted valuation.

When looking at a cloud company, here are some factors to consider:

- *Cost/revenue drivers.* Most cloud companies help customers reduce their costs because of automation of work flows. This is certainly a great benefit, but there could be more. A cloud company can actually help companies find ways to improve revenues. This is something that always gets the attention of customers.

  One example of this is athenahealth. The company developed a cloud-based platform that helps physicians collect more reimbursements. Athenahealth even collects a percentage of the increase in sales. In all, it has turned into a powerful business.

  You also want a cloud company that makes it easy to customize its software. To this end, Salesforce.com accomplished this by allowing third parties to create applications on its platform. It was similar to the iTunes concept.

  Finally, the sales cycle for the purchase of business software can be long. It can easily take over one year. So look for a cloud company that gets customers on board fairly quickly. Some of the new players in the market, like Dropbox, Box, and Yammer, have free versions that make it extremely easy to start using the product. Over time, these companies will upsell premium offerings.

- *Innovation.* Software customers expect certain core feature sets. These often include access to mobile apps, such as for smartphones and tablets. There is often a requirement that there be a social layer. If these are missing, then an investor should be cautious.

- *Average revenue per customer.* This is often not disclosed. But a cloud operator will probably disclose the customer count, perhaps for the past few years. In this case, you can divide the revenue amount by the customer count. If there is a steady rise, say 5 percent to 10 percent per year, then it is an indication that customers are likely paying for more usage of the software. Of course, if the number is declining, then there may be some inherent problems.

Social Networking

Major technology trends often need some critical drivers. This was certainly the case with the emergence of social networking, which got traction in 2003. At the time, broadband was much more prevalent, which made Internet access faster. The growth in digital cameras was also key because they allowed for uploading of photos. Another important factor was that people were getting more comfortable using the Internet, and this meant posting personal information about themselves.

In the early days of social networking, there were a variety of sites that grew quickly—but would eventually fizzle out. They included operators like Friendster, MySpace, Bebo, and tribe.net.

So why did Facebook become the dominant player in the space? There are some important factors. First, the company's CEO and founder realized that Facebook needed to constantly focus on its mission of making it easier for users to share their experiences. For example, when it launched Facebook Photos, the market was already saturated with these kinds of services. But Facebook focused on making it unique by allowing users to tag their friends in the pictures. It turned out to be a killer feature, and within a year Facebook Photos was the biggest photo-sharing site in the world.

With any type of technology company, especially one that focuses on consumers, it is a good idea to see how the product evolves. Is it aligned with its core mission? Does the company even have a mission?

Now, even though Facebook is the clear leader in social networking, there will still be more opportunities for other companies to exploit high-growth niches. For example, LinkedIn has built a $10 billion business in social networking for professionals. Then there is Yelp, which has become a leader in online reviews for restaurants and other local businesses.

At the core of a social network is the value of its data. Essentially, users provide information about themselves, which tends to be fairly accurate. Because of this, a social network can be a tremendous vehicle for advertising revenues. For example, on Facebook it is possible to target an ad to 20- to 25-year-olds who live in Seattle and like the movie *The Social Network*. No other advertising medium has provided this kind of detail.

But when looking at a social networking investment, it is worth keeping some things in mind. First, look for a company that has lots of engagement, which means that users keep coming back to the site. One way to measure this is with a metric called daily active users (DAUs). For Facebook, it was an astounding 526 million in the first quarter of 2012.

You should also look for a company that has multiple revenue streams. The fact is that advertising revenue can be volatile.

LinkedIn is a social network that has been versatile with its revenue streams; that is, the company has four of them: premium subscriptions, self-serve ads, sponsorships, and corporate recruiting services.

Mobile

Mobile technologies have been around for decades. But with the introduction of the smartphone, the industry has seen tremendous growth. The business has been key in making Apple the world's most valuable company.

Smartphones are essentially becoming a daily habit for people. Interestingly, though, it seems they are only occasionally used for making calls and instead are mostly used for other things like texting, taking photos, playing games, checking the weather, finding a review for a restaurant, and so on. In fact, the rate of adoption has been incredibly fast.

And it will definitely continue. Here are some notable projections:

- The number of mobile connected devices will reach 7.1 billion by 2015 (Cisco).
- The number of smartphone shipments is expected to go from 305 million in 2010 to one billion by 2015 (IDC).
- Wi-Fi–enabled devices are predicted to go from one billion in 2010 to three billion in 2015.
- Third-generation (3G) mobile communications represented 17 percent of the worldwide market in 2011 and are forecasted to go to 49 percent in 2015 (Informa Telecoms & Media).
- The number of mobile apps downloads is expected to surge from 8.2 billion in 2010 to 108 billion in 2015 (Gartner).

Tablets have also become another super-fast-growing mobile device. Of course, the spark was Apple's iPad in 2010. A year later, the market saw 63 million shipments, and the prediction is for 139 million by 2015, according to International Data Corporation (IDC).

With so much attention focused on mobile devices, the biggest money-making opportunity is likely to be advertising. The medium has some important advantages. First, it is possible to get more data on a person, such as in terms of location. For example, it is now possible to target advertising for a certain restaurant or store to users when they are nearby.

It is also easier to personalize a mobile experience. After all, people keep their phones with them throughout the day. What's more, by downloading apps, a company can be a part of that person's life. It is a powerful brand presence and can lead to ongoing usage and customer loyalty.

But over time, the smartphone will become a part of the purchase decision. That is, it will become common to use it as a way to make payments or use rewards.

Another monetization opportunity is in-app purchases. This is when a user makes a purchase while using an app (which was likely downloaded for free). A frequent use is games, such as by Zynga. But there are likely to be many other applications. According to Gartner, the market for in-app revenues is expected to go from $4 billion in 2010 to $52.3 billion in 2015.

Marketplaces

An online marketplace can be a powerful business. A classic example is eBay. In the mid-1990s, the company started as a hobby—but it quickly turned into a hugely profitable business.

It is important to focus on the leader. Usually, it will become the standard and, as a result, the rivals will quickly fade away. After all, when it comes to online auctions, eBay is still the dominant global player.

A key driver for the success of marketplaces is that customers can make a decent amount of side income. In the case of eBay, some people can make thousands of dollars each year from selling their unwanted stuff. With such an incentive, there is little need to go elsewhere. The result is that a successful online marketplace tends to have lock-in with its customers.

Over the past few years, the IPO market has seen some online marketplaces go public. One is HomeAway. The company went public in June 2011 and its stock rose nearly 50 percent on its first day of trading.

The company is the world's largest online marketplace for the vacation rental industry. It has leveraged Internet technology to make it easier to find renters as well as to manage the rental process, such as with background checks and credit card handling. When the company went public, it had about 560,000 listings of vacation rentals and its websites averaged 9.5 million unique monthly visitors. From 2005 to 2010, revenues soared from $8.4 million to $167.9 million.

Something that has been important to HomeAway is that it has created a trusted platform (this is crucial for any marketplace). To this end, the company was smart to have a dedicated customer support organization as well as a sophisticated system to catch fraudulent listings.

Security

Security has been a big pain point for companies. When there is a breach, the consequences can be devastating. One of the most notorious was when hackers accessed information on over 100 million credit cards from Sony's PlayStation.

Across the world, governments have implemented compliance requirements to protect information. Thus, violations can result in onerous fines and ongoing audits.

All in all, data security threats continue to get worse. Many involve sophisticated Mafia organizations. There are even cases of state-sponsored hacking. According to the U.S. Defense Department, this kind of activity may actually constitute an act of war.

Hackers are now focusing more on high-value targets, such as credit cards, Social Security numbers, intellectual property, and health care records. Such information can lead to identity theft, insurance fraud, and bank theft. It's all very chilling.

Here are some statistics:

- The year 2011 saw a 44 percent increase in cyber attacks (Ponemon Institute).
- Approximately $300 billion in intellectual property was stolen in the United States during 2011 (Gartner).
- The global market for hacked data is about $1 trillion (Joseph Menn, who is the author of the *Fatal System Error*).

Legacy security solutions—like firewalls and antivirus software—have generally not been able to deal with the new types of threats. But this has been a big opportunity for new companies that have broader approaches and deeper technologies.

The market is also massive. IDC says that the security software market was $27 billion in 2010 and will grow to $38 billion by 2014. In fact, many security software IPOs have been big winners for investors. Look at Fortinet, which went public in late 2009. The stock is up nearly 200 percent. Then there is Sourcefire, which had its IPO in March 2007; its gain is more than 250 percent.

Big Data

To allow for megatrends like the cloud and mobile, there needs to be a sophisticated infrastructure. Legacy systems were simply not designed to handle the huge amounts of data. In fact, this has led to the emergence of a new category of technology: big data.

There are two main forms:

1. *Human-generated content.* This includes data created by people, such as documents, Short Message Service (SMS), video, photos, and social media. No doubt Facebook has been a big driver of this information.

The problem is that the data is usually not in a standardized format, which makes it difficult to analyze.

2. *Machine data.* This is created by software applications and mobile devices. Examples of the data include log files, call records, clickstreams, and geo-location information.

Based on the research from IDC, the amount of data is expected to grow at an annual rate of 45 percent from 1.8 trillion gigabytes in 2011 to 7.9 trillion gigabytes in 2015.

Tracking and understanding this data is crucial. It can help detect security breaches or issues with a website (such as a page not working). For some companies, big data has become a key competitive advantage. Consider that Zynga processes huge amounts of data to understand user behavior. It has been extremely effective in making its games more engaging, which often means more revenues.

According to Gartner, the market opportunity for big data is about $18.6 billion. Essentially, this type of technology will eventually uproot older approaches, such as business intelligence software and web analytics.

One of the first big data companies to go public was Splunk. In April 2012, the company issued shares at $17 and ended its first day of trading at $35.48.

Splunk has developed a platform that allows companies to analyze machine data in real time. It generally helps to reduce costs, mitigate security risks, and improve business decision-making.

From fiscal 2010 to 2012, revenues went from $35 million to $121 million. The company had over 3,700 customers, which included major companies like Bank of America, Comcast, and even Zynga.

With the surge in big data, there will definitely be more IPOs in the sector over the next decade. But they may not be public for the long haul. Big data is likely to be a strategic asset, which will attract acquisitions from major tech companies like Oracle, IBM, and EMC Corporation.

Evaluating a Tech IPO

When thinking about investing in a tech IPO, it is important to consider the following:

- *Continuing research and development (R&D).* R&D is absolutely crucial in high-tech growth. Although large expenditures reduce current earnings, over the long term R&D can result in tremendous gains.

As a general rule, you want to see a company spend at least 7 percent of its revenues on R&D. But spending the right amount on R&D is not the only factor to check. That money must also be spent wisely. One way to gauge the effectiveness of R&D efforts is by examining several years historically. Suppose the company spent $5 million five years ago on R&D to build a product. Was the product released within a few years of that expenditure? And how did it compare to similar products from the rest of the industry?

- *Revolutionizing a traditional business.* If you're lucky enough to spot a company that's truly changing an industry for the better, you've probably found a winner. FedEx revolutionized a very old business, the delivery of packages, by guaranteeing overnight service. Amazon.com has revolutionized bookselling by bringing its shelves online and building a tremendous website.

- *Creating the standard.* A company that becomes a real industry touchstone can essentially capture a market. A classic example is Microsoft. The company had the foresight to predict that personal computers would need a standardize operating system. By focusing on DOS, the company created a cash cow. It provided resources to build other products, such as for computer networking and its Office Suite. But Microsoft realized that a standard must evolve. To this end, the company moved toward a graphical user interface with Windows in the mid-1990s.

  It also looks like Facebook may essentially be a standard. That is, it has become the core platform to allow for social networking. Consider that thousands of companies build applications on the system. Some of them have created billion-dollar franchises, like Zynga. Facebook has also become the standard way for many web services to register and log in.

- *Multimarket potential.* Look for software products that can be used for many different markets. It is common for tech companies to have systems that are really useful only for small niches, so breaking into new markets is often expensive and risky.

- *Management.* You want a CEO who is considered a visionary in the industry. True, they may get some things wrong, but they still understand the important trends and focus on them. Companies like Microsoft, Oracle, and Dell would have likely been small-time operators if it were not for their well-respected CEOs.

- *Beware of massive infrastructure plays.* These are ventures that spend huge sums to build communications networks. During the late 1990s, there were many of these companies, like Global Crossing, which were investing in fiber-optic cables to allow for broadband systems. They required frequent issuances of shares and debt.

But there were some problems. First, the competition resulted in rapidly declining prices. True, this was good for consumers but horrific for companies.

Next, the funding environment dried up. When this happened, many of the infrastructure operators went bust.

Conclusion

Although there are many success stories for high-tech IPOs, they do not provide a guaranteed road to riches. In fact, some of the worst-faring IPOs have been high-tech companies. A company may be king one day and dethroned the next. To invest successfully in high-tech IPOs, you need to actually understand the innovation. It requires a lot of work, but the financial rewards may be worth it.

Reference

Menn, Joseph. 2010. *Fatal System Error*. New York: Public Affairs.

CHAPTER 13

Biotech IPOs

Biotech is a relatively new industry, dating back only to the mid-1970s. The underlying science involves the development of drugs using the DNA code. There might be, for example, a genetic defect that causes a certain disease; scientists will then endeavor to isolate the defect and to create a drug to cure the ailment.

The result can be huge gains for investors but it often takes a prolonged period of time. This was the case with Amgen Inc. George Rathmann started the company in 1980 by getting a round of venture capital of $8.5 million. A year later, he snagged $19.4 million more.

But it was still not enough. By 1982, the company was running out of money.

Rathmann believed that a better way to finance the company was to have an initial public offering (IPO). It was certainly a gutsy decision since Amgen had no revenues.

The company issued 2.35 million shares at $18, raising $42.3 million. But the offering was far from easy. The stock price plunged to $10 but was able to recover to $16.75 by the end of the day's trading.

Keep in mind that it would take roughly nine years for Amgen's first drug, called Epogen, to come on the market. But it was worth the wait. Here's what the revenue ramp was for the company:

Year	Sales	Profits
1988	$19.1 million	−$8.1 million
1989	$19.1 million	$199.1 million
1990	$34.3 million	$381.2 million
1991	$97.9 million	$682 million
1992	$1.1 billion	$357.6 million

Some analysts believe that the biotech industry today is where the computer industry was 30 years ago—poised for substantial growth.

If biotechnology lives up to expectations, it could revolutionize modern medicine and, in the process, create significant opportunities for investors.

Because of the highly technical nature of the industry, it's difficult to pinpoint the companies and products that will be the first to emerge.

Factors fueling the growth in biotech include:

- *Revolutionary approaches.* Traditional pharmaceutical companies develop chemical-based drugs. But for the most part, these types of drugs only treat the symptoms; they do not cure the disease. The genetic drugs created by biotechnology companies are designed to prevent the cells of a disease from mutating or to kill the cells that are creating the disease.
- *Wider applications.* The biotech industry has the brainpower and scope of research to develop cures for such intractable diseases as cancer, heart disease, AIDS, Alzheimer's, and even manic depression. But there are other applications. Biotech may help create alternatives to fossil fuels or help clean the environment by creating microbes that eat radioactive wastes. There are also attempts at creating computer chips out of DNA structures.
- *Growth.* From 2010 to 2020, health care spending in the United States is expected to go from $2.6 trillion to $4.6 trillion. This translates into an annual growth rate of 5.8 percent. Consider that about 11 percent of spending is expected to be for prescription drugs.

   A big factor will be the aging of the population, which will ultimately become eligible for government programs like Medicare and Medicaid.
- *Patent cliff.* This describes when a pharmaceutical company's drug sales plunge because the patents expire. The reason is that there will generally be a variety of generic drug operators that will provide cheap alternatives.

   The problem is that pharmaceutical companies have had many difficulties over the past decade creating new drugs. In other words, the patent cliff is likely to mean a big hole in revenue. So to deal with this, one strategy is to fund and acquire biotech companies. According to the research from Evaluate Pharma, the six biggest-selling drugs in the world will be biotech formulations by 2014.
- *Orphan drugs.* In 1983, Congress passed the Orphan Drug Act. The goal was to provide financial incentives for biotech companies to create drugs for diseases that impact small populations. This has certainly provided a boost to the biotech industry. Consider that there are thousands of diseases that fit the requirements for the law.

- *National Institutes of Health (NIH).* This government organization spends $30 billion per year in early-stage research on medical treatments. No doubt this has been a key source of innovation and the foundation for many strong biotech companies.
- *Academic research.* At the same time, the U.S. university system has some of the world's best researchers. It also helps that these institutions can generate licensing revenues from the drugs developed.
- *Margins.* Besides the potential for high revenue growth, biotech companies often have high gross margins. It's not uncommon to have levels reaching 80 percent or even higher. A key reason is that the company will have strong protection for the product because of its patents.
- *Risks.* Despite all these benefits, investors still must understand that the biotech industry involves lots of failed drugs. The scientific process is complex and highly unpredictable. Besides, the U.S. Food and Drug Administration (FDA) is the most rigorous in the world.

  According to the Pharmaceutical Research and Manufacturers of America (PhRMA), for every 5,000 compounds in the lab, only five go on to human testing. Of these, only one will get FDA approval.

  This failure rate adds a huge amount to the overall cost of developing a drug. For the most part, the average is $500 million and the time to market is a decade or more.

FDA Approval

Understanding the Food and Drug Administration (FDA) approval process is crucial for investing in biotech companies. Before a company can sell a drug to the public, the FDA must be convinced that it is safe. Thus, if there is no approval, there is no product and there is zero revenue. It is primarily for this reason that biotech stocks are so volatile and often go bust.

Here is a simplified version of the steps a biotech company must take to receive FDA approval:

- *Preclinical testing (six months to one year).* When a drug is first developed, the company conducts preclinical tests (all tests are governed by the FDA, which, unfortunately, leads to long lead times for approval). The drug may be tested on cells of animals to evaluate its safety. If the drug appears to be effective, the company will file an Investigative New Drug (IND) application with the FDA to get approval to test on humans. Success in preclinical testing does not mean the drug is the next Rogaine or Viagra. In fact, many of the drugs that get preclinical approval from the FDA fail when testing is done on humans.

- *Phase I: testing on humans (one to two years).* This phase typically involves testing on approximately 25 paid volunteers. In some cases, these volunteers are prisoners or terminally ill patients. The tests involve variations in dosage in order to determine the safety and side effects of the drug.

- *Phase II: wider testing (one to two years).* This phase is conducted on a much larger group of people, about 100 to 1,000. It takes months to plan and to set up Phase II, which involves determining the efficacy of the drug based on several different doses. This phase determines how much of the drug can be administered and also measures the effect on the illness of various doses.

  In many ways, this is the most critical phase of the approval process. About 50 percent of the drugs that have success in Phase II ultimately reach the market.

- *Phase III: final phase (two to three years).* Thousands of people are tested in Phase III, which includes placebo-control, double-blind tests. That is, one group is given a placebo (which is a sugar pill), and the other is given the drug. Double-blind means that neither the patients nor the doctors know who is getting the placebo and who is receiving the real drug. Basically, this test determines whether the drug is better than a placebo.

If the drug is approved at Phase III, the stock price of a biotech company will usually soar. But the process is still not over! The company then files an FDA application for marketing approval. This can take about one year, after which the company is free to market and sell the drug to the public.

But even after all this, there still may be risks; that is, there may be unanticipated side effects. If so, the FDA may require that the drug be taken off the market.

Analyzing Biotech IPOs

Analyzing biotech IPOs is extremely difficult for most of us. As you read biotech prospectuses, you will notice some highly technical terms, such as nucleotides, amino acids, monoclonal antibodies, and antisense oligonucleotides. It's almost as though you need to be an MD to understand the terminology. In fact, many Wall Street analysts who follow biotech stocks are MDs.

Since most biotech IPOs have drugs that are in the development stage, you are essentially analyzing the stock based on the potential outcome of pending research. So how do you value this research? How can you determine whether the company will pass the final phases of FDA approval? It's almost impossible for potential investors to know how a drug will fare in testing. What's more, when a biotech company's drug fails the FDA approval process, the results for the company can be severe. Even a delay can be a big problem.

For example, in November 2007, pharmaceutical firm ARYx Therapeutics went public and raised $50 million. The company was developing a drug to address gastrointestinal disorders.

Unfortunately, the FDA process was extremely tough and by 2011 there was a delay. While this was not necessarily a sign that the drug would fail to get approval, it was actually enough for ARYx's venture capital investors to pull the plug on the company, and the stock price went to $0.

This outcome is common in the biotech industry. As a result, the stock prices are often volatile. So for investors, exceptional stock-picking skills are critical.

Here are some strategies to help out:

- *Market potential.* Look for companies that have drugs aimed at major markets. For example, cancer treatment is a huge area (it is the second leading cause of death in the United States). Despite all the medical innovations, there has been only a modest decrease in the death rate from cancer since the early 1990s. According to the American Cancer Society, there are about 1.6 million new cases diagnosed per year and about 600,000 people will die from the disease. Based on research from the NIH, the direct medical costs exceed $100 billion.
- *Pipeline.* Look for companies with a minimum of two drugs under development and in at least Phase II of the process. If one drug fails to get approval, the company can focus on the other one.
- *Strategic partners.* Look for biotech companies with strong ties to major pharmaceutical companies. First of all, alliances provide biotech companies with much-needed capital. Most of these deals involve prepaid royalties on future sales, as well as direct investment. Second, alliances allow biotech companies to take advantage of their partners' resources, such as research, employees, and marketing. Finally, the strategic partnership validates the biotech company. In other words, a major pharmaceutical company believes there is potential in the biotech company's technology and is willing to put money and resources into it.

- *Debt.* When a biotech company goes public, it will usually not have much debt. But it may have another type of financing that has the same characteristics of debt: convertible notes. A convertible note allows an investor to convert the instrument into stock. But in the meantime, it also pays ongoing interest. If a company has a problem, the investor may have the right to demand payment of the convertible security.

  If you see a large amount of this, be careful. The biotech company could face some financing risks.

- *Burn rate.* It's ironic, but the more success a biotech company has, the higher the costs. After all, a company will need to spend huge sums for the clinical trials as well as hire new scientists.

  Because of this, a biotech company will sustain substantial losses. This is why investors should measure the burn rate. Essentially, this shows the quarterly net losses for the company. To calculate it, you first find the revenues for the current quarter (whether from the 10-Q or the 10-K) and then multiply the quarterly revenues by 4. This will give you a rough estimate of the annual spending.

  Next, you will get the cash on hand and then divide this by the annual revenue. For example, suppose a company has a quarterly loss of $25 million and $100 million in the bank. You would do the following:

$$\$25 \text{ million} \times 4 = \$100 \text{ million in annual revenue}$$
$$\$100 \text{ million}/\$100 = 1$$

  This means the company has about a year's worth of cash left. Unfortunately, this is a short runway. Most likely, a company will soon need to raise even more money, which will probably reduce the stock price. It's better to see a biotech company with about two years' worth of cash in the bank.

- *Experienced management.* As with any IPO, look for a management team with a track record. It is always reassuring if the management has been able to bring a successful drug to market previously.

  But there should be more than a strong group of PhDs. You also want to see a company that has some managers who understand the financing process. A biotech company is often raising capital.

  This was certainly the case with Amgen's Rathmann. He received a PhD in physical chemistry from Princeton University and then went over to 3M, where he quickly rose through the ranks. Then in the mid-1970s he joined Abbott Laboratories and soon became vice president of research and development (R&D). Over his career, Rathmann understood the tricky balance of great science and how to commercialize it. So by the time he helped to create Amgen, he had the right skill set to build a game-changing company.

Rathmann retired in 1990 but continued to help biotech start-ups. Unfortunately, he eventually got kidney disease—but it was Amgen's Epogen that helped keep him alive and well.

- *Scientific advisory board (SAB).* Most biotech companies have one. This is a group of researchers and experts who provide ongoing advice and feedback.

  You will find the bios of the SAB in the prospectus. As much as possible, you want to find members who have relevant experience and tremendous backgrounds. This includes not only scientists from elite universities but perhaps even Nobel Prize winners.

- *Research and development (R&D).* This is the core of any top biotech company. One way to get a sense of this is to calculate the following ratio and compare this to others in the industry:

$$R\&D \text{ expenditures} / \text{Total expenses}$$

  You'll use total expenses since there will likely be minimal—if any—revenues. Be wary of companies that spend substantial percentages on administrative costs.

- *Resources.* Before investing in any biotech IPO, take a look at the company's website. You're likely to see a wealth of information on the company, and perhaps you'll even begin to understand the science. Most important, you'll also see what drugs the company has under development and what stages of FDA approval they are in.

  There is also a website detailing FDA clinical trials called Center Watch (www.centerwatch.com), which has an abundance of useful information. You can also visit the FDA site at www.fda.gov.

Conclusion

Biotech does have a bright future. As the global population ages, there will be strong demand for new drugs. Besides, the traditional pharmaceutical industry is having trouble innovating, so the biotech industry is likely to see ongoing mergers and acquisitions.

Yet biotech IPOs can be extremely risky and require lots of research. But with so many resources on the Internet—and the help of the S-1—it is much easier nowadays to get a sense of a company's opportunity.

References

Binder, Gordon, and Philip Bashe. 2008. *Science Lessons: What the Business of Biotech Taught Me about Management.* Boston: Harvard Business School Press, 25–30.

Kavilanz, Parija. 2011. "U.S. Will Pay for Half of All Health Care Costs by 2020." *CNNMoney*, July 28. http://goo.gl/q4m8M.

CHAPTER 14

Finance Sector IPOs

David Bonderman, who started his career as a bankruptcy attorney, is now one of the world's top investors. He logs over 2,000 hours per year on his jet and scouts out investment opportunities for his private equity firm, TPG (which has $49 billion in assets).

He never flinches from taking big risks. Keep in mind that some of his biggest wins were with airline deals, such as Continental Airlines and Ryanair. He also structured a variety of deals in the aftermath of the savings and loan crisis of the late 1980s.

Yet 2008 turned out to be the time that Bonderman's magic touch got crushed. In April, he led a $7 billion investment in Washington Mutual. Bonderman got a juicy 25 percent discount on the valuation of the shares and snagged a board seat.

While Washington Mutual's mortgage portfolio was hemorrhaging, Bonderman was betting that the economy would stabilize. Besides, wouldn't the government save the bank?

Well, by September, Washington Mutual was sold to JPMorgan. Unfortunately, Bonderman lost 100 percent on his investment.

It was a huge embarrassment—and a stark reminder of the huge risks of financial services companies. After all, these types of companies have large amounts of short-term debt. So when there is a credit freeze, the consequences can be severe.

Despite all this, there are still opportunities for initial public offering (IPO) investors. But it is key to do lots of due diligence.

Banking

In the wake of the financial crisis, President Barack Obama and Congress passed landmark legislation called the Dodd-Frank Wall Street Reform and

Consumer Protection Act. In all, there are over 14,000 new regulatory requirements covering fees, capital requirements, and limitations on trading.

The result is likely to be lower profits as well as higher costs. Keep in mind that banks will need to spend much more on their own infrastructures and legal staffs. These burdens are likely to be even more severe for smaller banks.

At the same time, the reputation of the financial industry is under assault. Consumers generally have a low regard for these institutions, as seen with protests like Occupy Wall Street.

But even with all the grim developments, the banking industry may be poised for long-term growth—and this could spur moneymaking IPOs for investors. The new regulations should lessen the reckless behavior that crushed hundreds of banks. They will also likely encourage more confidence in the system.

But there are also some macroeconomic drivers. One is interest rates. Keep in mind that banks are intermediaries—they obtain money from depositors by paying them interest. They then take this money and lend it to consumers and businesses at a higher percentage of interest.

Since the financial crisis, the Federal Reserve has taken extraordinary actions to keep interest rates low—both short-term and long-term ones. Because of this, the margins for banks have been thin.

But over time, there will likely be a bigger spread between short-term and long-term rates, which will be a big boost for banks' profits. Yes, banking may go back to being a 3–6–3 business. That is, bankers will pay depositors 3 percent, lend money at 6 percent, and then tee off at 3 p.m.

Another key driver will probably be the rebound in real estate. This may seem unrealistic, especially in light of the current problems (such as with foreclosures).

But according to JPMorgan, the U.S. population is expected to increase by 30 million by 2020. This means there will be demand for 1.2 million housing units per year. In contrast, from 2008 to 2011 the rate has been half this amount. In fact, the net new housing units were only 250,000 per year during this time.

In other words, there will be lots of pent-up demand for housing, which will accelerate as the economy improves.

Another factor is that the affordability of a purchase is the best in 15 years. It's actually cheaper to pay a mortgage than to pay rent in many regions across the United States.

For IPO investors, there are historical precedents for a sharp rebound in real estate, which have fueled gains for banks. One is Texas during the 1990s, which had experienced a grueling depression because of the plunge in oil prices.

But over time, things started to improve. One of the beneficiaries was Southwest Bancorporation of Texas. When the company went public, the CEO, Walter E. Johnson, had more than 30 years' experience in the banking industry. From 1972 to 1988, he was president of Allied Bank of Texas, where assets reached $4 billion before it was bought by First Interstate Bancorp.

When Johnson took control of Southwest Bancorporation in 1988, the bank had $43.4 million in assets. By the end of 1996, he had built it up to $1 billion in assets. For the nine months leading up to September 30, 1996, the company increased its net income by 32.3 percent, to $7.4 million. The company went public in January 1997, issuing stock at $8.25 (adjusted for a stock split). Over the next 10 years or so, the stock would reach $37.

Yet even in a boom, investors need to be careful with their analysis. When investigating bank IPOs, focus on characteristics such as these:

- *Fee income.* Financial institutions have been shifting their revenues to fee-based sources—credit cards, mutual funds, insurance, annuities, and asset management. Fee income is desirable because it is less dependent on the pendulum swings in interest rates. A good rule of thumb is to have a financial company with at least 25 percent of its revenues derived from fee-income sources.
- *Franchise value.* You want a company that has a dominant position in its market. This should help protect a company from competition. It may also be attractive to a larger player. Over the past few decades, a key for growth for big banks has been acquisitions.

  However, it is usually not a good idea to buy a bank IPO solely for the potential of a deal. One case was BankUnited. The company was part of a rescue in May 2009 that involved a variety of private equity firms and support from the Federal Deposit Insurance Corporation (FDIC).

  To restructure its operations, BankUnited hired as its CEO John Kanas, who had over 35 years' experience in the banking industry. He even invested $23.5 million in the deal. All in all, things worked out quite well. By January 2011, BankUnited went public.

  But the ultimate goal was to sell the company to a major bank. While there was interest, the bids were not attractive. So Kanas took the company off the market.
- *Technology.* New innovations—online banking, ATMs, and iPhone apps—have helped banks cut costs. Automation means more money for the bottom line. So look for a bank that has been investing in new technologies. No doubt new innovations—like smartphones and tablets—are likely to be vitally important.

Asset Managers

An asset manager invests capital on behalf of institutions and individuals—which often involve equities, bonds, and perhaps even commodities. The traditional asset manager is the mutual fund. This is a vehicle that sells to public investors and must undergo Securities and Exchange Commission (SEC) regulations.

Then there are alternative asset managers, which are generally known as hedge funds and private equity firms (we cover the latter in the next section). Because these firms focus on institutions and wealthy investors, there is minimal regulation from the SEC.

A hedge fund will also engage in highly sophisticated investment strategies. These may include arbitrage, short selling, and complicated derivatives structures. In some cases, a hedge fund will make a bad bet and go bust. This happened with Amaranth Advisors in 2006. Because of an aggressive trade on natural gas futures, the fund lost $6 billion and had to be shut down.

While many mutual funds have gone public over the decades, it is only recently that hedge funds have done the same. Interestingly, more mutual fund operators are starting to create their own hedge funds.

However, here are some commonsense guidelines when evaluating an asset manager, whether a mutual fund or a hedge fund:

- *Invest in the portfolio managers.* Peter Lynch's tremendous success with the Fidelity Magellan Fund catapulted Fidelity into the stratosphere as it became the biggest mutual fund company in the world. This is an extreme example, but the principle holds up. Look for an IPO that has strong portfolio managers with consistently positive long-term performance records, regardless of the market environment.
- *Skin in the game.* To keep top managers, they should have strong ties to the firm. One way to do this is to allocate hefty allocations of shares to them. So when looking at an asset manager, look for those where management and the portfolio managers have heavy equity holdings.
- *Growth.* Look for growth in earnings and assets under management. The more money an asset manager has, the better, because compensation is based on a percentage of the assets under management.
- *Marketing.* A mutual fund needs to spend money on sales and marketing to increase assets under management. With thousands of mutual funds competing, sales and marketing are crucial to success. However, because of securities regulations, hedge funds are not allowed to engage in marketing.

Private Equity Firms

Private equity is a fairly young business, with its roots going back to the 1970s. This type of investment includes the purchase of businesses using heavy amounts of debt. Then after a few years—during which there is often a restructuring—the private equity firm will either sell the company or take it public. If done successfully, the returns can be substantial.

Over the past few years, a variety of top private equity firms have pulled off their own IPOs. These include the Blackstone Group, Kohlberg Kravis & Roberts Co. (KKR), and Apollo Global Management.

There will likely be more transactions as well. One reason is that private equity firms want a stable base of capital, which can make it easier to take a long-term view on deals. Other reasons include having enough capital to move into other investment categories and build infrastructure.

And yes, a private equity firm can be massive. One is Blackstone. Back in the mid-1980s, investment bankers Stephen Schwarzman and Peter Peterson launched the firm. Their start-up capital was $400,000.

But they were extremely aggressive and had a good sense for uncovering strong investment opportunities. Now Blackstone manages $160 billion in assets and would actually be ranked No. 7 on the Fortune 500 if it combined all of its portfolio companies.

When looking at a private equity IPO, here are some strategies:

- *Diversity.* The private equity business is highly cyclical. Consider that there have been several periods—such as in the late 1980s and 2008 to 2009—that saw horrendous markets. It was not uncommon for some private equity investments to get wiped out.

  Because of this, it is important for investors to focus on those private equity firms that have businesses in diverse categories. These may include hedge funds, real estate, debt investments, merger advisory, and wealth management. It is also a good idea to look for those private equity firms that have investments across a broad section of countries as well as industries.
- *Returns.* It is critical for private equity firms to show good returns. If there has been underperformance for the past couple of years, this could be a big problem. It will likely make it tougher for the firm to raise more money, and the profits are likely to decline.
- *Volatility.* The stock prices of private equity firms can be extremely volatile. The reason is that the earnings are tough to predict. After all, a big part of a firm's profits comes from the fees generated from transactions like IPOs and acquisitions.

- *Reputation.* This is vitally important for private equity firms. The top-tier operators will get an opportunity to see the choice deals. They also have the credibility to get the necessary financing, such as with bank loans and junk bond offerings.
- *Regulatory risk.* The typical structure for a private equity fund is the carried interest. This means it will receive a 1 percent to 2 percent fee for the money under management as well as 20 percent to 25 percent of the profits from the investments.

But there is something controversial about the carried interest: taxes. Carried interest has been taxed at the long-term capital gains rate of only 15 percent rather than at the short-term capital gains or ordinary income rate (up to 35 percent). It should be no surprise that this has become a hot political issue and there has been pressure to change this, especially as the United States has continued to show slow growth and the budget deficits remain high.

Online Brokerages

Discount brokerage firms were introduced in 1975. Before then, brokerage commissions were fixed. But when Congress deregulated commission rates, it sowed the seeds of today's financial revolution. Firms like Charles Schwab and Quick & Reilly were the first to offer customers low commission rates, which led to much higher trading volumes.

Of course, the other key factor for the growth in discount brokerage was the Internet. During the 1990s, a variety of these firms, such as E*Trade, went public in hot IPOs.

Over the past few years, the online brokerage industry has undergone more innovation, which has resulted in new IPOs. That is, new firms have entered other categories.

One is FX Alliance, which has benefited from the growth in the foreign exchange market. To increase efficiencies, the company developed an electronic trading platform that helped to automate transactions, audits, and posttrade recording.

It was a market in need of a change. FX Alliance's CEO and co-founder, Philip Weisberg, formerly worked at JPMorgan and had seen firsthand the antiquated processes. For the most part, traders used telephones and faxes to pull off their trades.

Weisberg also picked a huge market opportunity. The global FX market is the largest market and includes a myriad of players like large banks, asset managers, hedge funds, central banks, broker-dealers, corporations, governments, and retail investors. The volume comes to about $4 trillion per day.

By the time of the IPO in 2011, FX Alliance had over 1,000 institutional clients and processed over $62 billion average daily volume. It was also a highly profitable business. In 2010, the company generated adjusted earnings before interest, taxes, depreciation, and amortization (EBITDA) of $46.6 million on revenues of $99.1 million.

Even with the high growth in next-generation online brokerages, there are still some risks. One is market volatility. A decrease in trading volume can result in reduced transaction revenues and a decrease in profitability. This is a bigger problem for those firms that focus on a single market.

Another issue is price competition. History shows that trading inevitably becomes more and more efficient. Some of the reasons include better technologies as well as competition.

Yet there are still opportunities for IPO investors. But before making a purchase, here are some factors to consider:

- *Technology.* To remain competitive, a broker needs to constantly invest in its platform so as to get higher transaction speeds. This means focusing on those companies with a focus on R&D spending and top technology veterans in the senior management ranks. Another key is if the company has been getting patents to protect its technology.
- *Value-adding resources.* A successful online brokerage will provide useful tools to help its customers. Often, these will lead to more trading. In the case of FX Alliance, the company was smart to develop its own online content properties like DailyFX. They get over 2.2 million unique visitors per month.
- *Distribution agreements.* Online brokerages want customers, customers, and more customers. Because fees are low, achieving a critical mass is necessary for success. This means spending millions to get exclusive placements on high-traffic sites like Yahoo! These arrangements shut out other online brokerages, making it more difficult for them to compete.

Insurance

One of the keys to the success of Warren Buffett was his entry into the insurance industry. The business model was highly lucrative: People paid money on a consistent basis for protection from problems of health, disability, and unexpected death. However, the payment of claims was many years in the future, so Buffett was able to use the large amounts of incoming cash to invest in the bond and stock markets. Because of this, he created a fortune of over $40 billion.

While insurance IPOs are not common, they are usually noteworthy. For the most part, the insurance companies going public are well-established operations and have large customer bases. Their IPOs will also usually raise substantial amounts.

When perusing the IPO prospectus of an insurance firm, look for factors that point to the following:

- *Brand name.* Look for an insurance company that has strong customer loyalty and brand recognition. For the most part, insurance is a commodity business, and one type of life insurance policy is not much different from another company's. All in all, the biggest difference is the price of the policy. To compete in this environment, insurance companies must have a strong brand name in order to attract new customers without having to reduce prices and, thus, margins.
- *Reserves.* Look at the risk factors in the prospectus and see if the insurance company has sufficient reserves. Focus on those companies that have a high credit rating (such as AAA from Moody's Investors Service). As seen with the financial crisis, even large insurance companies—such as American International Group (AIG)—can be vulnerable to failure.
- *Cost cutting.* Look for an efficient organization. Are the administrative costs rising faster than the revenues? If so, such unbalanced spending will hurt profitability and the stock price.

Specialized Online Financial Services

Over the past few years, there have been a growing number of online companies that focus on specialized segments of the financial services industry, such as mortgages, credit cards, or banking. As the Internet and smartphones become more popular, consumers have increasingly used these platforms for their financial needs.

Two notable examples are Zillow and FinancialEngines.

Zillow

Richard Barton and Lloyd Frink started the company in 2005 with the goal of revolutionizing the real estate business. They thought all consumers should have access to home sales information—not just Realtors.

According to the founders, "the Zillow name evolved from the desire to make zillions of data points for homes accessible to everyone. And, since a home is about more than just data—it is where you lay your head to rest at night, like a pillow—'Zillow' was born."

Zillow's database would include information from existing sources but also rely on the feedback of users. There was also a sophisticated set of algorithms that would create a valuation for a home. It would become known as a "Zestimate."

Over time, the database grew to include over 100 million homes. But Zillow was smart to expand into other categories, like mortgages and rentals. There was also early development of mobile apps for the iPhone and Android devices. During December 2011, close to 100 million homes were viewed from these apps.

In 2011, Zillow posted $66.1 million in revenues, up 117 percent over the prior year.

FinancialEngines

In 1990, William Sharpe won the Nobel Prize in economic sciences for his pioneering work on portfolio management. But he thought his theories could be helpful to ordinary investors. So in 1995, he created an online financial analysis company, called FinancialEngines.

The service essentially automates the process of putting together a comprehensive financial plan—dealing with complex things like risk and asset allocation. In fact, it is available for portfolios of any size.

It took a while for FinancialEngines to get traction. But the company pursued a smart go-to-market strategy—that is, by focusing on the 401(k). Of course, these vehicles have become a key part of retirement planning, but participants usually have a tough time getting professional advice. The main reason is their account balances are usually not large enough to attract financial planners.

FinancialEngines also added another follow-on service, which allows for people to effectively take money out of their retirement accounts. Consider that starting in 2011 more than 10,000 baby boomers turned 65 every day. And this trend will continue for the next 19 years.

Conclusion

The financial industry is diverse. Investors should weigh the advantages and disadvantages of each sector and realize that these segments of the industry do not behave exactly alike. However, with the growth of U.S. investments, the prospects for finance company IPOs look bright as long as the stock market doesn't take a major tumble.

References

JPMorgan. 2011. Shareholder Letter. http://goo.gl/05mW2.
Sidel, Robin. 2012. "BankUnited Gives Up Plans to Sell Itself." *Wall Street Journal*, January 19, http://goo.gl/31hpR.

CHAPTER 15

Retail Sector IPOs

Some of the greatest initial public offering (IPO) fortunes have been made from retail companies. The main reason is scalability, the ability to sell large quantities in many geographic markets. Once you have the blueprint for one store, it is easy to duplicate it across the United States and perhaps even the world.

Consider that Walmart went public in 1970 by issuing 300,000 shares at $16.50 each, raising about $4.95 million. The company was mostly a regional operator with 38 stores. But it was growing quickly. From 1969 to 1970, sales had spiked from $12.6 million to $21.3 million.

But the company needed to pull off the IPO because it had little capital for expansion. Walmart required about $500,000 for each new store, and the company's legendary founder, Sam Walton, had the single-minded goal of creating the world's largest retailer.

Of course, the IPO was a good choice. As of now, Walmart has over 10,100 locations in 27 countries and sales of $443 billion. The market value is a whopping $208 billion.

True, finding the next Walmart is no easy task. The retail industry is rife with competition and reels from the rapid changes in consumer tastes. So to be successful with retail company IPOs, you need to do your homework and have a bit of luck, too. Here are the factors to look for in your analysis.

Brand

A key asset for any retailer is brand. A brand helps to create customer loyalty and also differentiates a company from its rivals.

Yoga apparel retailer lululemon athletica is a powerful example. In 1998, Dennis "Chip" Wilson, a former snowboard and surfing entrepreneur, saw that there was a void in the yoga apparel market and set out to build a leading brand in the category. He realized this when he started taking yoga classes.

At the core, Wilson focused on cutting-edge design as well as new clothing technologies to allow for better performance. But he also wanted to create a compelling in-store environment. He had employees go through extensive training to become experts. He even put chalkboards in fitting rooms that made it easy for customers to provide feedback.

Another key was creating a vertical platform. That is, lululemon controlled the design and manufacturing of its products. This would allow for better quality control and responsiveness to consumer trends.

With a strong brand, lululemon has been able to command tremendous pricing power. Keep in mind that its pants rarely go on sale and have price points that range from $78 to $128.

When the company went public in July 2007, lululemon disclosed strong financials. From fiscal year 2004 to 2006, revenues went from $40.7 million to $148.9 million.

By 2011, revenues had hit $712 million. The stock also soared from $18 at its IPO to $75.

Disruptive Threats

E-commerce players like Amazon.com have transformed the traditional retail space, as seen with the collapse of chains like Borders. From 2000 to 2011, online sales have gone from 2 percent of total sales to 8 percent.

The mobile revolution is also having an impact. In fact, Target has sought help from its suppliers to deal with an emerging trend of so-called showrooming. This is when shoppers go to a store to check out products and then make purchases on their smartphones.

To deal with these developments, a retailer must have unique merchandising strategies and a strong customer experience. There should also be a solid digital business. If not, there could be erosion in growth and margins.

A company that has been able to evolve with the dynamic changes in the retail landscape is Mattress Firm. It may not be an exciting business—selling mattresses and related accessories—but the business has been strong. When the company went public, it had a sterling track record of positive comparable-store sales growth of 24 consecutive months. The initial stock price for its offering was $19, and the stock has since climbed to $39.

Mattress Firm has been smart to have a wide array of models, including cutting-edge ones. For example, the company got an exclusive on YuMe, which adjusts the temperature.

Another important factor in Mattress Firm's success has been its Red Carpet Delivery Service. The company provides same-day delivery about a quarter of the time, which is unique in the industry.

But perhaps the most distinguishing characteristic of Mattress Firm is its store format. Its Comfort by Color system is a creative way to help customers shop for the most suitable mattress. A customer will first try out four surface options: firm, plush, pillow top, and contoured. Each type has its own color. In other words, once customers decide on the right type, they can shop for the best choice by just "following the color," and this system has been critical in simplifying the shopping experience.

Major Consumer Changes

From time to time, there are major changes in retail trends. One of the most recent came about from the financial crisis of 2008. With persistently high unemployment, consumers wanted to find deep discounts on everyday products.

This opened up a big opportunity for the dollar stores. One was Dollar General, which launched its IPO in November 2009. At the time, the company already had 8,577 stores. But there was still much room for growth since much of its footprint was in 35 states.

The company's business has proved resilient in any economic environment. For 20 years, Dollar General has posted annual same-store growth. A big reason for this has been the attractive store economics. Opening a store has usually required low capital investments. In fact, a typical new location would generate cash flows within the first year of operation.

Timing

There are always new retail concepts. While they may be interesting and innovative, they will probably not get much traction with consumers. Keep in mind that it is extremely difficult to change behavior patterns. Often, it can take many years to do so, which could make it tough for an IPO to show gains.

This happened with Webvan. Launched in the late 1990s, the goal of the company was to revolutionize the grocery industry. To this end, it would allow consumers to buy their groceries online and receive same-day delivery. There was a wide selection of offerings like hand-cut meats, fresh fish and live lobsters, chef-prepared meals, fine wines, and premium cigars. Shipping was also free for orders over $50.

Yet the costs of creating the sophisticated distribution centers were extremely high. There was also a need to operate a fleet of high-end trucks, which had to be refrigerated. Such things were ominous since the traditional grocery business operates on thin margins of 2 percent to 3 percent.

The business plan could have worked out, but there was a big problem: Webvan's forecast for consumer demand was wildly optimistic. Unfortunately, consumers were not interested in changing their shopping habits any time soon. Hey, they often liked to check out fruits and vegetables before making a purchase, right?

So after its IPO, Webvan continued to sustain massive losses. In about two years, the company was bankrupt, having gone through over $1.2 billion in invested capital.

Instead, to get consumers to adopt a new concept, it is key to solve major frustrations. This was the key for Netflix. Reed Hastings started the company because he got hit with a $40 late fee from Blockbuster.

He wondered if a better approach would be to charge a monthly sub-scription and to send out DVDs via the mail. To see if it worked, he actually sent several DVDs to himself. This little experiment showed that this would be a viable channel.

Hastings wasted little time. He raised venture capital and built out the infrastructure, such as warehouses. When he launched the service in 1999, the company would generate $5 million in revenues. Two years later, it would reach $75.9 million.

In May 2002, Neflix went public at $15 and raised $82.5 million. The S-1 gave a clear-cut explanation of the value proposition: "We believe our growth has been driven primarily by our unrivalled selection, consistently high levels of customer satisfaction, rapid consumer adoption of DVD play-ers and our increasingly effective marketing programs."

Along the way, the company built out an online video service. It also turned out to be a big hit, as the stock hit an all-time high of $304. However, by the end of 2011, the stock had come under lots of pressure because of the growing competition.

Check Out the Store

It's a simple thing to do but it can be helpful. Is the merchandise attractive? Do you see good amounts of traffic? And are you noticing that people are buying stuff?

And what about the employees? Do they offer help and answer your questions? Is the store clean? Do you always see big discount bins?

This kind of approach is one of the hallmarks of legendary investor Peter Lynch. He managed the Fidelity Magellan Fund from 1977 to 1990, during which he racked up annual average returns of 29 percent.

He liked to invest in retailers because he could investigate the stores. It meant uncovering some huge winners, such as his 100x return on Levitz.

In his book *One Up on Wall Street*, he writes: "If you stay half-alert, you can pick the spectacular performers right from your place of business or out of the neighborhood shopping mall, and long before Wall Street discovers them."

Financial Metrics

There are myriad ways to measure the performance of retailers. But here's a look at the main ones:

- *Sales per square foot.* This shows the efficiency of a retailer. You want to see a figure that is higher than the competition—and that is growing over time.
- *Same-store sales.* This is perhaps the most important indicator for a retailer's success. This metric—also known as comparable-store sales or comps—shows the performance of store locations that have been around at least one year.

You want to see growth in same-store sales on a year-over-year basis. Hopefully, it will be in the double digits.

This was the case for Michael Kors, which is a top luxury retailer. At the time of its IPO in December 2012, the same-store sales were a sizzling 48 percent. The stock went on to go from $20 to $47.

If there is negative growth in comparable sales, then it is probably best to avoid the IPO. This trend probably is caused by rising competition and problems with the merchandising.

Narrow Base

It is common for retailers to have operations focused in a certain area of the country. The problem here is that if there is a downturn in the local economy, the company can be severely affected. It's better to focus on retailers that have at least some regional diversification.

Many retailers use the capital earned from an IPO to expand their markets. If a company you are looking at has a narrow geographical focus, check the IPO prospectus for diversification plans.

But it still may not be enough. An example is Duane Reade, a pharmacy that had most of its locations concentrated in the New York City metropolitan area. The company went public in February 1998 and raised $92.5 million.

Unfortunately, union disputes, a local recession, and destruction of the best-performing store in the 9/11 attacks had a severe impact on the company, and the stock price plunged.

Conclusion

For every Walmart there are many more duds in the retail space. But investors still have an opportunity to get some nice profits. Perhaps the best advice is to take Peter Lynch's approach: visit the stores.

References

Lynch, Peter. 2000. *One Up on Wall Street.* New York: Simon & Schuster, 194.

Mattioli, Dana. 2012. "Lululemon's Secret Sauce." *Wall Street Journal*, March 22. http://goo.gl/qtOcq.

Trimble, Vance. 1990. *Sam Walton: The Inside Story of America's Richest Man.* New York: Dutton, 130–140.

Zimmerman, Ann. 2012. "Showdown over 'Showrooming.'" *Wall Street Journal*, January 23. http://goo.gl/vn64W.

CHAPTER 16

Foreign IPOs

Marc Rich, who as a kid escaped from the Nazis, would eventually become a top commodities trader. He started his career at Philipp Brothers, where he created the global spot market for crude oil. It meant that he had to cut deals with a variety of governments like Iran and Cuba. Despite the dangers, he made huge amounts of money and went on to create his own firm. It became Glencore.

However, in the early 1980s, the U.S. federal prosecutor, Rudolph Giuliani, brought tax evasion charges against Rich, who then fled the United States and was eventually granted a pardon by President Bill Clinton in 2001.

While Rich was a fugitive, his company actually continued to thrive and ultimately became the largest commodities trader in the world. In 2011, revenues hit $144 billion and the company went public. But instead of listing on the U.S. markets, Glencore had its initial public offering (IPO) in London and Hong Kong. Such a move was a big blow to the New York Stock Exchange, which usually snagged mega offerings.

But the fact is that there are growing opportunities for IPOs in foreign markets, especially in China and other parts of Asia. Consider that other top brands also recently listed in Hong Kong, including Prada and L'Occitane. Even Rovio, the developer of the mobile app Angry Birds, was considering a similar move.

When looking at the Hong Kong, Shanghai, Shenzhen, and Taiwan markets, these markets had 423 public offerings in 2011. The total amount raised came to $81 billion, compared to 102 offerings in the United States for a total of $27.5 billion. In fact, about $7.8 billion of the latter offerings were from foreign countries.

In other words, IPO investors have big opportunities in foreign markets. So let's take a look.

Advantages of Foreign IPOs

When it comes to investing in foreign markets, Mark Mobius is one of the pioneers. Since the late 1980s, he has been a portfolio manager at Templeton and was one of the early investors to capitalize on the growth opportunities in countries like China and India. A key part of his strategy has been to constantly travel across the world.

Interestingly, you can follow him on his blog at mobius.blog.franklin-templeton.com. It's a great way to get a sense of the exciting developments in emerging markets. And yes, Mobius is still bullish on the long-term prospects.

Here are some of the takeaways:

- *Strong fundamentals.* While the United States and Europe struggle with slow growth and deficits, this is certainly not the case with emerging market countries. Often, they have solid budget surpluses and large amounts of foreign exchange reserves. The banking systems are also fairly conservative, which adds stability. Keep in mind that countries like Brazil and China recovered quickly after the financial crisis of 2008.
- *Large markets.* The perception is that emerging markets are focused mostly on low-end manufacturing. But this is certainly beginning to change. After all, a key to Apple's success has been its relationships with companies in China, such as Foxconn.

  Because of the migration to skilled labor, the emerging markets are seeing the growth in their middle classes. This will mean more sustainable growth.
- *Frontier markets.* These are countries that may become the next members of the emerging markets. Some of the prime examples are in Africa, South America, and the Middle East.

  One key driver is actually the Internet, which has spread ideas like capitalism, human rights, and democracy. As seen in 2011 with the Arab Spring, this has led to the downfall of authoritarian governments in Tunisia, Egypt, and Libya. Over time, the liberalization should allow for political stability and economic growth.

  Already, there are signs of strong growth in frontier markets. Consider Africa. One bright spot is Nigeria, which has a population of 150 million people and has been growing its economy at 7 percent to 8 percent for the past decade.
- *Commodities boom.* As the world continues to grow, there will be continued demand for commodities like oil, aluminum, copper, nickel, and iron ore. This has been a boon for many emerging and frontier countries because they usually have large amounts of untapped resources.

- *Privatization.* When a government owns a business, the motives of the company are more political than economic, resulting many times in poor management. But once a company is privatized, it is free to compete and to innovate. Privatization can lead to higher profitability through reduced cost structure, and it provides incentives for managers and employees to have a greater stake in the company's success.

  Many foreign nations have been and will continue privatizing their main industries. And IPOs are at the very center of this process, because issuing stock to the public facilitates privatization. When a company goes from being a nationalized business to being a private one, there is a lot of immediate potential for IPO growth.
- *Diversification.* International investing can also add diversification to your portfolio, because foreign markets are not always in sync with market cycles in the United States. When the U.S. market is down, a variety of foreign markets will be up. The stocks in these nations, too, sometimes sell at very low valuations compared to the historically high valuations in the United States.
- *Growth opportunities.* The United States is still the center of tremendous innovation, having been the launchpad of breakout companies like Cisco, Microsoft, Starbucks, and Facebook. But this dominance is starting to diminish. Over the years, emerging market countries have invested heavily in education. In other words, they are starting to create their own breakout companies. So yes, the next Facebook may come from China or India or even Vietnam.

Risks

In addition to opportunities, there are also major risks associated with investing in foreign companies.

Risk of Political Strife

Emerging nations are susceptible to wrenching political chaos, which inevitably harms stock prices. Mexico is a prime example. In 1994 there was a violent peasant revolt in Chiapas. Presidential candidate Luis Donaldo Colosio Murrieta, who was to succeed the current president, was assassinated. The discord caused investors to pull their money out of the country, and the stock market collapsed.

But political risk is not limited to riots or assassinations. Perhaps the more common type of political risk is the influence of government policy, such as heavy taxes, a lax monetary policy, or harsh trade restrictions.

However, the most serious threat to investors is when a foreign government nationalizes businesses. When a government takes over a private business, investors lose everything.

While investors may think this type of action is a thing of the past, there are still stark examples. One was Yukos, which was a highly successful oil company. Yet it was perhaps getting too much power—at least so it seemed to Vladimir Putin—so the company suddenly received a tax bill of $27 billion in 2003 and the Russian government froze the assets. Since it could not pay the huge bill, the company's properties were sold for pennies on the dollar to Russian-controlled entities. Mikhail Khodorkovsky, who was the owner of Yukos, was convicted of fraud and sent to prison. In the end, public shareholders were left with worthless stock.

Currency Risk

When investing in foreign stocks, the transactions are usually made with the country's currency. This means that the investment will fluctuate based on the foreign currency and the U.S. dollar. It's actually possible that the value of the stock will go up and you may still lose money. This is because the currency may have been devalued even more.

There are financial techniques to reduce the currency risk, called hedging. But hedging is too expensive for individual investors; it's more suitable for institutional investors.

Copycat IPOs

A company may try to leverage the hype of an emerging technology. This happened with a variety of Chinese offerings in 2010 and 2011. Youku.com was proclaimed the "YouTube of China" and Dangdang Inc. was the "Amazon.com of China."

Oh, and yes there was a version for Facebook: Renren. In May 2011, the company went public in a spectacular offering. The stock price quickly went from $14 to $24.

But if investors took the time to read the S-1, they would realize that Renren was nowhere near the scale of Facebook. Consider that it posted a loss of $64.2 million in 2010 and had generated revenues of only $76.5 million. The company also had its audit committee chairman resign because he was embroiled in a scandal with another high-flying company.

The S-1 even had a typographical error. It misstated the monthly unique log-in user base. Instead of being 7 million, it was 5 million.

A year after its IPO, the shares of Renren were trading at about $5.50.

Aftermarket Support

The U.S. market has the most advanced financial distribution centers in the world. In a week, this system can handle billions of dollars in IPOs; the same is not true in other countries. There is a greater likelihood that foreign IPOs, over time, will fall in price. The reason is that these countries do not have many financial institutions to help support the stocks, such as institutional investors, analysts, and even the financial media.

Fraud

The U.S. securities markets have the most thorough laws for disclosure of information. Disclosure requirements in the foreign markets tend to be very lax, almost nonexistent. Different accounting systems and standards, too, can make analysis confusing.

This can even be a problem for foreign companies that list on U.S. exchanges. In 2011, the Securities and Exchange Commission (SEC) cracked down on a variety of Chinese companies for lack of disclosure on key areas like cash balances, revenues, and receivables.

Many of these companies actually went public through a process of a reverse merger. This involves a company merging into an existing public entity that is a corporate shell. It is a quicker way to go public and usually means less disclosure.

The SEC has tried to improve matters. For example, it now requires that foreign companies may no longer keep their prospectus private until a couple of weeks before the IPO. The goal is to give investors a better sense about the conflicts and issues about the disclosures.

Yet the risks remain. True, the SEC wants better disclosure requirements, but it will likely take much time to get foreign companies to agree to these requirements.

Risk of Default

A default on government debts can have a devastating impact on stock prices. Again, this was the situation in Russia during a global financial crisis in 1998. The country was suffering from slow growth because of a costly war in Chechnya as well as the weakness in crude oil prices. Russian leader Boris Yeltsin began to consolidate his power by sacking a variety of high-ranking officials. But this caused even more uncertainty; interest rates continued to soar and the ruble came under tremendous pressure. From January to August, the Russian stock market lost a grueling 75 percent of its value.

To deal with this, the Russian government devalued the ruble and defaulted on its international debt. These actions sent ripples across the global financial system. It actually resulted in the failure of one of the largest U.S. hedge funds, Long-Term Capital Management, and stalled the IPO of Goldman Sachs.

IPO Process for Foreign Deals

When a foreign company goes public in the United States, there are some differences from the typical process. Essentially, the rules are less onerous in terms of the disclosures in the prospectus and also corporate governance. In addition, there are relaxed requirements for ongoing reports when a foreign company is public.

The Securities and Exchange Commission (SEC) has a guideline for these types of companies, which are known as foreign private issuers. To meet this guideline, a company needs to pass two tests. One is the location test, which means that less than a majority of the executives and directors are not from the United States. What's more, less than 50 percent of the assets must not be within the United States.

Then there is the ownership test. This is where less than 50 percent of the outstanding voting shares are owned by non-U.S. residents.

Even if a company meets these tests, this does not mean it will provide less disclosure. In fact, some companies will provide the same types of disclosures in a typical S-1 so as to build more credibility with U.S. investors.

But if a company does elect to be a foreign private issuer, it will file an F-1 registration document with the SEC. While the F-1 is similar to an S-1, there is actually less disclosure for executive compensation, pension assets, lease commitments, and exposures to derivatives. Depending on the circumstances, a company may have to report only audited balance sheets for the two most recent fiscal years and audited income and cash flow statements for the three most recent fiscal years.

However, the F-1 requires disclosures on matters like the holdings of the existing shares and the tax impact on nonresident shareholders.

The NASDAQ and the New York Stock Exchange also have relaxed rules for foreign private issuers. That is, there are exemptions for the audit committee independence rules.

Once a company is public, it will report its annual report on Form 20-F. And while it does not have to file a Form 10-Q, it will have to disclose a Form 6-K if the country requires quarterly filings.

Other requirements that foreign private issuers are exempt from include short-swing trading restrictions for executives and board members, proxy solicitations (such as for a vote on a merger), and reporting of insider sales.

American Depositary Receipts

American depositary receipts (ADRs) are the best and easiest way for U.S. consumers to invest in foreign markets. An ADR issued by a foreign company is actually listed on a U.S. stock exchange, making it much easier to get price quotes—even for IPO shares. Furthermore, ADRs do not require dealing with an overseas broker; rather, a U.S. full-service or discount broker can handle trades.

Technically, ADRs are not really stocks. Here's why: Suppose you want to buy 100 shares of the XYZ ADR. It is listed on the New York Stock Exchange and trades at $10 per share. You call your broker, who phones another broker in Hong Kong, who buys the shares. The foreign broker then deposits these shares in a U.S. bank, and the bank issues a certificate, called an ADR, to your local broker.

When you decide to sell, you call your broker, who calls the Hong Kong broker. That broker sells the shares, and you receive your money.

Even though you receive your money in U.S. dollars, there is currency risk involved in buying ADRs. In fact, the foreign broker is actually exchanging U.S. dollars with foreign currency. This is why there is often a price difference between ADRs and the real stock as it's listed on the foreign exchange.

It sounds a bit convoluted, but ADRs have been around for decades and have proven to be quite sound. And yes, they can present lucrative opportunities for IPO investors.

One example is the offering of Baidu, which was masterminded by the Chinese national Robin Li. During the 1990s, he quickly became a top person in the emerging industry of search engines. By 2000, he had come back to China and launched Baidu. He wanted to create the country's top search engine (the site now has over 80 percent of market share and is ranked No. 2 in the world).

In August 2005, Baidu went public at $27 and shot up to $122.54 on its first day of trading. In the company's F-1 filing, it reported massive growth with a compound annual rate of 224 percent.

Direct Investments in Foreign IPOs

While it can be tough to get in on IPOs in the U.S. markets—that is, at the offering price—this is not necessarily the case with foreign markets. Actually, it is often fairly easy to get shares in new foreign offerings.

But this means buying shares that are listed on foreign markets. True, it may sound scary but it is now much easier to purchase shares listed on foreign exchanges. Top brokerages like E*Trade and Charles Schwab have strong trading platforms for this, which also include lots of research.

Yet the fees can be high, say 1 percent to 2 percent per trade. So it's a good idea to try to negotiate this. It's always worth a try.

U.S. brokerages may also not cover certain markets, especially the smaller ones. But these may hold some of the best opportunities. To this end, you can set up an account with a foreign-based brokerage.

The first step is to do a Google search and focus on those brokerage firms on the first page. Then do some research on each one. What are the fees? What about their research? Is the site even in English?

You should also check out the website of the country's stock exchange. If the brokerage is a member, then this is a reassuring sign of the firm's stability.

Once you find a firm, it will be easy to set up an account. It will be similar to the process in the United States. However, you will need to wire a minimum deposit to the brokerage. The fee will likely be about $40 to $50.

In fact, you might want to set up a bank account in the country as well. This may be required if a stock pays dividends. Keep in mind that a U.S. bank will probably not cash these dividend checks.

You should also get a tax adviser to make sure you fill out and file the right forms with your tax return. Keep in mind that the Internal Revenue Service (IRS) does not care where you earn your income. Rather, your worldwide income is taxed.

When investing in foreign stocks, you'll notice that many companies will report their financials every six months, not on a quarterly basis. In addition, the disclosures may be less comprehensive than what's required in the United States. There may also be different conventions. For example, the financials may report numbers as $1.000,00, not $1,000.00.

Conclusion

While the United States still has lots of innovation—and this will likely continue to be the case—there are still many opportunities across the world. Emerging markets like China, Brazil, and Russia offer great investments. The good news is that some of the top foreign companies do come public in the United States. By purchasing an ADR, you can get easy exposure to these opportunities.

We've also seen how it has become easier to invest directly in IPOs of foreign markets. In fact, these may present even bigger opportunities. But of course, it is a good idea to take things slowly. Understanding the nuances of a foreign market can be challenging.

CHAPTER 17

Energy IPOs

Over the years, some of the best-performing initial public offerings (IPOs) have been in the energy sector. With high oil prices, these companies have shown strong margins and growth rates. Here are some top performers:

Company	Date of IPO	Return
Hornbeck Offshore Services	March 2004	220%
EV Energy Partners LP	October 2006	224%
Continental Resources	May 2007	545%
Concho Resources	July 2007	730%

Before investing in an energy IPO, it is a good idea to understand the main categories in the industry. Here's a look.

Crude Oil

Crude oil is at the source of some of the world's largest corporations, such as Exxon Mobil, Chevron, and Royal Dutch Shell. In fact, many of the majors are state-owned operations, such as in the Middle East.

Even though the industry is dominated by global operators, there are still many small companies, and they do come to market through public offerings. Even with the push for alternative sources of oil, the fact remains that the world remains highly dependent on crude oil. And this will likely be the case for decades.

No doubt the price of oil can be volatile. One of the biggest drivers is geopolitics. In 1973 and in 1979, the world suffered from oil shocks because of war and instability in the Middle East.

Another important factor about crude oil is the peak oil theory. The origins go back to the 1960s when a geophysicist for Shell Oil did extensive analysis of oil fields and realized that after a certain point, the production would reach its peak and decline thereafter. According to his analysis, he predicted that the U.S. oil supply would reach this point in the early 1970s. It was controversial and attracted much criticism, but he was ultimately proved correct.

The big uncertainty is whether the Organization of Petroleum Exporting Countries (OPEC) nations are approaching peak levels of production. Interestingly, analysis from the International Energy Agency says that they actually have reached that point.

If so, it could mean that crude oil prices will remain high for the long haul. While this may be bad news for consumers—and may even slow down the global economy—it could make crude oil IPOs lucrative.

Natural Gas

Natural gas is made up mostly of methane and is usually found close to fossil fuel and coal deposits. It has become an attractive source of energy because it tends to be cheaper than crude oil and it does not have the same levels of carbon emissions.

A major development in the natural gas industry has been fracking—that is, hydraulic fracturing—of shale deposits. Consider that there are heavy concentrations of natural gas in rock and shale formations but the gas has been extremely difficult to extract. The 1990s brought the development of innovative technologies, such as horizontal drilling. As a result, there now appears to be a huge amount of potential natural gas in the United States.

Yet there are some concerns, especially from environmentalists. They believe that the use of water injection may harm local water supplies.

All in all, the price of natural gas has several drivers. One is the weather. If the winter is unusually warm, then there may be less demand for natural gas. What's more, hurricanes can have a big impact on the price.

Keep in mind that there has been a massive glut of natural gas in 2011 and 2012. Companies were too aggressive with their production, and demand also lagged.

But looking at the long term, the prospects for natural gas look bright. Exxon Mobil did its own analysis of the market and predicts that natural gas will account for 26 percent of the world's energy by 2030. In light of this, it should be no surprise that in 2010 the company purchased a top shale natural gas company, XTO Energy, for $31 billion.

Coal

Coal has many forms. The higher-quality ones, like anthracite, have higher energy levels, whereas those with high concentrations of sulfur and ash, such as lignite, have much less energy.

There is a large supply of coal in the United States, which has made it attractive as a source of energy. But of course the environmental impact is horrible. Because of this, the US has imposed stringent regulations on coal, which has increased the costs of production. Yet this may not be a problem. Countries like China have a huge need to create steel, which means finding supplies of metallurgical coal. It means they will likely have no choice but to pay higher prices.

Alternative Energy

Even though billions of dollars have been invested in this industry, it is still fairly small when compared to crude oil, coal, and natural gas. But over the next couple of decades, there will likely be lots of growth potential—and yes, IPOs. The public markets have already seen a variety of alternative energy deals. Yet they have generally underperformed. Why?

First, it can be extremely expensive to create new energy sources. Doing so could mean creating new plants and distribution systems. Besides, the fact remains that traditional energy sources are still incredibly efficient.

Next, alternative energy may not necessarily be adopted. This has been evident with electronic cars. Even though companies like Ford and General Motors have launched strong models, consumer demand has still been light. The fact is it takes a while to change buying behavior.

There are many types of alternative energy, but the following are some of the main categories.

Solar

Solar energy has been around for over 60 years and has turned into a global business, especially in China. The typical approach is photovoltaics, which involves solar cells that are known as polysilicon.

There are several important benefits for solar energy. Perhaps the most notable is that it is based on free fuel. No doubt the sun is essentially a massive nuclear power plant and will provide lots of power for millions of years.

Solar energy is also environmentally friendly. There are no carbon emissions or left-over wastes.

Despite all these factors, there are some major drawbacks. Solar energy is highly dependent on the weather. Thus, it is not appropriate in cloudy climates.

The industry is also highly dependent on government support. In fact, with budget deficits in the United States and Europe, this has meant cutbacks in solar energy programs.

Ethanol

Ethanol is fuel that is primarily based on corn. It has turned into a stable source of energy and is environmentally friendly. But producing ethanol may actually result in shortages of food supplies. This became a huge political issue in 2008 and 2009. There were even food riots in various third world nations.

Ethanol has also proven to be subject to gluts, which happened again over the past few years. The result was the bankruptcies of various producers.

Geothermal Energy

It sounds kind of like science fiction; that is, geothermal energy is based on the molten magma from the earth's inner mantle. Like the sun, the center of the earth is also a great source of energy. The problem is that it can be extremely costly to reach it.

But geothermal energy has little waste. It is mostly just steam. The plants to process geothermal energy are also relatively small.

Biomass

Biomass has an interesting source of fuel—garbage, animal waste, and plants. Consider that these things absorb the sun's rays, which means they store energy. With sophisticated equipment, it is possible to harness that energy. No doubt it is a good way to solve the problem of what to do with waste!

However, like many other alternative energy sources, it is expensive to process.

Wind Power

Since the late 1880s, wind power has been a way to generate electricity. As of now, it is a key source of energy for countries across the world. A breakthrough innovation is the turbine, which allows for the storage of the energy.

But there are some environmental hazards like loud noise and the killing of birds (that run into the windmills). Also, some climates do not have much wind.

Types of Energy Companies

The ecosystem for the energy industry is extensive. This means there are various types of companies. The main ones include the following:

- *Exploration companies.* These are also called upstream companies. They tend to be small operators and can spend many years trying to find new energy deposits. Often, the search results in nothing. While you can occasionally buy an exploration IPO on NASDAQ or the New York Stock Exchange, the market that has many of these offerings is the Toronto Stock Exchange (TSX).
- *Oil services companies.* These companies help with the process of extracting energy. They also usually have sophisticated equipment, like drill bits, as well as software.
- *Refiners.* These companies have plants that turn crude oil and other energy sources into gasoline, fuels, and even chemicals. There are few refiners in the United States because of the extensive regulations.

  What's more, refiners usually have low margins and can easily lose substantial amounts of money when oil prices surge. Over the past few years, there have been several plant shutdowns of refineries.
- *Pipelines.* These companies operate the storage and transportation infrastructure to move energy. They tend to be fairly stable and pay strong dividends.

Evaluating an Energy Company IPO

When looking at an energy company, there are some factors to consider. Here's a look:

- *Production.* This is a key factor. You want a company that has a history of being able to grow its production over time. If there are declines, it is usually a bad sign. It could be more than a temporary issue, especially if energy prices are high. In such an environment, wouldn't a company try to increase production?
- *Financials.* Because of the high costs of exploration and extraction, energy companies usually have high levels of debt. But some companies are too leveraged. You want to make sure that there is three to four times enough cash flows to meet the interest expenses and any upcoming debt payments.

Often, a company will issue more stock to raise capital. But this can put pressure on the value.

- *Cost metrics.* You want a company that has a competitive cost-per production level. For example, if its cost per barrel of crude oil is $25, then this is definitely attractive when the prices are $100.

- *Reserves.* This is crucial for an energy company. Reserves are the total amount of a natural resource it currently owns. If the reserves are running out, a company will often look for deposits near existing fields—known as "brown fields"—where the chances of finding new sources are much higher. At the same time, a company may purchase new fields or even buy other companies. But such options are far from ideal and can be costly.

So if a company is unable to meaningfully increase its reserves, it will face the bleak prospect that production will eventually plunge, as will the revenues and profits. And, if there are high levels of debt, the outcome could be bankruptcy.

Reserves are really based on estimates (there are no clear-cut numbers). There are three approaches:

1. *Proven and probable.* This approach is based on extensive third-party feasibility studies and is the most accurate by far.
2. *Measured and indicated.* While this involves analysis, it is not as detailed. So, the reserves could easily be off base.
3. *Inferred.* This number is speculative and should not be relied upon.

If the price of a natural resource increases, this often will mean that stated reserves will increase. Why? The reason is that it will become more economical to extract those deposits that are deeper.

Master Limited Partnerships

Over the past few years, master limited partnerships (MLPs) have become a popular ownership structure in the energy industry. In fact, there have been dozens of these types of IPOs.

For the most part, MLPs are for pipeline companies for either crude oil or natural gas. They tend to have steady growth regardless of the prices of the underlying commodities. Part of the reason is that pipeline companies will have long-term contracts in place.

At the same time, there is usually little competition. After all, it is extremely expensive to build a pipeline. This makes it easier for pipeline companies to charge premium rates.

Because of the tax advantages, MLPs will distribute much of their earnings as dividends. Actually, the yields can be substantial, such as 5 percent to 10 percent. So in a low interest rate environment, MLPs have become a popular investment for investors seeking consistent income streams.

When evaluating an MLP, here are some factors to consider:

- *Dividend track record.* Look for a company that has increased its dividends every year, say for a decade or more. You also want to make sure that cash flows are increasing at roughly the same rate. Keep in mind that some MLPs may raise debt to maintain their dividends, which is not sustainable.
- *Yield.* Do necessarily pick an MLP with the highest yield. The reason is that the core business may be having problems; for example, there could be a need for substantial capital investments. If interest rates increase or it becomes more difficult to raise financing, the consequences could be severe.

  Instead, focus on those companies with attractive growth prospects. While their yields may be lower—say 4 percent to 6 percent—they should still be good sources of income.
- *Taxes.* Taxes can get complicated for investors, so it is a good idea to get some help. For example, owners of MLPs will receive a Schedule K-1 tax document after the end of the tax year, usually in February or March. It shows your income distribution as well as other tax factors. However, depending on some complex rules, the gains may be ordinary income or even deferred.
- *Funds.* If you do not want to engage in stock analysis, there are several exchange-traded funds (ETFs) that invest in MLPs. One is the ALPS Alerian MLP ETF (AMEX:AMLP), which has assets of about $3 billion. The expense ratio is a reasonable 1.40 percent and the annual yield as of mid-2011 was 6 percent. The ETF is based on an index that consists of 25 stocks, most of which are in the energy sector.

  In terms of taxes, investors will receive a Form 1099, not a K-1.

Conclusion

The energy business should be a source of many lucrative IPO opportunities. As the global population continues to grow, there will be a continued focus on finding traditional sources as well as look at solar, biomass, wind power, and geothermal energy producers. True, these types of companies have struggled in the IPO market. But this difficulty will likely be short-lived as new energy sources turn into major industries.

CHAPTER 18

REIT IPOs

Until 2007, the U.S. real estate market looked like a sure thing. Many people were making fortunes from flipping properties. There were even reality television shows that covered the topic.

But of course, the bubble popped and led to one of the worst economic downturns since the Great Depression. In its wake, many mortgage companies and home builders went bust.

In light of all this, it may seem strange to invest in real estate initial public offerings (IPOs). But the fact is that there should still be many opportunities. After all, valuations are much lower now.

A great way to invest in real estate is through a real estate investment trust (REIT). In this chapter, we look at how to invest in these kinds of deals and how the IPOs work. But first, let's take a look at some of the trends for the real estate market.

Trends in the Real Estate Market

Without a doubt, the real estate market is huge and has many sectors. So when looking at the potential investment opportunities, it is better to look at the main categories:

- *Commercial real estate.* This covers many areas like office buildings, hotels, and retail. Actually, there was not necessarily a bubble in these markets. Instead, they sustained losses because of the difficulties in getting credit and the slow growth in the U.S. economy.

  However, this means the level of investment in new supply has been fairly low—and this should bode well for the next decade. Keep in mind that the recent slump was the first one in modern history that was not caused by oversupply.

- *Apartments (or multifamily housing).* The prospects look bright for the apartments sector. In terms of demographics, there are 89 million echo boomers, who were born between 1977 and 1996. This group represents a quarter of the U.S. population and is the largest generation. It also tends to have a high tendency to rent. The group has been impacted by other trends like higher unemployment and tougher mortgage standards. This has led to an increase of shared households—that is, adult children coming back home to live with their parents (31 percent of those between 18 and 34). Yet this group will eventually begin to leave over time and likely rent apartments.

   In terms of supply, it has not been strong. According to RCG Economics (an independent research firm) and the U.S. Census Bureau, there were about 198,000 multifamily permits issued in 2011. This is down from 455,000 in 2005.

- *Residential real estate.* The residential real estate market may still be fairly weak for a while. This market was hit the hardest by the financial crisis.

   Besides, there appears to be changes in attitudes about home ownership, especially with echo boomers. It is not necessarily considered a must-have. After all, millions of Americans have gone broke because of foreclosures.

   Recently, the home market has seen extremely low levels of construction. So even if demand does not increase much, there could still be opportunities for growth.

- *Mortgages.* The mortgage market includes lenders and servicers. The loans created are often issued to investors through the bond market, who get periodic cash distributions from interest and principal payments. Based on research from Inside Mortgage Finance, there are about $10.3 trillion residential mortgages in the United States.

   The financial crisis has had a major impact on the market, such as with the surge in foreclosures and delinquent loans. This has led to higher underwriting standards, which should provide for safer investments.

Basics of REITs

There are two types of REITs. First, there is the mortgage REIT, which invests primarily in fixed-income securities. These are specialized vehicles and can be highly volatile, especially when interest rates change. If rates increase, the values of the portfolios will usually decline, whereas portfolio values will increase if interest rates fall. With interest rates at historic lows, there could be some major risks for mortgage REITs.

Then there is the equity REIT, which has ownership in real estate properties. Much of the income is in the form of ongoing rent.

In fact, equity REITs have historically been a strong hedge against inflation. Keep in mind that these were some of the top performers during the 1970s.

In times of high inflation, investors focus on hard assets as a way to protect their wealth. And one of the best ones is real estate. Besides, the rents usually include escalation clauses, which allow for higher income.

True, inflation has been moderate since the mid-1980s. But again, this may change in the future. With higher budget deficits and loose monetary policies across the world, this may become a big problem in the future.

Finally, a REIT does not use an S-1 filing. Rather, it will use an S-11. This is similar to an S-1 for the most part, but there are some key differences. For example, the document will have extensive disclosures on the properties that the REIT owns, including the rents, occupancy rates, and ownership positions.

Yields

Congress created the REIT structure back in the 1960s so as to increase investment in the real estate industry. With the country growing at a rapid pace, this was a much-need move.

The core rules for being a REIT have remained the same:

- At least 75 percent of the assets must be in qualifying real estate.
- At least 75 percent of income must come from rents or mortgage interest.

But perhaps the most important one is:

- If a REIT distributes a minimum of 90 percent of its income as dividends, there are no federal taxes owed.

As a result, this type of investment has been a key source of attractive yields for investors, which can easily range from 3 percent to 6 percent or so.

However, investors must understand that there is a downside: only 40 percent of the yield is taxed at the lower dividend tax rate of 15 percent. Because of this, investors often put REITs into their individual retirement accounts (IRAs), which provide tax-deferred gains.

Analyzing REITs

For most IPO investments, the focus is on earnings. If earnings continue to grow for the long term, the shareholder returns can potentially beat the market.

But when it comes to REITs, the earnings are not necessarily a good metric. How? Let's take an example. XYZ is a REIT that owns 10 apartment buildings in California for which it paid a total of $150 million.

But the company is required to take depreciation charges against the apartment buildings. Suppose the annual amount is $5 million.

So yes, this will be a big hit to the earnings each year. But the fact is that there has been no cash outflow; depreciation is a noncash expense.

This is why investors use another metric when looking at the earnings of a REIT: funds from operations (FFO). Essentially, this is the income plus the depreciation. You'll find FFO in the footnotes of the S-11.

But FFO is far from perfect. For example, if a company buys a new property, there will be a major outflow of cash. To account for this, there is the adjusted funds from operations (AFFO) metric. This will subtract the capital expenditures, which gives a better idea of the cash flows. Analyzing the AFFO is a good way to get a sense of whether the REIT can continue to pay its dividends.

There's something else that is important: depreciation will reduce the carrying costs of the assets of a REIT. This means that the book value could understate the true value of the real estate assets.

To continue our example, let's say that after 10 years, the stated value of XYZ's buildings is $70 million because of the depreciation charges. Yet during this period, the real estate market has been strong. According to generally accepted accounting principles (GAAP), however, the company cannot change the value of the buildings.

In this case, investors will have their own estimates. Consider that the typical way to value real estate is with the capitalization rate (cap rate). This is compared to the general return in a local market.

The cap rate essentially capitalizes operating income. The formula is:

$$\text{Cap rate} = \text{Annual net operating income/Cost of value}$$

Thus,

$$\text{Value of property} = \text{Operating income/Cap rate}$$

If the operating income on a property is $1 million and the cap rate is 5 percent, then the value of property is $20 million. The lower the cap rate, the higher the valuation.

Finally, here are some other factors to look at when investing in REITs:

- *Trends.* Over the years, look for a REIT that is showing consistent growth in occupancy rates and rental income. What's more, it is important that a company has a track record of acquisitions. Have these deals worked out? For the most part, the key to growth for a REIT is through acquisitions.

  It is also important to understand some of the key economic drivers in the local economy. As the old saying goes, success in real estate is about "location, location, location."
- *Debt.* REITs have large amounts of debt. It is not easy to determine the point at which it becomes unmanageable. But there is one thing an investor should look at: the amount of debt that has floating rates. These are interest rates tied to some underlying index rate. If interest rates increase over time, this could become a problem for the REIT.
- *Upgrades.* Though upgrading can add to current costs, a REIT can generate higher rental rates when it improves its properties.

Funds

In his 2011 annual shareholder letter, Warren Buffett apologized because he was "dead wrong" about his forecast of the comeback of the real estate market (although he is still bullish on the long term). Yes, even the world's best investors have a tough time figuring out real estate investments.

Now REITs can help out. They have professional management and some tax advantages.

Despite all this, the analysis can be difficult. Besides, a REIT may be too focused on a certain region or state. So, if there is a downturn in the local economy, the consequences can be severe.

Thus, a better option may be to invest in a fund of REITs. Some good ones include:

- *CGM Realty.* The portfolio manager, Ken Heebner, is one of Wall Street's best stock pickers. But he also has a long background with real estate. During the past decade, his REIT fund has generated average annual returns of nearly 19 percent.
- *iShares Dow Jones US Real Estate.* This is an exchange-traded fund that invests in 80 REITs, mortgage companies, and even timber operators. In 2012, the dividend yield was an attractive 3.70 percent.
- *Cohen & Steers Realty Shares.* The portfolio managers, Martin Cohen and Robert Steers, have been managing this fund since the early 1990s. For the

most part, their approach is to focus on properties that have relatively low values. But they also want to be in areas that have strong growth trends, such as health care properties.

Conclusion

After the financial crisis, it does seem scary to invest in real estate. But then again, valuations are much more reasonable now and there are various sectors that look promising, like apartments and commercial properties. The REIT structure also provides for competitive dividends that are certainly attractive in a low-yield environment.

PART IV

Other IPO
Investments

CHAPTER 19

IPO Funds

With more than 10,000 mutual funds on the market, it seems only natural that some would invest heavily in initial public offerings (IPOs)—and there are several that do. After all, as stated in the Introduction, mutual funds buy a large percentage of all IPO shares. It is actually a good way to juice a mutual fund's performance. In fact, legendary portfolio managers—like Fidelity Magellan's Peter Lynch—have gotten allocations of IPOs. The larger the fund, the bigger the chance the portfolio manager will get shares, especially for hot deals.

However, there are some mutual funds that will buy shares even before a company goes public. That is, they will participate in venture capital rounds of financings. Some of the well-known players include T. Rowe Price, Fidelity, and Legg Mason. For example, by the end of 2011, T. Rowe Price had $400 million worth of Facebook stock. It had also invested in other pre-IPO companies like WorkDay, Twitter, Zynga, and Groupon.

Keep in mind that T. Rowe Price has spread these shares across various funds so as to reduce the risk. Also, the firm manages a substantial amount of assets, which came to $489 billion by the end of 2011. Besides, T. Rowe Price will generally invest when a company reaches a certain critical mass. You will certainly not find any raw start-ups in the portfolio.

So in a way, you may be invested in IPOs and not even realize it.

For individual investors, a mutual fund can be a good way to play the IPO market. Here's a look.

Types of Funds

A fund is a pool of money that has one or more portfolio managers. There will also be an objective; that is, the fund will focus on a certain type of market or investment strategy.

Another key aspect of a fund is the net asset value (NAV). This is calculated as follows:

(Total investment assets − Expenses)/Number of shares outstanding

A fund will usually make this calculation at the end of each day of trading. The exception is exchange-traded funds (ETFs), whose NAVs are calculated continuously.

There are some important benefits of investing in funds:

- *Diversification.* A portfolio manager has the capital to purchase many types of investments, including IPOs. Even if a few are duds, that should not make a huge difference, as the other investments should help to offset the losses. To manage this level of diversification yourself would be quite costly.

  Diversification does not always work, though. This is the case during times of extreme market stress, such as what happened during the recent financial crisis. For the most part, just about all investments across the world plunged during this time. But these situations are exceedingly rare.

- *Professional management.* Portfolio managers have education and investment experience that individual investors usually do not have. They also have a staff to help with the legwork. Besides, a large mutual fund will have the time and clout to get access to allocations of IPO shares.

- *Legal protections.* At least for mutual funds, exchange-traded funds, and closed-end funds, there are extensive federal government regulations. After all, these investments are focused primarily for the general public, and the Securities and Exchange Commission wants to reduce fraud as much as possible. This means that mutual funds must not only provide substantial disclosures but also segregate investors' funds. At no time will portfolio managers have possession of the capital.

There are also a variety of structures available. They include the following.

Mutual Funds

The mutual fund is the most common type of fund (it is also known as an open-end fund). Whenever an investor buys more shares, the mutual fund will issue new shares. Or, when there are sales (also known as redemptions), the fund will reduce the number of shares. Because of this, the share price of the mutual fund will always equal the NAV.

The minimum investment requirements are usually reasonable, such as under $10,000 or so.

But there are some limitations. First of all, you can purchase or sell shares only one time during a trading day. Also, a mutual fund may have lots of problems if there is a spike in redemptions. It will force substantial amounts of selling of the stocks in the portfolio at possibly disadvantageous prices, which can worsen the returns.

Fees for mutual funds can also be hefty. This is definitely the case for specialized funds, such as those that focus on narrow categories like IPOs. Some of the fees to look out for include:

- *Loads.* This is a commission to the broker who sells you shares in the fund. Some loads are charged when you buy into the fund. For example, if you put $1,000 into a mutual fund and it has a 4 percent load, you will pay $40 in commission. So in order just to break even, your fund will have to increase by 4.16 percent. There are also back-end loads, which are charged when you sell your fund shares. The longer you have held the shares, the less the commission is.

    If you are doing your own research, you should not select a fund with a load.
- *12b-1 fee.* This is also known as a distribution or marketing fee. It is a sales commission that is deducted every year you hold the shares in fund. The maximum that can be charged is 1 percent of your investment. Again, pick a fund without one.
- *Management fee.* Even if you buy a no-load fund, you still need to pay this fee. It covers research expenses, such as buying subscriptions to investment services and paying salaries for portfolio managers. For a specialized fund, expect to pay something that is 1 percent to even 2 percent of the NAV.

Another big issue for mutual funds is performance. All in all, the majority of portfolio managers underperform their relevant indexes. There are several reasons for this. Academics have pointed out markets are highly efficient and it is nearly impossible to beat them over the long term. Only a few outliers exist, like Warren Buffett.

Then there is compensation. When compared to hedge funds, the portfolio managers in the mutual fund industry usually get much lower compensation. In other words, it is tough for these funds to attract top-notch talent.

Finally, mutual funds can have unexpected tax consequences. For example, they might distribute large annual gains. If you buy soon before this, you'll owe tax on the whole amount. This may be the case even though you have lost money on the investment!

This situation is common for mutual funds that engage in heavy trading. You can get a sense of this by looking at the turnover ratio. This shows the percentage of a fund that has been traded during the year. If it is over 200 percent, then the portfolio is quite aggressive.

A way to deal with the tax bite is actually to put a mutual fund in an individual retirement account (IRA) or a 401(k). But of course, this means keeping the investment there until you retire (unless you want to pay a 10 percent penalty).

The most notable IPO mutual fund is the IPO Plus Fund. The sponsor is Renaissance Capital, which provides IPO research to institutions. The database has proprietary research on over 5,000 IPOs.

The IPO Plus Fund got its start in 1998. It purchases shares in the secondary markets, from IPO allocations, and in the aftermarket. In 2012, some of the fund's top holdings included General Motors, GNC Holdings, Jive Software, Kinder Morgan, and LinkedIn. The minimum investment is $5,000 for regular accounts and $2,500 for IRAs.

The portfolio manager is Linda R. Killian, who has spent 21 years as an analyst of IPOs. Some of her areas of expertise include health care, retailing, telecommunications services, consumer products, and media.

Another IPO mutual fund is Direxion Long/Short Global IPO Fund (DXIIX). It takes a hedge fund approach to investing. That is, it will go either long or short on IPOs. Let's face it: some IPOs can be duds. So why not make money on those, too?

Exchange-Traded Funds

This is a recent phenomenon, with the first exchange-traded fund (ETF) hitting the markets in the early 1990s. But during the past decade, there has been explosive growth in this space.

In most cases, an ETF will not have portfolio managers. Instead, the investments will be based on a certain index, such as the Standard & Poor's (S&P) 500. This means that the costs of an ETF are usually low.

What's more, an investor can buy or sell an ETF at any time of the day. In other words, it is like any other stock traded on an exchange.

This is certainly a nice benefit for active traders. For example, they can use trading strategies like limit orders and stop-loss orders. It is also possible to short an ETF.

Because of its structure, there are usually no distributions of taxable gains. All in all, an ETF is highly tax efficient.

An ETF can be effective for playing themes. For example, let's say there have been numerous IPOs in the solar industry. But you believe that many of these companies are of low quality and the market has reached bubble level. You think it will soon pop. In this case, you can short the Guggenheim Solar ETF.

Or suppose the biotech sector has languished for some time. But over the past quarter, there has been a pickup in biotech IPOs. This may actually be a sign that investors are getting excited about the sector. So yes, you might want to buy shares of a biotech ETF. Yet you might want to focus on one that has an index that includes smaller companies, which are likely to see more appreciation if there is a rebound.

If you want to boost things even more, you can look at a leveraged ETF. This uses sophisticated strategies like futures and options to double or triple the returns. Thus, if you have a 2x ETF, this means that it will increase by 2 percent if the underlying index increases by 1 percent. Conversely, a 1 percent drop will result in a 2 percent fall in the ETF.

Be careful with leveraged ETFs. They can quickly eat into your returns if you make a bad bet.

Here are some IPO ETFs:

- *First Trust US IPO Index Fund (NYSE:FPX).* This ETF is based on an index of 100 of the largest IPOs in the United States. It waits until seven days after launch to buy a new IPO so as to avoid buying when there is intense trading and buzz. The fund will also sell the shares after 1,000 days. To help improve diversification, no stock can represent 10 percent of the overall portfolio.

    The fund has benefited from breakout IPOs like Visa and MasterCard. For the past three years (as of April 2012), the compound average annual return was close to 28 percent.
- *Global X Social Media ETF (NYSE:SOCL).* The fund is based on an index that focuses on social networking companies, such as LinkedIn, Zynga, Groupon, Yelp, Pandora, and Angie's List. There are also investments in foreign countries, with a major focus on China.

Closed-End Funds

A closed-end fund will get its start by raising money through an IPO on an exchange, such as the New York Stock Exchange or NASDAQ. Some foreign exchanges have large numbers of such funds as well. One is the Toronto Stock

Exchange, which has many closed-end funds that focus on mining companies, and these funds often have investments in IPOs.

Because a closed-end fund is publicly traded, the number of shares outstanding is fixed. Consequently, there will often be a difference between the stock price and the NAV. In fact, quite often the NAV will be at a discount. One strategy is to buy shares when this discount approaches 15 percent to 20 percent.

Why the discount? There are several reasons. First of all, there may not be much trading volume in a closed-end fund, which can result in a lower valuation. At the same time, the fees can be hefty, say over 2 percent of the NAV.

Over time, the gap should close. However, be wary of a closed-end fund that is trading at a premium.

A key advantage is that there is no redemption risk. That is, a closed-end fund does not have to return any of its funds to investors. This is very important for funds that invest in risky investments like IPOs and pre-IPO shares.

Here are some closed-end funds:

- *Keating Capital (NASDAQ:KIPO).* The fund invests primarily in pre-IPO companies. The investment criteria are:
  - A company with over $10 million in trailing 12-month revenues.
  - An IPO expected within 18 months.
  - Potential return expectation of 2x over a three-year holding period.

  Some of the companies in the portfolio include LifeLock, SilkRoad, Truecar, and Zoosk.

  The portfolio manager, Timothy Keating, has been investing in early-stage companies since in 1997. He also worked at Bear Stearns and Kidder, Peabody & Co.

  However, there are big risks when investing in pre-IPO companies. After all, some companies may never come public because of problems with the company or the industry. Keep in mind that one of Keating's portfolio companies, BrightSource, had to withdraw its IPO in 2012.
- *GSV Capital Corp. (NASDAQ:GSVC).* The company buys pre-IPO shares, usually in emerging industries like cloud computing, clean tech, mobile, software, and social networking. Some of its holdings include Zynga, Dropbox, Facebook, and Twitter.

  The portfolio manager is Michael Moe, who is a veteran of Silicon Valley. No doubt this has helped to get access to early-stage investment opportunities. He also has a strong board of directors, with Intuit chairman Bill Campbell and Hewlett-Packard PC head Todd Bradley.

Moe wrote a book called *Finding the Next Starbucks: How to Identify and Invest in the Hot Stocks of Tomorrow.* He also co-founded ThinkEquity, which is an investment banking firm that is focused on tech companies.

Yet buying hot pre-IPO companies can be risky. Consider that Moe purchased Groupon's stock at $25. The company came public at $20 and fell to $12.

So it should be no surprise that the GSV Capital has been volatile.

• *Harris & Harris (NASDAQ:TINY).* The fund invests primarily in pre-IPO shares of nanotechnology companies. This industry deals with manipulating particles at an atomic or molecular scale. By doing this, it is possible to create better materials. In some cases, there may be applications for categories like health care, energy, and electronics. However, a problem is that the technology has been slow to result in commercial products, which has meant few IPOs.

But one way to get returns has been acquisitions. And the nanotechnology space has been active. In 2011, several of Harris & Harris's portfolio companies were purchased. One was BioVex, which Amgen acquired for $425 million.

In fact, with the cash from these kinds of transactions, a closed-end fund like Harris & Harris may reinvest the capital into more companies or even provide a dividend for its shareholders.

Hedge Funds

People often get confused about hedge funds. After all, the word *hedge* is misleading. Essentially, a hedge fund includes any type of investment fund that is for large investors such as institutions, as well as wealthy individuals. Now, there are some mutual funds that try to emulate hedge funds, but there are only a handful of them and they usually have high minimum investments, such as over $25,000. And they will probably have little or no exposure to IPOs.

Some of the world's best investors are hedge fund operators. They will often use complex strategies, such as short selling, leverage, and derivatives. While the risks can be high, so can the returns.

The fees are also high. Keep in mind that hedge funds get a performance fee of 20 percent to 25 percent of the profits from the fund as well as a 2 percent ongoing management fee. So if a hedge fund manager has standout returns, he or she can make huge sums. For example, in 2011 Bridgewater

Associates' Ray Dalio earned $3.9 billion. Then again, he was able to generate a 25 percent return during a tough year. He did this with investments in gold, short selling strategies, and currency plays.

Most hedge funds have a high-water mark. That is, no performance fees are owed if the performance is lackluster. Let's take an example. Suppose XYZ fund drops by 15 percent. In this case, the fund manager will not get any performance fees until this loss is recouped.

However, this protection is not foolproof. Keep in mind that it is common for a fund to close down when there are big losses. The fund managers will then go on to create a new fund!

Actually, even if you are wealthy, you still may not be able to invest in a hedge fund. There are some that have closed their doors to new investors or that will be highly selective.

Even if you can get a piece of a hedge fund, it still may be a bad deal. There are many fund operators whose returns have been consistently lower than the relevant benchmarks.

There are also lockups. These prevent investors from redeeming their shares for a period of time, say one or two years. In times of financial distress—such as during 2008—this can be a huge problem for investors who have a need for liquidity.

And yes, there are examples of fraudulent behavior with hedge funds. It is actually fairly easy for frauds to occur because regulations are loose.

In 2011, the federal authorities brought securities fraud charges against the operator of a hedge fund in Florida. He had claimed that he had pre-IPO shares of hot companies like Facebook, Groupon, Twitter, and Zynga. As a result, he raised at least $12.6 million. However, about half of the funds were used to pay for things like cars, tailored clothes, and a yacht.

So before investing in a hedge fund, do as much due diligence as possible on the portfolio managers. It is also a good idea to get the help of a financial adviser.

Fund Strategies

Here are some tips for investing in mutual funds, ETFs, and closed-end funds that have large exposures to IPOs:

- *Use dollar-cost averaging.* Many mutual funds have systematic investment programs: you can have the fund automatically deduct a certain amount, say $100 or $1,000 or more, from your bank account each month or each quarter. This way, you will not be exposing all of your funds at once but will instead be gradually and steadily investing your money. This strategy is called dollar-cost averaging. When the shares are selling at low prices, you will be buying a lot of shares, but when the share prices are high, you will be buying fewer. In effect, you are buying low. This is a good strategy for investing in IPOs, since there is a high degree of volatility and the market is difficult to predict.

Reinvesting capital gains and dividends is another great way to use dollar-cost averaging, and most funds allow such reinvestment. But keep in mind that even if you put the capital gains and dividends back into the fund, you are still taxed on them.

- *Read the prospectus.* Just as every IPO has a prospectus, so does every mutual fund. The documents are similar. You'll see information on past performance, the management team, fees, and the fund's objective. There are also some helpful web resources like Yahoo! Finance and Morningstar.
- *Ask for help.* Most mutual funds have an 800 number. You should use it whenever you need information on the fund, an explanation of fund performance, or even industry trends. Also, ask how much of the fund's assets are invested in IPOs.
- *Look at the mutual fund's website.* In fact, the site for Renaissance Capital at www.ipohome.com is rich with resources on IPOs.
- *Read the proxy statements.* A mutual fund must get shareholder consent to make any major policy changes. This is done via a proxy, a document sent to shareholders. Read these documents and vote; it can make a difference. Perhaps the biggest thing to look for is a change in the objective of the fund. For example, suppose you invest in an IPO mutual fund whose objective is to invest 80 percent of its funds in IPOs, and suddenly it wants to lower this to 50 percent. These are things that investors should know. You should also pay close attention to changes in fees.
- *Correctly monitor performance.* Compare your fund to others like it. For the most part, IPO funds are micro-cap funds. It makes sense to weigh your IPO fund against other such micro-cap funds instead of against the Standard & Poor's 500 index, which has larger, more established companies and would not provide an accurate comparison.
- *Know your fund manager.* You are investing not just in the fund but also in one or more portfolio managers. These people decide what to buy and sell. If a respected, successful portfolio manager leaves the fund, then you may want to leave, too, unless the new manager has an investment philosophy you believe in.
- *Know the fund's holdings.* You can request information from the mutual fund that shows the top holdings. What types of companies does the fund

own? Are IPOs in the top holdings? If so, are they the types of companies you feel comfortable investing in?

Conclusion

For those who do not have the time to research stocks, funds are a great alternative. The good news is that there are many options to choose from, such as mutual funds, exchange-traded funds, closed-end funds, and even hedge funds. They should all be part of a diversified portfolio.

However, a fund that is focused on IPOs will still likely be risky, even though there is a portfolio of stocks. As a result, such a fund should still represent a small part of your portfolio, say less than 10 percent.

References

Moe, Michael. 2006. *Finding the Next Starbucks: How to Identify and Invest in the Hot Stocks of Tomorrow.* New York: Portfolio.

Rothfeld, Michael. 2011. "Florida Man Is Accused of Fraud." *Wall Street Journal*, November 18. http://goo.gl/SP6xe.

CHAPTER 20

Spin-Offs

When a company (called the parent) sells all or a part of a subsidiary or division to the public, creating a new, independent company, the result is a spin-off. When a company is spun off, shareholders have stock in two different companies. Typically spin-offs come from large corporations, such as Viacom, AT&T, or General Electric, because they have many divisions.

Spin-offs can be very lucrative. An academic study published in 2004 from professors John J. McConnell and Alexei V. Ovtchinnikov analyzed 36 years of data. The conclusion was that on average the returns for spin-offs were 20 percent higher than the Standard & Poor's (S&P) returns for the three years after the transactions were complete. The authors pointed out the example of Lucent, which was a spin-off of AT&T. The original price was $27 and within three years the price per share reached $230.

Of course, this does not mean that all spin-offs will do well or that this out-performance will continue. Besides, a few high-return deals can skew the data.

Yet there are some compelling reasons why spin-offs can be attractive investments.

The Basics

In a spin-off, the stock price of the subsidiary is based on the exchange ratio. The exchange ratio is a percentage of the current stock price of the parent company. For example, suppose that XYZ decides to spin off its Z subsidiary. The parent determines that it will issue 0.92 (or 92 percent) shares of Z to existing shareholders. So if the current price of XYZ is $100, shareholders will be issued initial public offering (IPO) shares at $92 per share in Z.

There are a variety of reasons why parent companies will spin off divisions.

- *Enhance shareholder value.* This is usually the main reason for the transaction. The belief is that investors like pure plays, not conglomerates.
- *Get new customers.* A prime example is Lucent. When it was part of AT&T, a variety of customers did not want to do business with Lucent because the customers were competitors of AT&T's other divisions. After the spin-off, business soared for Lucent.
- *Unload.* Sometimes parent companies consider a subsidiary to be a nonessential (or even failing) business and want to sell it off to the public, ideally for a good price. This is a particularly popular practice when the IPO market is very strong. The parent company may even transfer debt from its balance sheet to the subsidiary's. Investors beware.
- *Meet legal regulations.* A parent company may spin off a division because it is in violation of the antitrust laws. This was basically the case with AT&T when it spun off its Baby Bell companies during the early 1980s.
- *Create easier valuation.* After a spin-off, it becomes much easier to value the parent and the subsidiary. In fact, analysts typically upgrade their evaluations of both when there is a spin-off.
- *Remove "rich uncle syndrome."* A subsidiary that is part of a major corporation can sometimes be shielded from the demands of competition. By doing a spin-off, the subsidiary will, ideally, be invigorated by participating in the market.

There are actually four basic types of spin-offs:

1. Traditional spin-off.
2. Spin-off with equity carve-out.
3. Split-off.
4. Tracking stock.

Traditional Spin-Off

The traditional spin-off occurs when the parent company distributes 100 percent of the subsidiary to existing shareholders on a pro rata basis. Outside shareholders are not given an opportunity to obtain shares—that is, until the shares trade in the aftermarket.

For example, if company XYZ decides to spin off its Z subsidiary, the shareholders of XYZ get, on a pro rata basis, 100 percent of the shares of the

Z subsidiary. However, the XYZ shareholders do not have to pay for these Z shares. Why? Because the company is being divided into two pieces. Once this is done, the shareholders of XYZ can sell their Z stock to the general public.

Spin-Off with Equity Carve-Out

A spin-off with equity carve-out is created when the parent distributes a minority position in a subsidiary to the public.

For example, XYZ decides to distribute 20 percent of Z to the public in an IPO. The remaining 80 percent is then distributed to existing shareholders. Why 20 percent? Because if it were more, the transaction would not be tax free. In fact, to make sure the transaction is tax free, the parent corporation needs to get a tax ruling from the Internal Revenue Service (IRS).

A main reason parent companies like doing carve-outs is that doing so raises cash by offering the IPO to the public. When a company issues 20 percent of Z, the public must pay for the 20 percent, while the remaining 80 percent is owned by the parent corporation.

Split-Off

A split-off happens when existing shareholders have the option to swap all or a part of their existing shares for new shares in the subsidiary based on an exchange ratio set by the parent company. In this type of transaction, no money is raised for the parent company (since the company is merely being divided). A split-off is equivalent to a stock buyback. The parent corporation will attempt to make the exchange ratio attractive enough for shareholders to swap stock in the parent corporation for stock in the subsidiary. The result is that there are fewer shares of the parent company left.

Tracking Stock

A tracking stock is very similar to a traditional spin-off. Basically, tracking stocks are a separate class of a company's common stock that is used to track the performance of a certain business unit. They are not considered spin-offs, though, because tracking stocks continue to operate completely within the parent company. Typically, a major company will issue shares in a division to shareholders, and in many cases the parent company will raise money in the process.

This was actually a big trend during the dot-com boom as traditional businesses wanted to get more value from their Internet assets. Companies like General Electric, Barnes & Noble, and Disney issued tracking stocks. However, they turned out to lose huge amounts for investors.

Actually, subpar performances are common with tracking stocks. After all, a tracking stock conveys absolutely no ownership rights to the shareholders. In fact, tracking stocks are often called "fictional stocks"—if the company goes bust, you have no claim to any assets. There are other potential problems, such as conflicts of interest. In a tracking stock, the board of directors is the same for both the parent and the subsidiary company. So when the board makes decisions it is difficult to determine whether it is favoring the parent or the subsidiary.

Investing in Spin-Offs

After announcing a spin-off, a company may take six months to a year, or even longer, to make Securities and Exchange Commission (SEC) disclosures. It is possible to purchase shares in the parent company before the disclosures, although this is risky, since it is advisable to read the disclosures before investing in a spin-off. So to play this game wisely, you need some patience.

The SEC disclosure document for a spin-off is the Form 10-12B, which has most of the information needed to make an investment. Some companies will file the information in an 8-K instead (but this is fairly rare).

Usually, the Form 10-12B will go through several amendments. So make sure you have the latest document. The document is like a prospectus, but usually shorter.

You should also get the company's other financial statements, such as the annual and quarterly reports. If a spin-off represents a large percentage of the parent company, there is also a requirement to file a proxy statement, so that shareholders can vote on the transaction.

Such documents can be several hundred pages long, but you don't have to read everything. Instead focus only on certain parts, such as the following:

- *Big name in the new company.* Look to see if a top-notch CEO will head the spin-off. When Marriott decided to spin off its hotel properties into a new entity called Host Marriott, the then-CEO of Marriott, Stephen Bollenbach, decided to become the CEO of the new Host Marriott company. He obviously saw a lot of upside to this new company. What's more, management was motivated with 20 percent ownership of the stock. Within four months of the spin-off, the stock tripled.
- *Timing.* It's usually a good idea to wait a week or so to buy stock of a spin-off. The main reason is that the institutional investors will usually sell off their

shares because the company may be too small or these investors really want to own just the parent. There may also be automatic selling from index funds.

In fact, the firm Bespoke Investment Group conducted a study on the matter. It analyzed spin-offs from 2001 to 2011 for those companies with valuations of $100 million or more. In the first week of the spin-off, the company had an average decline of 3.4 percent. But after this, the performance was much better. Within three months, the average return came to 5.2 percent, and it grew to 9.7 percent after six months.

- *Growth potential.* Look for spin-offs that have huge parents. All in all, these divisions probably did not get much resources or attention. But by being independent, they can better pursue the growth opportunities.
- *Toxic debt.* In some cases, a parent may push a large amount of debt and other obligations on the spin-off company. No doubt this could be crippling. So make sure to look at the balance sheet.

There is an exchange-traded fund (ETF) that focuses on spin-offs: Guggenheim Spin-Off Fund (NYSE: CSD). It is relatively new but has posted a strong track record. Between 2010 and 2012 the annual average return was 27 percent.

The fund tracks the Beacon Spin-Off index, which usually includes about 40 stocks or so. For the most part, the ETF can be a good approach to play spin-offs without having to do the extensive stock research.

Conclusion

Spin-offs can be great investments. But it is probably better to focus on traditional ones, not variations like tracking stocks. And timing can be critical. As indicated, it is usually best to wait a week before buying the stock. You'll probably get a better valuation.

References

Bespoke Investment Group. 2012. "Spin Offs Back in Style." February 15. http://goo.gl/24qwF.

McConnell, John J., and Alexei V. Ovtchinnikov. 2004. "Predictability of Long-Term Spinoff Returns." Academic paper, March 28. http://goo.gl/GFxSk.

CHAPTER 21

Fad IPOs

Manias and fads often drive the initial public offering (IPO) market, which loves to highlight the "next big thing." But in the long term, fads eventually fizzle out, leaving loyal investors with huge losses.

A fad is a gigantic trend that sweeps the nation, if not the world. As described in Charles Mackay's classic book, *Extraordinary Popular Delusions and the Madness of Crowds*, sometimes people stampede to buy a product that is of questionable value. But a fad is short-term, lasting several years at most. The masses eventually become bored and move on to something new.

This reality does not mean that you should never invest in fad IPOs. After all, you have the potential to make a lot of money very quickly. In fact, you can profit from fad IPOs even after the fad has become quite prominent.

One fad that made considerable cash for its investors was Crocs. The company got its start in 2002 with innovative shoes made out of a special plastic that retailed from $30 to $60 a pair. The company quickly saw huge demand. By the first nine months of 2005, sales had surged from $8.1 million to $75 million. There was also net income of $12.8 million.

In February 2006, the company pulled off its IPO. Issued at $21 per share, the stock spiked by 48 percent on its first day. Within less than a year, the shares would double.

However, with the financial crisis, demand started to lag. It also looked like the Crocs fad was fading. By late 2008, the shares were trading at $1.20.

So yes, be cautious: the high rate of return on a fad IPO will usually last a year or two. Then the consumer moves on, and the stock plunges.

In other words, it is crucial to be very quick when investing in fad IPOs. These are definitely not buy-and-hold investments.

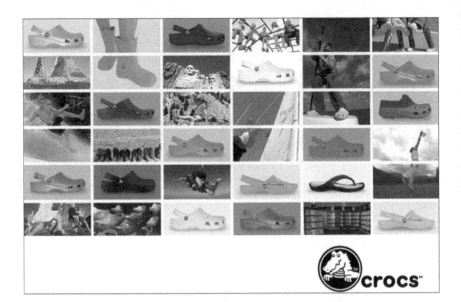

MAJOR FADS OF THE PAST 20 YEARS

Cabbage Patch dolls	Rubik's Cubes
Baseball cards	Pet rocks
Bagels	Wine coolers
Mighty Morphin Power Rangers	CB radios
Pokemon	Beanie Babies

Spotting the Fads

Sometimes a fad is not a fad at all. For example, when McDonald's went public in 1965, many thought fast food was the craze of the moment and would quickly fizzle. Instead, fast food met a consumer need that has lasted for decades.

Fads also tend to take some time to develop. For example, even though baseball cards have existed since the late 1800s, it took until the 1980s for them to become a full-fledged fad.

Or consider wine coolers. These fruity wine drinks were created in the mid-1970s but did not reach fad status until the early 1980s.

So the point at which a product transforms from a mere product into a consumer phenomenon is by no means predictable. And perhaps because of the proliferation of mass media, the past few decades have seen more than their share of fads.

But there are some categories that tend to be fad-rich. Let's take a look.

Consumer Technologies

In the consumer technology world, there is always a short fuse. After all, technology is constantly improving as products quickly become obsolete. If anything, it is a constant stream of fads. Some of the early ones included the Atari game console and Sony's Walkman.

Unfortunately, it is extremely difficult for technology companies to replace their products. They often become too dependent on their revenues and fail to come up with new concepts.

This phenomenon is known as the "innovator's dilemma" (the phrase came from an article co-written by Clayton Christensen in 1995). It describes the process of disruptive technologies that change markets and how such technologies can result in the doom of the current leaders.

Yet there are standout examples of companies that have been able to deal with this, such as Apple. No doubt the company could have fizzled if it had not moved beyond the iPod. But Apple kept pushing innovation, which led to the iPhone and the iPad. By 2011, Apple had become the world's most valuable company, with a market value of over $600 billion.

But this is an exception. Unfortunately, there are many consumer technology fads that quickly flame out and destroy companies.

This often happens during booms, and was especially the case when the Internet became hugely popular.

During the late 1990s, investors wanted to find the next eBay or Amazon .com. And yes, Wall Street minted hundreds of dot-com IPOs to satiate the demand. The capital from the offerings would help to build consumer brands by such means as heavy spending on commercials.

But many of these companies were just fads. Keep in mind that it often takes a while to create a strong, enduring consumer brand.

One of the most notable dot-com me-too companies was eToys. This was an online e-tailer of children's products, including toys, software, and videos. The company had its IPO in May 1999, and the stock went from $20 to $86 per share within a year. Actually, eToys had a market value twice that of Toys "R" Us.

But the fundamentals of the company were terrible. In fiscal 1999, the revenues were only $34.7 million and the losses came to a stunning $73.9 million.

In March 2001, eToys filed for bankruptcy and KB Toys bought the assets for $5 million.

Restaurants

The restaurant industry is prone to fads. It's a highly competitive space, and entrepreneurs are always looking to create the next must-have concept. An innovation usually attracts a good amount of competition.

This is why it is important for a restaurant operator to create a top brand as well as build a strong infrastructure. It also should identify a real long-term consumer trend.

So far, this has been the case with Chipotle Mexican Grill, Inc. Since going public in 2006, the stock has soared by over 940 percent.

In the S-1, you would have noticed that Chipotle was certainly a unique restaurant. In fact, it declared that it was "not a chain." The focus was to serve food fast but not make it a "fast food" experience. This involved the use of high-quality raw ingredients, classic cooking methods, and a distinctive interior design. Essentially, Chipotle created a new category in dining called "fast casual," which became the fastest-growing segment in the restaurant business.

When Chipotle went public, it had nearly doubled revenues over the prior two years.

But such a company does not come around often. The fact is that many restaurant IPOs are really just fads.

Some warning signs to look for include:

- *Celebrity endorsements.* While a theme based on a hot name in entertainment may get some initial buzz, it usually flames out. This was the case with Planet Hollywood, which signed marquee names like Demi Moore, Bruce Willis, and Arnold Schwarzenegger. As should be no surprise, it became a hot spot as locations opened up across various major cities.

  With such fanfare, the IPO performed fantastically. The offering price was $18 per share, and the company raised $200 million. The stock hit a high of $28 in 1996. But by late 2000 the stock was trading at $2 per share. All in all, the food was not very good.
- *Business not defensible.* Millions of people love to eat bagels. To capitalize on this, a variety of bagel companies went public back in the mid-1990s.

  But the problem was that they could not differentiate themselves. For the most part, a bagel is a bagel. Does it really matter where you buy one?

  At the same time, the barriers to entry were very low. Setting up a bagel shop is relatively inexpensive, and, as a result, many people got into the business at once. With so many bagel shops, there was fierce price competition and not enough profits to go around.

In the end, many of the bagel company IPOs plunged in value and went bust.

Toys

You will often find fads in the toy business. The product life cycle for most toys is notoriously short. True, there are notable exceptions, such as Mattel's Barbie doll, which has been the all-time best-selling toy for the past 30 years.

But for the most part, toys are essentially fads. A prime example was Coleco's Cabbage Patch dolls, which every kid seemed to want in the mid-1980s. As the craze died, so did the company.

A recent example is Build-A-Bear Workshop. A former retail executive, Maxine Clark, launched the company in 1997. She opened a store in the Saint Louis Galleria that essentially was an assembly line where kids could create custom teddy bears.

In November 2004, Build-A-Bear went public at $20 and the stock soared 48 percent on its first day of trading. The company had grown its store base from 14 to 165 stores since 1999, and revenues hit $213.4 million.

The company would grow for a few more years, but Build-A-Bear's market eventually became saturated and demand started to tail off. By early 2009, the share price was below $5.

Apparel

Apparel is another market that has its share of fads, which can make it extremely difficult for companies to build sustainable businesses. True, some have found ways to innovate—like lululemon and Calvin Klein—but they seem to be fairly rare.

One interesting case of an apparel flameout is Heelys, Inc. The company went public in December 2006 and the stock soared 44 percent on its first day of trading to $30.30 per share.

Heelys was the creator of shoes that had wheels, which were extremely popular with kids. The company even had patents on the technology.

But it did not matter, because Heelys' customers quickly got bored with the shoes. Another problem was that schools and stores started to ban the shoes because of health and accident concerns.

By August 2007, the company was already reporting weak financial results as the stock plunged to $9. It would reach $2.50 by the end of the year.

Knowing When to Get Out of Fad IPOs

The real key to investing in fad IPOs is knowing when to sell. Again, there is no exact science. Many fad stocks are extremely volatile and subject to periods of profit taking. But here are some sell signals to watch for:

- *Mounting competition.* This is perhaps the best indicator that it's time to sell a fad IPO. Snapple, for example, did extremely well after its IPO, but it didn't take long for the major soft drink companies to enter the market. Several Snapple clones appeared on the scene at a rapid pace, quickly eating away at Snapple's market share.

  The baseball card fad fizzled, too, after too many competitors tried to get in on the game. Because of the success of the original Topps baseball cards, many other companies entered the market, such as Classic, Score, Upper Deck, and Action Packed. There was a flood of baseball cards on the market, and, as a result, consumers did not know which ones to buy. The market eventually collapsed, as did the stocks.

- *Major drop in earnings.* When analysts are shocked by a fad IPO's poor earnings report, a large drop in the stock price is probably not far off. This is usually a good time to sell, because in many cases the news only gets worse.

- *Drop in prices.* If a company announces plans to lower its prices, this is a major danger sign. It may mean that the company has large amounts of inventory that it cannot sell.

- *Backlash.* Another telltale sign that a fad is burning out is when it becomes a topic of ridicule. For example, this happened to Crocs shoes, which became a target for an episode on *Saturday Night Live.*

  Or, in some cases, the product will become hated by high-profile people. This happened with Ugg boots when Pamela Anderson realized they were made from animal skin.

Conclusion

IPOs are prone to fads. After all, such a company is often showing tremendous growth, which should get the attention of investors. Unfortunately, as seen with companies like Heelys, a fad can quickly fade and crush shareholders.

While there are no clear-cut ways to spot a fad, there are some helpful techniques. Basically, be concerned if there are recent drops in pricing, accumulation of inventory, and rising competition.

References

Bower, Joseph L., and Clayton Christensen. 1995. "Disruptive Technologies: Catching the Wave." *Harvard Business Review*, January–February.

Christensen, Clayton. 1997. *The Innovator's Dilemma.* Boston: Harvard Business School Press.

Mackay, Charles. 1841. *Extraordinary Popular Delusions and the Madness of Crowds.* New York: Harmony Books, 1980.

CHAPTER 22

Secondary Markets, Angel Investing, and Crowd Funding

In the early 1980s, David Cheriton joined Stanford University as a professor in the computer science department. While there, he made significant breakthroughs in areas like communications and distributed systems. But along the way, he also created several companies, such as Granite Systems, which eventually sold to Cisco for $220 million.

Then in 1998 he met two Stanford students, Sergey Brin and Larry Page. He liked their idea for a search engine, called Google, and even invested some money in the company. Yes, it turned out to be one of the most successful transactions in history. In fact, Cheriton's investment, which came to $100,000, turned into more than $1 billion.

But this was not a fluke. Cheriton also made early-stage investments in companies like VMware.

Cheriton is part of a group known as angel investors. These are generally successful people—such as executives, entrepreneurs, and even professionals like doctors and lawyers—who invest in the start-up phases of companies. No doubt the rewards can be great, but so are the risks. There are also some key regulations involved.

With the Internet, as well as changes in regulations, it is becoming easier for investors to join the angel crowd and get an opportunity to invest in pre-IPO opportunities.

Pre-IPO Funding Process

To understand how angel investing works, it is important to get a sense of the key stages of financing for a company.

The first funding is called the seed round. This often involves friends, family, and angels. The amounts can range from $10,000 to over $1 million.

The capital is to essentially test the business concept by building an initial product. There will also be some hiring of the core team.

If the product looks like it could be a winner, a company will then put together a Series A round. This will involve one or more venture capitalists (VCs) and perhaps some angels. VCs are large funds that focus on early-stage companies. In the Series A round, the total amount can be $5 million to $50 million or more.

After this, a company may have a Series B, C, and so on, depending on how the company is performing. What's more, in later rounds, a company will usually expand the investor base, such as by including hedge funds, private equity funds, and even mutual funds.

Assuming a company has the ability to be profitable and show sustained growth, it will probably then decide to go public.

Accredited Investor

Except for crowd funding deals, you must be an accredited investor to participate in pre-IPO investments. This is a classification set forth by the Securities and Exchange Commission (SEC) under Regulation D.

Why is this important? The main reason is that if a company can raise money under Regulation D there is no need to file a registration statement. As seen in Chapter 3, this can be time-consuming and expensive.

Under Regulation D, a company can have an unlimited number of accredited investors. However, there can only be up to 35 who are nonaccredited investors.

An accredited investor is presumed to be sophisticated and understand the risks of an early-stage investment. To qualify, the SEC requires the person have at least one of the following:

- Net worth—or joint net worth with a spouse—that exceeds $1 million. This excludes the value of the primary residence.
- Income exceeding $200,000 in each of the two most recent years or joint income with a spouse exceeding $300,000 for those years. There should

also be a reasonable expectation that these income levels will continue in the current year.

How to Become an Angel Investor

If you want to be an angel investor, you need to find ways to get deal flow. This means you will frequently receive e-mails or calls about companies that are seeking funding. Interestingly, a great way to get deal flow is to make a couple of initial investments. Keep in mind that the angel world is close-knit and word will spread quickly that you're someone who is willing to do deals.

But there are some more organized approaches. Here are two to consider:

1. *Angel group.* This is an organization that will cover a major city. An angel group may have 10 to 100 members or so. For the most part, every month they will meet to see pitches from companies that are seeking to raise capital. An angel group will have certain requirements, say to invest a minimum of $50,000 per year.

   An angel group has several important advantages. First, you can lower your risk since other angels will likely participate in the financing. It also means you can invest in a variety of deals.

   Next, an angel group will benefit from the members' backgrounds and experiences. This can be crucial in spotting quality investments. It can also be helpful when conducting due diligence.

2. *AngelList.com.* This is a top portal that connects angels with companies looking for capital. With it, an angel can review many investment opportunities. Keep in mind that each company will have a profile, which includes an executive summary. There may be other helpful resources, like videos. You can follow a profile—like Twitter—and contact the entrepreneur.

   AngelList.com has some of the top angel investors, such as Chris Sacca, Marc Andreessen, Dave Morin, and Fred Wilson. As a result, the site generally has many high-quality deals.

Angel Deal Structures

When investing in an angel deal, you may receive either equity or debt in the deal. Often, it does not matter which one; consider that over time, the debt will be converted into equity anyway. Besides, if a company fails to pay off the debt, the company will be wiped out. There will be little money or assets left.

But if you receive equity, it should be preferred stock. This provides more protections for the investor and voting rights.

Or, if you get debt, then it should be a convertible note. This is essentially a bridge. You are lending money to a company that will then eventually get a larger round of financing. When this happens, the convertible note will be converted into stock. And make sure this is preferred stock.

You should also get a discount on the conversion. This means you convert the stock at a lower valuation, say 30 percent of the next round. This is a way to get a benefit for taking the risks of being an angel investor.

Strategies for Angel Investing

Angel investing is not easy. Simply put, you will have little information on which to base your decision. A company will likely not have a product. And if it does, it is probably crude (it's probably just a prototype). So throw out anything you learned in business school. And get rid of your spreadsheets; they won't help.

In other words, you are taking a big leap of faith in the founders and the market opportunity. For some investors, this is invigorating. It's really fun to be part of the early stages of a company.

But for other investors, it is a nightmare. After all, the founders are likely to be in their twenties and have little or no experience creating companies.

In fact, the original idea for the venture is likely to change. This is known as a pivot. Take a look at Instagram. It was originally a mobile app for users to check into locations like bars and restaurants. But it went nowhere. The founders then changed the focus to sharing photos. It was a smart move, as the app soared in popularity and in April 2012 Facebook purchased the company for $1 billion even though it had zero revenues.

So to be a successful angel investor, you need to have a good knack for identifying standout founders. Unfortunately, there are no guidelines for this. Instead, it is about having experience with start-ups—and yes, lots of luck!

Despite all this, there are some things to help out the process.

Understanding Markets

When a sector is red-hot, there will be a surge in angel fundings. This will boost the valuations and create lots of competitors. Unfortunately, it will usually mean returns will be low for angel investments.

A better approach is to look for deals when the markets are cold, such as was the case in 2002 and 2003 and from 2008 to 2010. If you invested during these periods, you would have likely had a much higher success rate.

Advice

Get a lawyer to help with the funding documents. This can avoid many problems. Let's face it; start-ups can be messy—and founders may do things against their investors.

When retaining a lawyer, make sure he or she has experience with angel investments.

Valuation

Again, don't use any finance theory here. The valuation is the result of a negotiation between the angel and the founders. For angel rounds, the amount can range from $100,000 to $10 million or more. It depends on the team and how hot the market is. A valuation may escalate if there are already notable angels involved in the deal.

It's important to understand the jargon about valuation. There are actually two types: premoney and postmoney. The premoney valuation is the value of the company before any investment is made. The postmoney valuation, in turn, is the amount after the investment.

Example: XYZ Corp. is an early-stage company but has a strong team and the prototype definitely has promise. Based on this information, the premoney valuation is $5 million.

If the company raises $1 million, then the postmoney valuation will be $6 million. This is the premoney valuation plus the infusion of capital.

Thus, when talking to the founders, it's important to be clear on what valuation is being used. It can make a big difference!

Dilution

Unless you keep investing in the venture, your ownership position will decline over time as a percentage of the company. This is known as dilution and it is inevitable. But as long as a company keeps growing, it should not matter much.

For example, when Reid Hoffman and Mark Pincus invested in the angel round of Facebook, they had a substantial equity stake. But by the time of the IPO, it had fallen to less than 1 percent. But did it really matter? Each had a stake worth over $400 million by the time of the IPO—not bad for an investment of less than $100,000.

Market Opportunity

It is okay if a company initially targets a niche market. In fact, this can be a smart strategy. It will test the business and help to get a foothold. After all, Facebook started as a site for Harvard University students.

But the venture needs to be able to move beyond the niche. This means the market potential should be $1 billion or more.

Why? The reason is that for an angel to make money, it is necessary to exit eventually by means of either an acquisition or an IPO. Each exit method generally requires that a company has a major market potential.

Executive Summary

A business plan is not necessary. It's really overkill. But a venture should still have an executive summary, say a couple of pages. There should also be an investor presentation, which will include 10 to 20 slides, known as an investor deck. This should provide enough information to get a sense of the opportunity.

When looking at these materials, make sure they cover the following aspects of the business:

- *Target market.*
- *What makes the company's product different.* More importantly, is it enough to get the interest of customers?
- *The competition.* By the way, be wary if the founders say there is "no competition." This is almost always wrong, so making such a claim can be a big red flag.
- *Projections.* The first year usually has monthly numbers and then there are two years of annual numbers.

The revenue projections are always wrong; don't pay attention to them. But the expense items should be detailed. You want to know how the money will be spent. It will also give you an idea of when the company will need to raise extra money.

The actual costs are still likely to be more than expected. A good rule of thumb is to multiply the expected expenses by 1.5.

Go-to-Market Strategy

The market strategy is often neglected, but make sure there are reasonable strategies to spread the product and acquire customers. How much will it cost to get customers? Will there need to be distribution partnerships?

Due Diligence and the Term Sheet

Once you feel comfortable with the investment opportunity, the next step is to do due diligence. This is not usually time intensive because the company is in the early stages. But some of the important things to check are the following:

- *Documents.* Ask for all the key legal documents. These include:
  - Articles of incorporation and bylaws.
  - Board minutes.
  - Stock purchase agreements.
  - Stock option plans and agreements.
  - Employee list.
  - Employee handbook.
  - Investor list.
  - Financials, tax returns, and bank statements.
  - Any material contracts.
- *Competitive analysis.* Do your own evaluation of the target market and the competition. Can the venture truly beat out the rivals? Or will there need to be much more work?
- *Intellectual property.* It is always good that a company has some technology. It's even better if there are patents. But does the company own this intellectual property? In some cases, the founders may have created the technology while working for their former employer. In this case, the employer may own the intellectual property.
- *References.* Ask for these. But find your own. You can look at the LinkedIn profiles of the founders and call some of their contacts. This can provide invaluable information.

If the venture passes muster with the due diligence, you will then provide a term sheet (it can be one to 10 pages). This sets forth the key elements of a proposed investment. At the minimum, it will indicate the investment amount and the valuation, but there are some critical elements an investor should negotiate.

There are a variety of term sheets on the web, such as Y-Combinator. They are a good way to start.

When negotiating with the founders, you should try to get the following:

- *Liquidation preference.* A liquidation can be bankruptcy, but it usually means an IPO or acquisition. With a liquidation preference, you want to maximize your return. At a minimum, you want to get back your initial investment before the founders and employees get anything. This means you will have a 1x preference. Thus, if you invest $1 million in the venture and it eventually sells for $1 million, you will get all the proceeds.

  You may be able to negotiate a higher liquidation preference, such as 2x or 3x.

  At the same time, you could negotiate for a participation clause. With this, you can get the liquidation preference and also upside on the deal. Continuing with our example, let's say that the company sells for $2 million and your equity interest is 50 percent. You will get the $1 million from the liquidation preference and $500,000 from the participation clause.

- *Dividend.* This can range from 5 percent to 10 percent. In most cases, a company wants to keep the cash so it will accrue the dividends. Then, at the time of a liquidation, the angel investor will get all dividends in arrears before any cash goes to anyone else. This is a way to boost the return on an investment.

- *Antidilution.* This will protect your investment if there is a subsequent round of financing at a lower valuation. This is called a "down round" and can result in substantial dilution for existing investors.

  To avoid this dilution or reduce it, you can have an antidilution clause in your term sheet. The math can get complicated, but for the most part, the type of antidilution clause that is most investor friendly is the full-ratchet antidilution provision. This means the original angel investor will get the same price as the new investor.

- *Reverse vesting.* This should be mandatory. Reverse vesting means that at the time of a financing, the founders do not receive ownership of the stock. Instead, they will need to earn it over time. This is usually based on a vesting schedule in which the founder will wait one year to vest the first 25 percent of the stock, and then the vesting will be on a monthly basis for the next three years.

  Reverse vesting is extremely helpful because you do not want to fund a company and then have one of the founders leave the firm with a chunk of stock. That would be unfair not only to the investor but also to the rest of the co-founders.

- *Veto powers.* Make sure the founders do not have carte blanche with your capital. To this end, you can have veto rights on major areas like borrowing money, paying dividends, and issuing new shares.

Keep in mind that a term sheet is not an offer. Rather, it is an agreement to agree. But once there is a final term sheet document, it is rare for the angel investor or the company to back out. The next step is to put together the main documents of the funding, such as the shareholder agreements. The process can take a few weeks. But once it is done, the angel investor will wire the investment amount to the company.

Secondary Markets

More leading-edge technology companies are remaining private longer. Where a company might have taken four to five years to go public in the 1980s and 1990s, now the period of staying private is more likely to be double this.

There are many reasons for the delay. As pointed out in Chapter 2, the expenses and regulatory requirements for going public are onerous. Companies also do not want to be subject to the quarterly whims of Wall Street investors and analysts.

But staying private longer has its disadvantages. Perhaps one of the biggest is providing liquidity for employees who have stock options. Keep in mind that they typically take lower salaries to get the equity compensation. So at some point, they want to see a reward for this effort.

To provide this liquidity, a new industry has emerged over the past few years: secondary marketplaces. These are online exchanges that allow employees and existing investors to sell their shares.

All in all, the business has surged. According to research from NYPPEX, the volume doubled in 2011 to $9.3 billion.

However, the growth rate may taper off. The main reason is that shares in Facebook accounted for a large amount of the trading.

Consider that, although there are still transactions from wealthy individuals in amounts of $150,000 to $200,000, the typical investor in secondary markets is usually an institutional investor and a transaction is generally $1 million or so.

And yes, some are massive transactions. Look at Saudi Prince Alwaleed bin Talal. In 2011, he made a $300 million secondary transaction in the shares of Twitter.

For investors looking for pre-IPO opportunities, secondary markets are certainly a good alternative. But there are definitely some risks.

Let's take a look.

The Operators

The main companies in the secondary markets include:

- *SharesPost.* Founded in 2009, the company operates an online bulletin board where people can list their shares. There is no need for approval from the companies.

    SharesPost has a group of transaction specialists, experts who can help buyers and sellers with the transaction process. What's more, all research reports are free.

    The company charges a minimum fee of $5,000 for a transaction up to $100,000. After this, there is a fee that can be as much as 5 percent.

    SharesPost also has a platform for private placements. This means it will raise capital on behalf of companies by selling shares in privately held companies. The first transaction was in late 2011. The company was TrueCar, an online auto provider, and it was able to raise $20 million in a private placement.

- *SecondMarket.* The company got its start in 2004 with a focus on trading in the distressed debt market. But in 2008, a Facebook employee contacted the firm to sell some of his shares. SecondMarket was able to pull off the transaction—and realized there could be an opportunity for a great business.

    In 2011, the company completed $558 million in transactions, up 55 percent over the prior year. The most popular companies were Facebook, Twitter, Foursquare, Dropbox, and Yelp.

    SecondMarket works directly with each company. This means it has access to the audited financials, which are available from a secure website.

    For each transaction, SecondMarket charges a commission that ranges from 2 percent to 5 percent. The percentage depends on the complexity and amount of the purchase.

- *Other marketplaces.* There have been a variety of financial firms that have moved into secondary markets. They include Knight Capital Group, Liquidnet, Cantor Fitzgerald, and GFI Group.

The Process

The typical secondary transaction can take anywhere from 30 to 45 days. The main reason is the right of first refusal (see next subsection).

Of course, a transaction involves a variety of legal documents. These include:

- *Purchase agreement.* This will be sent via e-mail, and both parties can sign it online. The contract will allow for the transfer of the ownership rights to the shares involved in the transaction.
- *Escrow.* This involves a bank or other financial institution that will hold the purchase money in an account. It will not be released until the new stock certificates are sent to the buyer.

No doubt the process can get complicated and the documents can have much legal jargon. Because of this, it is important to get the help of an attorney.

The Risks

What are the downsides to purchasing shares on a secondary marketplace? Let's take a look:

- *Volatility.* It can be wrenching. A *New York Times* piece pointed out that the shares of Facebook went from a valuation of $141 billion in January 2011 to $71 billion a month later. Then a few days later, the valuation was up to $87 billion.
- *Liquidity.* Once you buy shares on the secondary market, you will be subject to the lockup period. This means it could easily take more than a year until you can sell them. That's a long time to tie up your capital.

    Consider Groupon. Six months before its IPO, the shares were valued at $20 billion. But then six months after the IPO, the valuation was $7 billion.
- *Disclosure.* Unless a company has filed an S-1 with the SEC, the buyer in a secondary market transaction is likely to have access to little if any financial information. Instead, there will only be some analyst reports, which are based on best guesses.

    The result could be overvaluations of the securities. After all, if a certain company is getting lots of media exposure, it may attract many investors. And since the trading activity is fairly light in the secondary markets, it does not take many transactions to push up the stock price.
- *Litigation.* So far, there have been few lawsuits. Then again, the trading in secondary markets has been mostly on well-known tech companies. And once they have gone public, the stock prices have done well.

    But as time goes by, it is likely that investors will look at early-stage companies. These will likely have lower valuations. Yet if they do not go public—or, even worse, they wind up going broke—there will probably be a rash of lawsuits.

- *Right of first refusal (ROFR)*. Some companies are trying to take more control of secondary stock trades. The CEO of Twitter, Dick Costolo, said the activity is a distraction.

  One way to help things is a ROFR. This is a clause in a shareholder agreement that allows the company to either buy shares at the current bid or find an alternative buyer. It is a way to keep shares in the hands of friendly investors.

  But this can be frustrating for secondary market investors. The ROFR process can take 30 to 45 days. Thus, an investor may spend lots of time—and some fees—only to have the shares sold to another buyer. In fact, this is actually fairly common.

Crowd Funding

Crowd funding is when a company uses the Internet to raise money from the public. Until 2012, this was limited because of the federal securities laws.

Before 2012, there were three main approaches to crowd funding. First, there were donation sites. With these, a company may request funds for a charity or the development of a play. For this, the users may get some credit or a T-shirt. One of the top donation sites is Kickstarter.

The next approach was a prepurchase site. With this, a company will raise money for a project, such as to develop a new shoe. Each funder will get one or more of the items produced.

Finally, a company could borrow money from a peer-to-peer lender. However, the principals need to have a strong credit rating and the amounts are also limited at $25,000.

But the JOBS Act has made a huge change in the crowd funding market. That is, companies can now issue stock to the general public without the need to file a registration statement.

There are some requirements, though. For each year, a company can raise no more than $1 million.

There are also limits for investors. They are based on income levels:

- *Less than $100,000.* An investor can invest the greater of $2,500 or 5 percent of income or net worth each year.
- *Over $100,000.* An investor can invest the greater of $10,000 or 10 percent of income or net worth each year.

A company will also need to provide some disclosures, such as an executive summary and financials. If the capital to be raised is up to $100,000, the documents must be certified by an officer of the company. Amounts between $100,000 and $500,000 will need to have the disclosures vouched for by a certified public accountant. For any amounts above this, a company will need to obtain an audit.

There are already hundreds of crowd funding sites. The number will likely continue to grow over the years.

But investors need to be wary. Early-stage deals are extremely risky. While a few will become breakout successes, many others will fail.

And even if a company turns out to be successful, it can still take five to 10 years to make any money from the investment. Generally, liquidity will come either from a sale of the company or from a public offering.

Besides, why would a company even want to use crowd funding? Could it be that it is having difficulties finding top-notch angels or venture capitalists? Interestingly, these types of investors are likely to avoid companies that take this capital. The main reason is that they do not like dealing with many retail investors.

Fraud

When it comes to pre-IPO investing, due diligence is extremely important. You will not have the many protections that a public offering provides, such as extensive filings with the SEC.

Unfortunately, early-stage ventures are highly prone to fraud. While federal authorities have tried to combat this, it is far from easy. And even if the perpetrators are caught, they are usually broke.

For example, in late 2011, the federal prosecutors and SEC brought charges against a Florida-based financial, John Mattera. The charges included counts for securities fraud, conspiracy, wire fraud, and money laundering.

He allegedly attempted to sell pre-IPO shares in companies like Facebook, Groupon, Twitter, and Zynga. But according to federal charges, he had no ownership of the shares. Yet he was able to receive $12.6 million in gains, which he used to buy fancy cars and a boat.

Here are some of the signs that a pre-IPO investment may be a fraud:

- *High-pressure tactics.* Never be rushed into an investment. An early-stage deal financing can easily take several months. There should be enough time to evaluate the investment opportunity and think about the decision.
- *Hyped language.* If a person says the deal is the next Facebook or Google, then you should walk away. A professional investor does not make these kinds of statements. If anything, they are a violation of the federal securities laws.

- *Background checks.* At the very least, do a Google search on the principals of the deals. If you find any issues, then bring them up with the company.

    It is a good idea to do a more official background search, such as on potential criminal histories. There will be a fee for this, but it will be worth it. After all, if you are prepared to invest $50,000 or more on a venture, this is good insurance.
- *Too slick.* Okay, this sounds a bit vague. But if a person is trying to show how wealthy he is—such as with fancy cars and dinners—you should be a bit wary.
- *Promises.* If a person says that it is guaranteed that the deal will increase 10 times over or will be bought by Google or Apple, then pass on it. These claims are illegal.
- *Cold calling.* If you get a call from a broker who claims that he or she has an allocation of shares in a hot company, then hang up. If it's a hot deal, there would be no need for cold calling; instead, the broker would allocate the shares to top investors.

Finally, even if the deal is not a fraud, the risks of pre-IPO investing are extremely high. It's perhaps one of the riskiest asset classes. Because of this, you should not put too much of your portfolio in these types of investments—say no more than 10 percent.

It's true that there are some angels who invest in hundreds of start-ups (it's called the "spray-and-pray" approach). Yet consider that those who are successful at it—like SV Angel's Ron Conway—have a long history of angel investing. Plus, they also have high net worths and can afford to take the risks.

Conclusion

If you want to invest in pre-IPO companies—whether as an angel or through the secondary markets or crowd funding—keep in mind that the risks are substantial. There is a good chance you will not see any return for five to 10 years. True, the returns can be substantial; you possibly could make millions. But then again, many pre-IPO businesses fail. In other words, it is crucial not to put too much of your net worth in these types of investments.

CHAPTER 23

The 100x IPO

It's the ultimate dream for an initial public offering (IPO) investor—that is, getting a deal that returns 100 times the original investment. So if you invested $10,000, you will have made a cool $1 million.

Of course, this is pretty rare. But if you do get such an IPO, it can certainly be a life changer. In fact, the world's top investors often owe much of their standout returns to a few great trades.

A 100x IPO also does not happen overnight. In general, it takes at least a decade. And it could easily take more than 20 years, as seen with Walmart and Apple.

Here's a look at some of the notable 100x IPOs (assuming you bought $10,000 in shares on the first day of trading):

Amazon.com	$1.3 million
Dell	$1.5 million
Apple	$1.7 million
Microsoft	$3.5 million
Walmart	$10.3 million

So how can you spot a 100x IPO? There are no hard-and-fast rules. Perhaps luck is the deciding factor.

But there are some things to look for. To this end, let's take a look at the case of Amazon.com.

The Amazon.com IPO

On May 15, 1997, Amazon.com went public, with the stock increasing 30 percent on its first day of trading. The company raised roughly $54 million.

At the time, there was much controversy. Here's a look:

- *Competition.* At the time of the IPO, there were several online bookstores, such as Book Stacks Unlimited and CUC International. Barnes & Noble and Borders were also planning on launching their own websites. There was even the possibility that larger tech players, like Microsoft and America Online (AOL), would enter the market.

  Such concerns are common for new businesses. How can they really compete against larger operators?

  Yet when there are new technologies or trends, it is actually the new players that are the winners. They have the advantage of being quicker and can also try new businesses models. Existing companies have a much harder time disrupting their current revenue and profit streams.

- *Losses.* Investors do not like to see losses, but they are common in the early stages of a breakout company. After all, if a company wants to dominate an industry, it will need to invest heavily in building infrastructure. But it can be scary. Here's what the Amazon.com S-1 said:

  > Accordingly, the Company intends to invest heavily in marketing and promotion, site development and technology and operating infrastructure development. The Company also intends to offer attractive pricing programs, which will reduce its gross margins. Because the Company has relatively low product gross margins, achieving profitability given planned investment levels depends upon the Company's ability to generate and sustain substantially increased revenue levels. As a result, the Company believes that it will incur substantial operating losses for the foreseeable future, and that the rate at which such losses will be incurred will increase significantly from current levels.

  It was a risky strategy. But it was necessary for Amazon.com to become the dominant player in e-commerce.

Why Amazon.com?

Keep in mind that all breakout companies have been controversial. There were many doubters. If anything, controversy is necessary. It's a sign that the company is truly attempting something that is unique.

So for investors, it means that you need to filter out the noise, especially from the media. Again, focus on the S-1 and look for some of the following factors.

Revenue Growth

Revenue growth needs to be extremely strong. And the growth should have started early in the company's history. It's a sign that it is truly tapping into a megatrend.

This was evident with the growth ramp at Amazon.com:

Q1 1996	Q2 1996	Q3 1996	Q4 1996	Q1 1997
$875,000	$3,200,000	$4,200,000	$8,500,000	$16,000,000

During this time period, the quarterly sales growth rate was a stunning 100 percent and average daily visits went from 2,200 to 80,000. Repeat customers accounted for more than 40 percent of orders.

Fad or Real Business?

This is a tough question. As seen in Chapter 21, some businesses are really just fads and will quickly fizzle out.

The same could have been said about e-commerce. But Amazon.com's S-1 pointed out some compelling reasons why it was a real opportunity. That is, Amazon.com would offer the following key benefits to consumers:

• Wide selection of products.
• Ability to shop 24/7.
• Easy to search for books.
• No need to drive to a store.
• Lower prices.

Visionary CEO/Founder

This is incredibly important. Companies like Dell, Microsoft, and Facebook would not have been great companies without Michael Dell, Bill Gates, and Mark Zuckerberg. The creative abilities of one person can move mountains.

A biography will give little sense of this. Take a look at the founder of Amazon.com, Jeff Bezos. Before founding the company in July 1994, he had worked in the financial services industry. He also had gotten a BS in electrical engineering and computer science from Princeton University.

But as you read through the S-1, you can sense Jeff's vision and creativity. He set forth a great plan for being the world leader in e-commerce.

Land and Expand

A breakout company will often initially focus on a niche. By doing this, the company will learn about the market dynamics and the essential drivers for growth. Then the company can build on this and expand the market potential.

This was the case with Amazon.com. By starting with books, Amazon .com was able to build a strong business and get lots of initial traction. It could better compete against traditional bookstores because of the following:

- *Lower cost.* A traditional bookstore is capital intensive. It involves costs for real estate and inventory purchases. Amazon.com, in contrast, would have the advantage of leveraging centralized distribution centers. This made it possible to offer much lower prices.
- *Customer data.* While a traditional bookstore may have a loyalty program, it is limited. But a website can track the clicks of all its users. Are there some books that are getting searched more? In fact, Amazon.com would recommend books based on user behavior, such as prior purchases, which helped to increase purchases.
- *Ideal product.* Books are easy to sell online. They are essentially commodities and do not need customers to try things on.

Amazon.com was also smart to invest in a department that created engaging content to help sell the books.

Oh, and the typical book buyer was also likely to be on the Internet.

Innovation

Innovation is absolutely critical. And from the start, Amazon.com had a focus on innovation. True, it had some flubs, but this is the nature of experimentation.

By the time of its IPO, Amazon.com had already created the Associates Program, which allowed third parties to sell books from their sites. It turned out to be a big moneymaker—and helped to boost the brand.

Of course, Amazon.com would eventually move on to many other markets. In some cases, these markets were probably not even anticipated by the Jeff Bezos. Did he really think Amazon.com would have the Kindle?

Brand

To dominate a category, a company needs a tremendous brand. It becomes something that builds trust and repeat purchases.

To this end, Amazon.com had already become a leading brand on the Internet. But it realized it needed to continue to invest in its brand. As a result, the company would spend aggressively on marketing.

Conclusion

Again, it's not a good bet that you'll get a 100x IPO. But hey, you may get one that is 10x or 20x. And such returns can make a huge impact on your portfolio. As seen in this book, it is something that does happen in the IPO market.

Conclusion

Initial public offerings (IPOs) are investments that truly get the blood pulsing. They are almost always exciting and risky. As with most things that have the potential for a very high upside, uncertainty is an inextricable variable in the overall investment equation. As discussed previously, the words *hype* and *IPO* are often used in the same sentence. It is not uncommon to see an IPO soar 20 percent or more on the first day and then, in some cases, sink back to its beginnings in a matter of days or weeks.

If I could point to two factors that will make the biggest difference to an IPO investor, I would name patience as the most important trait, and research as the single most vital task for successful investing.

Patience, although a virtue, is more a practical matter when investing in IPOs. The first day of an offering is not always the best time to buy shares of an IPO, because the excitement of the offering can lead to wild price volatility. And even if you get the opportunity to buy an IPO at the offering price, there is no guarantee that the stock price will rise. Look at the case of Facebook. Even though it was a widely anticipated deal, it ended up flat on its first day. Then on the second day of trading, the stock plunged 11 percent. It was a shock to many investors across the world.

If you're looking for a long-term investment, it's possible to spare yourself from the initial roller-coaster ride by simply waiting a month or so for the price to settle down. Keep in mind that you could have waited a year before buying stock of companies like Walmart, Starbucks, Amazon.com, and Microsoft. And yes, you would have still made a fortune if you held on to the shares for the long haul.

However, before you seriously consider buying any IPO, you need to do the research. Much of this book explains the research process, but it's important enough to reemphasize. The best source of information on any IPO is its prospectus (it's also a good idea to check out the road show at RetailRoadshow, www.retailroadshow.com). As discussed in Chapter 5 in detail, the prospectus is chock-full of useful information. Here is a recap of the main points to concentrate on:

- *Underwriters.* Make sure the underwriters are top players in the industry, like Goldman Sachs, Morgan Stanley, JPMorgan, and so on. If the underwriters are small, then it's probably best to stay away from the deal. A good company should have no trouble attracting top-notch backers.
- *Business model.* Has the company been profitable or close to making money? If not, be careful. Some of history's best IPOs, such as Microsoft and Oracle, have had a history of profits.

  At the same time, look for factors for why the business will withstand competition. Is there an extensive infrastructure, like Amazon.com has? Does the company have an embedded product that is required for millions of businesses, such as Microsoft has?
- *Venture capital.* According to academic studies, venture capital (VC) backing can be very important for the success of an IPO. A VC firm not only provides the needed capital to the company but also brings alliances and helps to create the strategic vision. Also, if you find that top-name VC firms have invested heavily in the company, you can be confident that they've done extensive research and are satisfied with the company's chances for success.
- *Exchange.* Focus on IPOs from a national exchange, whether the New York Stock Exchange or the NASDAQ. Smaller exchanges are often the sources of companies that have unproven business models. In some cases, they may even attract frauds.
- *Use of proceeds.* What does the company plan to do with the money raised from the IPO? If it is using more than 50 percent of the cash to pay off debt, it will not have as much capital to expand its operations. Also, be careful if a majority of the cash goes to pay off insiders. It may be that they are bailing out of the company.
- *Management.* You want a CEO who has lots of credibility in the industry. Such a person will be critical for keeping up the growth and dealing with the inevitable problems. You also want a management team that has public company backgrounds, especially the chief financial officer and the chief operating officer.
- *Market potential.* Look for companies that have a product line that addresses a large opportunity. At a minimum, the target market should be at least $1 billion. If not, it will be difficult for the company to sustain its growth.
- *Industry.* Research the industry as much as possible. Do you know the main drivers? The technology threats?

- *Financial analysis.* In Chapters 6, 7, and 8, we took a deep dive into understanding financial statements. While financial analysis helps spot breakout companies, it is also helpful in avoiding money losers. Some of the red flags with financials include:
  - Sales growing much faster than profits, say by 25 percent or more.
  - An unexpected drop in free cash flows.
  - Aggressive acquisitions.
  - Operating cash flows consistently below net income, say by more than half.
  - Inventory growing more than sales, perhaps by more than 20 percent.
- *Auditor.* Pay attention to this firm's report. If you see that the auditor has given the company a going-concern determination, the company may wind up in bankruptcy.
- *Timing.* There are several things to keep in mind with an IPO's timing. First, there is the expiration of the quiet period 40 days after the IPO. After this, the underwriter's analysts can post research reports, which are often bullish. As a result, many investors will buy shares a week ahead of this date so as to get a quick gain.

  Next, there is the expiration of the lockup period six months after an IPO. Insiders are then allowed to start selling their shares, which can put pressure on the stock price. Often, this can be a good time to buy into an IPO.
- *Capital-intensive companies.* These may have lots of promise, such as to create a huge infrastructure, but the risks are extremely high. As seen with companies like Global Crossing and Clearwire, there is usually a need to raise more and more capital, which puts pressure on the stock price.
- *Customer concentration.* If a customer accounts for more than 20 percent of the overall revenues, it is probably a good idea to stay away. Even if the customer stays, that customer will likely still be able to get better terms when the contract is renewed.

Investing in IPOs is a relatively new opportunity for individual investors. With time and practice, the analysis and research required will become easier and feel more familiar. Start slowly, and focus on the companies you know the most about. Do the work before you invest; I assure you it will be worth your effort.

Appendix A: The Underwriting Process

As you invest in the initial public offering (IPO) market, you will see three types of underwriters:

1. *Majors.* These firms have global reach. They can easily do several billion-dollar deals in a month. They have thousands of brokers spread across the world. For the most part, you will not get a flaky IPO from a major. Examples of majors include Goldman Sachs, Bank of America Merrill Lynch, Morgan Stanley, JPMorgan, and Credit Suisse.
2. *Midsize.* These firms specialize in a certain industry or region. They have several hundred brokers. It is possible to find some very good prospects with midsize firms because they often have special knowledge about a local firm. Some examples include Jefferies, Raymond James, and Stifel Nicolaus.
3. *Small.* Be wary of the very small, unknown firms. An IPO requires numerous resources for which small firms tend to be inadequately equipped. Unfortunately, the deals often do not get much traction and can result in big losses for investors.

Underwriting Options

There are two main types of underwritings: firm commitment and best efforts.

Firm Commitment

This is when the lead underwriters essentially guarantee funding with an IPO. However, the guarantee is usually not in effect until one or two days before the IPO.

To understand how a firm-commitment IPO works, let's take a look at an example. In April 2012, Tilly's went public. The company is a fast-growing specialty retailer of West Coast–inspired apparel, footwear, and accessories.

It priced its IPO at $15.50, which raised about $124 million. But there was an underwriting discount of $1.085 or $8,680,000. This amount went to the underwriters.

A firm-commitment offering will also usually have an overallotment option (also called a green shoe). This means that if there is tremendous demand for the IPO, the underwriter can issue additional shares—say, 10 to 15 percent of the total stock issued. In the case of Tilly's, the lead underwriters had an overallotment of 1.2 million shares.

In some cases, an underwriter may get warrants, although this is usually for small deals (say $25 million or lower). This is really a form of compensation for services. A warrant is the right to buy stock at a certain price—which is usually at a premium to the offering price, such as 20 percent—for a specific period of time (one to five years). The warrants may account for 10 percent of the offering. For example, if the IPO has an offering price of $10 per share with a 20 percent premium, the underwriter may get warrants to buy one million shares at $12 each.

A firm-commitment offering is risky for the underwriter. If it has problems selling the issue, the firm will be left holding large amounts of stock that no one wants.

Best Efforts

As the name implies, best efforts means the underwriter will try to sell the offering, but there is no guarantee.

You will see best-efforts offerings for very small companies that have difficulty raising money. Be very careful if you are considering a best-efforts offering. After all, it should be troubling if an underwriter does not have enough faith in a company to do a firm-commitment offering. Actually, the majors and midsize firms do not engage in such best-efforts offerings. Only the small firms do.

Self-Underwritten Offerings

A company may decide to forgo the services of an underwriter. This has been happening with greater regularity because of the growth of the Internet, which makes it easier for companies to pull off an offering.

Unfortunately, there have been very few successful self-underwritten offerings. As the old saying goes: "Stock is sold, not bought." It takes a lot of effort to get an investor to buy stock in a company. So the distribution channels of an underwriter can be extremely valuable, despite the fact that the firm will garner large amounts of fees.

Appendix B: Analyzing the Financial Statement Items

The financials can be overwhelming for investors. But by using ratio analysis, it is possible to make better sense of things. Here's a look.

Liquidity Ratios

Liquidity ratios show the ability of a company to pay its debts. The most common liquidity ratio is the current ratio, which is calculated as follows:

$$\text{Current ratio} = \text{Current assets}/\text{Current liabilities}$$

As a general rule, you want a company that has a current ratio of 2:1 or higher. There may be exceptions, which makes it important to look at the current ratios of other companies in the industry.

The next liquidity ratio is the quick ratio or acid-test ratio. This uses essentially the same formula as the current ratio, except that inventories and prepaid expenses are excluded from the math. The reason for deleting them is that these types of assets are often difficult to convert into cash.

The target number for the acid-test ratio is 1:1.

Activity Ratios

Activity ratios indicate the efficiency of a company to convert current assets into cash. There are three types of activity ratios:

1. *Inventory turnover ratio.* This ratio shows the relationship between the amount of goods sold and the inventory. This ratio is very industry specific. For the

most part, a very high inventory turnover ratio may mean that the company does not have enough products in stock. In contrast, a very low ratio might mean that the company is not selling its products. In general, the higher the ratio, the better, since a company is getting cash more quickly.

The ratio is calculated as follows:

Inventory turnover ratio = Cost of goods sold/Average inventory

To compute the average inventory, make the following calculation:

Average inventory = (Beginning-of-period inventory
+ End-of-period inventory)/2

2. *Accounts receivable ratio.* This indicates how fast a company is collecting payments from customers who are making purchases on credit. The calculation is as follows:

Accounts receivable ratio = Net sales/Average net accounts receivable

Strictly speaking, you should use net credit sales for the numerator. But most financial statements do not provide that number, so instead you must use net sales.

As for the average net accounts receivable, this is calculated as follows:

Average net accounts receivable = (Beginning balance of
accounts receivable
+ Ending balance)/2

The accounts receivable ratio shows how many times the accounts receivable have been turned into cash in one year. As a rule, the higher the ratio, the better, since a company gets cash more quickly.

3. *Days' sales ratio.* This shows how efficient a company is with its receivables. The calculation is:

Days' sales ratio = Ending accounts receivable/Average daily sales

To calculate average daily sales, divide net sales by 365.

Profitability Ratios

As the name implies, profitability ratios analyze the profits of a company. The two main ratios are:

1. *Return on assets.* This shows the operating efficiency of a company—that is, how well the company uses its total assets. The ratio is calculated as follows:

$$\text{Return on assets} = \text{Income before interest, taxes, and}$$
$$\text{other income/Average total assets}$$

2. *Return on equity.* This is a big factor for any investor. You want to make sure that management is getting the best returns possible from the equity invested in the company. The return on equity is calculated as follows:

$$\text{Return on equity} = \text{Net income/Average common stockholders' equity}$$

Average common stockholders' equity is calculated as follows:

$$\text{Average common stockholders' equity} = (\text{Beginning common equity} + \text{Ending balance})/2$$

Price-Earnings Ratio

The price-earnings (P/E) ratio is computed by taking the current price of the stock and dividing it by the earnings per share (EPS). For example, if XYZ is selling for $30 per share and has $1 of earnings per share, it will have a P/E ratio of 30 ($30 per share divided by $1 EPS). This is a technique commonly used by Wall Street analysts to measure relative valuations of companies. For example, suppose other companies in XYZ's industry have, on average, P/Es of 40. Thus, XYZ is selling at a discount of 20 percent to the industry average P/E. This may mean the company is undervalued.

However, in many cases, IPOs do not have any earnings (these will come several years later), so doing P/E ratios does not make sense.

Perhaps a better way to value the company is by the price-to-sales (P/S) ratio. Let's say XYZ, with 1 million shares outstanding, has sales of $10 million and a market capitalization of $30 million. Market capitalization is derived by multiplying the current stock price by the number of shares outstanding ($30 × 1 million shares outstanding). To get the price-to-sales ratio, we divide the market capitalization by the annual sales. In this case, the price-to-sales ratio is 3:1 ($30 million market capitalization divided by $10 million in sales). This means the company stock is selling at three times sales. Compare this to other companies in the industry to see whether XYZ is undervalued, overvalued, or fairly valued.

Debt Ratio

In itself, debt is not bad. In fact, if a company has low amounts of debt, this may indicate that the company is too conservative. Then again, high levels of debt can be very dangerous, especially if the company hits hard times and is unable to pay the interest and principal payments. The result can be bankruptcy.

The most common indicator of debt levels is the debt-to-equity ratio. It is calculated as follows:

Debt-to-equity ratio = Total long-term liabilities / Total stockholders' equity

Glossary

absorbed The condition of an initial public offering (IPO) that has been sold out.

accounts payable The money a company owes to its creditors, such as for raw materials, inventory, equipment, services, and taxes.

accounts receivable Money owed to a company by customers. If accounts receivable are increasing much more than sales, the company may be having problems collecting payments.

accredited investor A person who has a net worth of at least $1 million or has an annual income of $200,000 per year ($300,000 for married couples). These guidelines are set by federal regulations. It is typically accredited investors who put money into companies that have yet to go public. Because of the high income requirements, many individual investors do not participate in pre-IPO investments.

aftermarket performance An indication of how well a stock has performed after it has gone public. The gain or loss is measured against the offering price.

all or none A condition providing that if a minimum amount of capital is not raised, an underwriter can cancel the offering. This is usually the case with best-efforts offerings, not firm-commitment offerings.

allotment The amount of IPO stock allocated to each underwriter.

American depositary receipt (ADR) A foreign company traded on a U.S. stock exchange. In most cases, ADRs are major companies.

analyst A person who researches companies in a certain industry. Analysts work for brokerages, banks, underwriters, or other financial institutions. Because typical IPOs are small, usually only a few analysts cover an IPO company.

angel investor A person who invests in early-stage companies. In many cases, an angel investor is wealthy and has an entrepreneurial background.

arbitration A process in which two opposing sides resolve a dispute instead of going to court. Most brokerage accounts require arbitration when a customer takes action regarding possible fraud or misrepresentation about an investment.

auditor A firm that vouches for a company's financial statement.

bake off When underwriters pitch their services to a company to handle its IPO. In hot deals, the competition can be intense, as seen with IPOs for companies like Facebook.

balance sheet A list of assets, liabilities, and equity of a company at a certain point in time. The balance sheet is included in a company's prospectus and is a valuable tool for analysis.

bedbug letter A notification sent by the Securities and Exchange Commission (SEC) to a company to withdraw its IPO offering because the registration statement is not in accordance with the securities laws.

best-efforts offering An agreement stating that an underwriter will use its best efforts to sell shares of a company to the public. There is no guarantee of a minimum amount of capital for the issuer. Small companies normally use best-efforts underwriters.

blank-check offering An IPO that has yet to indicate the type of business it will enter. This kind of IPO is extremely risky.

block A large amount of stock—10,000 shares or more. Institutions purchase IPOs in blocks.

blue-sky laws State regulations for IPOs.

board of directors A group of about five to 10 members who make key decisions for a company, such as on major investments, acquisitions, and the hiring of the CEO.

bond A debt of a corporation. It is sold in a public offering but usually to institutional investors. A bond will have an annual interest rate and will mature after a period of time, say 10 or 20 years.

book Information maintained by an underwriter to track all buy and sell orders for a public offering.

bought deal *See* Firm-commitment offering.

bridge financing A loan to a company in anticipation of an IPO. Part of the proceeds of the IPO will then be used to pay off the bridge loan. This is a relatively common practice.

broken IPO An IPO whose share price falls below the offering price.

buy-in When a brokerage will require a short seller to cover a position.

calendar *See* Pipeline.

call option A contract that gives an investor the right to buy 100 shares at a fixed price for a period of time, usually three months. The investor makes money when the stock price increases.

capitalization The amount of equity and debt a company has.

cash flow statement A document that shows the net increase or decrease in the company's cash. It has three segments: operations, investing, and financing. This is also known as the statement of cash flows.

certification A part of the Sarbanes-Oxley law that requires the CEO and CFO to sign the company's financials.

cheap stock Common stock issued to certain people—usually executives and other employees—at prices much lower than what the public will pay.

clearing price The price at which the demand for and supply of shares is equalized. A new form of IPO distribution, called OpenIPO, uses an auction system that allows for IPOs to be distributed at the clearing price.

collar The lowest price acceptable to an issuer of an IPO.

comfort letter A letter from an independent auditor stating that the disclosures in the registration statement are correct.

commissions The biggest expense for an IPO. The commissions are what the underwriters and stockbrokers make from the IPO.

common stock The most basic form of ownership in a company. Each share will usually have one vote.

completion The completion of all IPO trades, which takes about five days from the start of trading. Before completion, an IPO can be canceled and the money returned to investors.

confirmation Correspondence sent to a client that gives details about a trade, such as the quantity, name of the security, price, and commission.

cooling-off period The period of time between the filing of a preliminary prospectus with the Securities and Exchange Commission and the offering of stock to the public.

cost of goods sold The expenses that are directly related to the creation of a company's sales.

covering a short Closing out a short sale transaction, which involves buying back the stock.

crowd funding A procedure that allows small companies to sell stock through a website. This was made legal under the JOBS Act.

current assets Corporate assets such as cash, government bonds, accounts receivable, and inventory that can be converted into cash in a year or less. Thus, current assets are an indicator of the liquidity of a company. After an IPO, a company will usually have a high amount of current assets because of the large infusion of cash from the offering.

current liabilities Corporate liabilities that come due within a year or less, such as accounts payable, wages, taxes owed, or interest payments.

current ratio A company's current assets divided by its current liabilities. As a general rule, a current ratio of 2:1 shows that a company can meet its debts.

daily active users (DAUs) The number of users who return to a website on a daily basis. It's a key metric of success.

date of issue The date on which an IPO begins trading on the open market.

deal flow The number of potential transactions an investor sees.

depreciation The loss in value of assets from wear and tear and obsolescence. Depreciation is a key part of accounting and must be disclosed in financial statements.

dilution Dilution is the difference between what existing shareholders (founders) and new shareholders (investors) will pay for shares. The existing shareholders usually pay a much lower price for the stock than IPO investors do.

direct public offering (DPO) Selling stock directly to the public without using an underwriter, a frequent practice of small companies that have difficulty raising capital. The success rate of DPOs has not been good, although the Internet might change that situation. A major problem with DPOs is lack of liquidity (that is, difficulty selling shares at a good price).

discount broker A brokerage firm that charges investors low commission rates. However, a discount broker will typically not provide any investment advice. Recently, discount brokers have been offering their clients the opportunity to invest in IPOs.

discretionary account The right of a broker to make transactions in a client account without authorization. This requires a signed power of attorney.

dividend A cash payment paid to shareholders, usually on a quarterly basis. However, since IPOs are usually small, dividends may not accrue for many years.

dual-share structure Types of stock, such as Class A and Class B. Class A shares usually have no voting rights and are issued to the public. The Class B shares may have 10 to 20 votes per share and are held by the founders to maintain control over the key decisions of a company.

due diligence An investigation of an issuer by the underwriter to determine the value of the company.

earnings before interest, taxes, depreciation, and amortization (EBITDA) A figure that gives a rough estimate of a company's cash flow.

earnings per share (EPS) The earnings of a company divided by the number of shares outstanding. This is a critical number that analysts will cover and base their research on.

eating stock An underwriter buying IPO stock for its own account because there is not enough demand in the open market. This is a very bad sign for an IPO.

EDGAR A comprehensive collection of the SEC filings from public companies. There are also prospectuses on EDGAR. You can access the site (www.sec.gov) for free. This is an extremely valuable tool for IPO analysis.

effective date The date on which the Securities and Exchange Commission allows a company to issue its shares to the public.

8-K A financial disclosure for public companies. It covers things like acquisitions or the departure of an auditor.

elephant A large institutional investor.

exchange-traded fund (ETF) A pool of money that tracks an index, such as the S&P 500. These are traded on the New York Stock Exchange or NASDAQ.

financial printer A specialized printing company that knows how to meet the rigorous federal requirements for printing disclosure documents for public offerings.

financial statements The balance sheet, income statement, and statement of cash flows for a company, all of which are disclosed in the prospectus.

firm-commitment offering An offering in which an underwriter writes a check to the issuer for a specified number of shares. The underwriter expects to sell these shares to the public at a higher price, thus generating a profit.

flipping Investors taking a quick profit when an IPO's value increases at the start of trading. Underwriters do not like flipping, since it places heavy selling pressure on the stock price.

float The number of shares the general public owns. Float does not include the stock the insiders own.

flotation cost The cost of issuing new stock to the public.

footnotes Details at the bottom of financial statements to indicate the risks or accounting policies.

full-service broker The traditional stockbroker, who provides financial advice but charges much higher fees than discount brokers. In most cases, it is full-service brokers who sell IPOs, although that situation is changing.

fully distributed An IPO that was fully sold to the public.

generally accepted accounting principles (GAAP) A large set of methods and requirements for companies to follow when putting together their financial statements. A company is required to use GAAP when going public.

going concern Before a company goes public, an auditor investigates the company's financial data. If the auditor has substantial doubts about a company's ability to continue operating, it will indicate this in the company's prospectus by using the phrase *going concern*, which should be a red flag for investors.

going public *See* Initial public offering (IPO).

goodwill An intangible asset. It is accounted on a company's balance sheet when there is an acquisition.

green-shoe option An agreement allowing an underwriter to increase the number of shares issued in an IPO. The typical amount is 15 percent of the amount of the issue. A green-shoe option is usually included when an IPO generates high demand. It is also known as an overallotment option.

group sales Block sales to institutional investors.

guidance A company's forecast for revenues and earnings. It will usually be for the next quarter and the full year.

hedge fund A pool of money that is mostly for wealthy investors or institutions. A hedge fund will often look at sophisticated strategies or may also invest in IPOs.

hot issue An IPO that trades at a substantial premium on the offering.

house of issue *See* Lead underwriter.

income statement A document showing a company's revenues and expenses. An income statement shows profits or losses and is a required disclosure in a company's prospectus.

indication of interest (IOI) A statement from an investor indicating how many shares of an offering he or she will buy. An underwriter collects the IOIs and determines the demand for the offering in order to set an appropriate price and number of shares to be issued.

initial public offering (IPO) A company selling stock to the public for the first time. Money from the offering can either go into the company or pay off existing shareholders—or a combination of the two.

insider A person who is an officer, a director, or an owner of 10 percent or more of a company. In terms of an IPO, there are a variety of restrictions on how much stock an insider can sell.

insider information When someone has material information about a company that has not yet been disclosed to the public. It is illegal to trade on this.

institutional investor A firm that trades substantial amounts of stock and other investments. Institutions include mutual funds, pensions, banks, and insurance companies.

in-the-money When the stock price is above the strike price for a call option or below the strike price for a put option.

inventory Raw materials, work in progress, and finished products that a company has not yet sold.

investment banker *See* Underwriter.

issue The stock sold by a company in an IPO.

issuer The company that is doing an IPO.

JOBS Act Passed in 2012, this legislation has made it much easier for smaller companies to go public because of the relaxing of key provisions of the Sarbanes-Oxley (SOX) Act. The Jumpstart Our Business Startups (JOBS) Act also allowed for crowd funding, which makes it possible for small companies to issue stock from a website.

lead underwriter An investment bank, such as Goldman Sachs or Morgan Stanley, that determines the price of an IPO and how many shares should be allocated to members of the underwriting syndicate. It is also known as a lead manager.

letter of intent An agreement between the underwriter and the company doing an IPO. It will set forth the responsibilities as well as the compensation amounts.

liquidity The ability to turn an asset (such as a stock) into cash quickly without suffering any loss of real value. For small IPOs, there may not be much liquidity.

load The commission on a mutual fund.

lockup period The 180 days after a company goes public during which officers and insiders are restricted from selling stock.

Management's Discussion and Analysis (MD&A) A section in a company's S-1 in which you'll find the core information about the business as well as the main drivers and recent challenges.

managing underwriter *See* Lead underwriter.

margin A metric that shows the percentage of a company's profit in terms of the overall sales. It provides investors with a sense of the value of a company.

margin account A brokerage account that allows an investor to borrow against his or her assets. A margin account is also required for short selling.

market makers Professionals who buy and sell stock for their own accounts and make profits on the difference between their purchase price and the selling price (called the markup). Strong market makers are crucial for an IPO. After the IPO, the market makers provide liquidity for investors to buy and sell the issue.

master limited partnership (MLP) A corporate structure for the energy business, usually pipelines. There are key tax advantages for this approach. MLPs also generally pay high dividends.

mutual fund A pool of capital with which money managers invest in stocks and bonds. Investors can purchase shares in the mutual fund. The biggest buyers of IPOs are mutual funds.

NASDAQ (National Association of Securities Dealers Automated Quotation System) A stock exchange that does not have a physical trading floor. Rather, the NASDAQ trading system is a huge network of phones and computers. Many of the companies that go public will be listed on the NASDAQ exchange. It is also called the National Market System.

net asset value The total value of a mutual fund's assets minus the liabilities and expenses. It is published at the end of trading each day.

net income The difference between a company's revenues and its expenses. If there is a gain, the company has a net profit; if there is a loss, the company has a net loss.

network effect A concept that shows the power of certain technologies. For example, one telephone by itself has zero value, but when a second one is added, there is value. If a third telephone is added, a network is created, and value increases even more. In other words, the more participants in the network, the more valuable the technology. This has happened with a variety of Internet technologies, including free e-mail.

new issue *See* Initial public offering (IPO).

offering *See* Initial public offering (IPO).

offering circular *See* Prospectus.

offering date The date of the IPO.

offering price The price that the lead underwriter determines for an IPO. This is the price that the original investors get (usually, it is high net worth individuals and institutions who can buy at the offering price).

opening price The price at which an IPO starts trading on the open market. In many cases, the price will be at a premium to the offering price. This is also known as the first-trade price.

organizational meeting After an underwriter is hired, it will have a meeting with the company to put together the timetable and strategy for the public offering.

out-of-the-money When the stock price is below the strike price for a call option or above the strike price for a put option.

oversubscribed When an IPO has more buyers than there are shares. Most offerings will have a green-shoe option, which allows the underwriter to increase the number of shares of the offering if it is oversubscribed. An oversubscribed offering is a good sign and typically means the IPO will trade at a premium on the opening.

penalty bid A fee charged by an underwriter if investors flip an issue. That is, a penalty bid is meant to curtail flipping, a practice that can put pressure on the stock price.

Pink Sheets Companies too small to be listed on NASDAQ. The National Quotation Bureau publishes the stock quotes of Pink Sheets. The Pink Sheets market tends to be very illiquid.

pipeline Companies that have filed to do IPOs but have yet to trade. This is also known as the calendar.

preferred stock Equity in a company whose owners get dividends before common stockholders, as well as preferences in the event of liquidation because of bankruptcy. An IPO is usually in the form of common stock, not preferred stock. Rather, preferred stock is normally issued to venture capitalists before a stock is offered to the public.

preliminary prospectus *See* Red herring.

premium The difference between the offering price and opening price of an IPO. It is also known as the pop.

price-to-earnings (P/E) ratio A company's stock price divided by the earnings per share (EPS). It is a way to get a sense of the overall valuation of a company.

private placement The sale of stock or debt to raise money for a company. However, the securities are sold not to the public but instead to high-net-worth investors and institutions.

pro forma earnings An earnings measure that is created by a company and is not based on generally accepted accounting principles (GAAP).

prospectus A document filed with the Securities and Exchange Commission for a company that wants to do an IPO. The prospectus is for investors and discloses all material information, such as risk factors, financial data, management, use of proceeds, and strategies.

public offering *See* Initial public offering (IPO).

public offering price *See* Offering price.

put option A contract that allows an investor to sell 100 shares of a stock at a fixed price for a period of time, which is usually three months. The value of a put option rises when the stock falls in value.

qualified purchaser An individual who has a net worth of at least $5 million or who is responsible for net investments of at least $25 million. Qualified-purchaser status is required for certain types of private investments, such as those offered by the online financial firm WR Hambrecht + Co.

quiet period The period after a company files its S-1 registration statement during which management is not allowed to make any statements that are not included in the prospectus. The purpose of the quiet period is to prevent the hyping of the IPO. The quiet period lasts until 40 days after the stock starts trading.

real estate investment trust (REIT) A company that invests in real estate properties. If the REIT meets certain federal requirements, it can take advantage of a variety of tax exclusions.

red herring A document filed with the Securities and Exchange Commission before the completed prospectus is filed. It's called a red herring because the front page is in red ink and indicates that certain information (such as the number of shares to be issued and the price) is subject to change. It is also known as the preliminary prospectus.

registration right This gives an investor the ability to compel a company to file to go public.

registration statement A document consisting of the prospectus (which is available to the public) and a statement of additional information (which is only for the Securities and Exchange Commission) that is filed with the SEC.

Regulation A offering A stock offering for a small company. The maximum amount that can be raised is $5 million. Some companies use the Internet to do Regulation A offerings, but the success rate of these has been low.

Regulation D offering A filing that outlines details of a private placement. This is a small offering—usually no more than $5 million—for accredited investors, who have high incomes and net worths. With Regulation D offerings, a company does not have to file disclosures with the Securities and Exchange Commission.

related-party transaction When a board member or executive has a conflict of interest with the company.

restatement When a company must adjust its financial disclosures. Wall Street usually gets worried when this happens.

restricted stock Stock granted to executives, employees, and private investors of the company before the company goes public. This stock is not registered with the SEC and must comply with a variety of regulations. Typically, this stock cannot be sold until two years after it was granted.

retained earnings The total amount of earnings since the start of a company.

revenue recognition This involves generally accepted accounting principles (GAAP) to see when a company can include revenues in its financial statements.

risk factors A list of potential problems for a company. They are disclosed in the S-1.

road show Visits of senior management to a variety of brokerages to give presentations to potential investors. Typically, the road shows will be in the major investment centers, such as New York City, San Francisco, and Los Angeles.

Sarbanes-Oxley Act (SOX) Act A law passed in 2002 to increase the disclosures and penalties for public corporations. The aim was to help prevent frauds like those of Enron and WorldCom. But SOX also made it more expensive for companies to go public.

SEC *See* Securities and Exchange Commission (SEC).

secondary market An online exchange that allows investors to purchase shares in pre-IPO companies. The main operators include SecondMarket and SharesPost.

secondary offering A stock issue after a company has already done an IPO.

Securities Act of 1933 The law that covers the regulations for the IPO market.

Securities and Exchange Commission (SEC) The federal agency that regulates securities such as IPOs and insider trading.

self-underwriting A company bypassing the use of an underwriter and doing its own offering. Small companies frequently underwrite themselves, with the size of the offering, in most cases, below $5 million. However, the success of these types of offerings has been spotty.

selling stockholders The officers or founders of an IPO company selling some or all of their positions. Heavy selling may indicate the IPO will not do well.

shelf registration This is for a large company that has already had a public offering. With a shelf registration, it can issue shares at any time.

short selling Borrowing stock and selling it simultaneously. The investor will hope to buy it at a lower price to make a profit. Thus, the trade makes money when the stock price falls.

short swing rule An insider is not allowed to make a profit on a trade on his or her own stock for a six-month period. Any gains must be forfeited.

S-1 A document filed with the Securities and Exchange Commission. The filing includes the prospectus, which is also known as the registration statement.

spin-off A company's subsidiary that becomes a separate company via a new stock offering. The stock is usually issued to shareholders of the parent company.

stabilization A lead underwriter intervening in the market by buying shares to prevent the stock from falling below its public offering price. This practice protects the stock and is therefore allowed by the SEC.

sticky deal An IPO that will be difficult to sell.

strategic investor A large company that invests in early-stage ventures.

stuffing the channel When a company sends unordered products to a customer to artificially boost sales.

syndicate A group of underwriters who will sell the offering to investors. IPOs are typically very large, requiring numerous underwriters. The syndicate is headed by the lead underwriter or lead manager.

10-K A financial disclosure that has an annual review of a company's developments and financials.

10-Q A financial disclosure that has a quarterly review of a company's developments and financials.

tombstone An advertisement for an IPO placed by the lead underwriter.

tracking stock A publicly traded security issued by a parent company to track the performance and/or earnings potential of a subsidiary. Or when a major company splits off a division to shareholders, which is what AT&T did when it created a tracking stock for its wireless division. However, a tracking stock is very different from a spin-off; with a tracking stock, the parent company retains much control.

transfer agent A firm that handles the exchange of stock certificates and ownership records.

underwriter A firm that helps companies organize an IPO.

use of proceeds A section in a company's prospectus that indicates what it will do with the money from an IPO.

venture capital (VC) Cash from firms accepted before a company goes public. The venture capital firms usually take a large position in the company.

waiting period The period of time between the filing of the registration statement and the time when the shares can be offered to the public.

About the Author

Tom Taulli writes about venture capital and IPOs for Forbes.com as well as the IPOPlaybook.com. He has been involved in the financial markets since the mid-1990s when he launched WebIPO. It was a place where investors obtained research and access to deals for the dot-com boom.

Besides his writings, Tom is routinely quoted in the media about upcoming deals from his interviews on CNBC and Bloomberg TV.

He can be reached at tom@taulli.com or on Twitter at @ttaulli.

Index